Asia Bible Commentary Series

1 TIMOTHY

GLOBAL LIBRARY

Asia Bible Commentary Series

1 TIMOTHY

Paul Trebilco, Simon H. Rae, and Deolito Vistar

General Editor
Andrew B. Spurgeon

Old Testament Consulting Editors
**Yohanna Katanacho, Joseph Shao,
Havilah Dharamraj, Koowon Kim**

New Testament Consulting Editors
Steve Chang, Brian Wintle

© 2023 Paul Trebilco, Simon H. Rae, and Deolito Vistar

Published 2023 by Langham Global Library
An imprint of Langham Publishing
www.langhampublishing.org

Langham Publishing and its imprints are a ministry of Langham Partnership

Langham Partnership
PO Box 296, Carlisle, Cumbria, CA3 9WZ, UK
www.langham.org

Published in partnership with Asia Theological Association

ATA
QCC PO Box 1454–1154, Manila, Philippines
www.ataasia.com

ISBNs:
978-1-83973-813-5 Print
978-1-83973-814-2 ePub
978-1-83973-816-6 PDF

Paul Trebilco, Simon H. Rae, and Deolito Vistar have asserted their right under the Copyright, Designs and Patents Act, 1988 to be identified as the Authors of this work.

All rights reserved. No part of this publication may be reproduced, stored in a retrieval system or transmitted, in any form or by any means, electronic, mechanical, photocopying, recording or otherwise, without the prior written permission of the publisher or the Copyright Licensing Agency.

Requests to reuse content from Langham Publishing are processed through PLSclear. Please visit www.plsclear.com to complete your request.

All Scripture quotations, unless otherwise indicated, are taken from the Holy Bible, New International Version®, NIV®. Copyright ©1973, 1978, 1984, 2011 by Biblica, Inc.™ Used by permission of Zondervan.

British Library Cataloguing-in-Publication Data
A catalogue record for this book is available from the British Library

ISBN: 978-1-83973-813-5

Cover & Book Design: projectluz.com

Langham Partnership actively supports theological dialogue and an author's right to publish but does not necessarily endorse the views and opinions set forth here or in works referenced within this publication, nor can we guarantee technical and grammatical correctness. Langham Partnership does not accept any responsibility or liability to persons or property as a consequence of the reading, use or interpretation of its published content.

CONTENTS

Commentary

Series Preface vii
Authors' Preface ix
List of Abbreviations xi
Introduction 1
Commentary on 1 Timothy 5
Concluding Remarks 165
Selected Bibliography 167

Topics

Custom and Gospel 17
Truth, Love, and Social Sensibilities 28
Praying for Rulers 36
Church Government and Leadership 62
Relations with Society and Society's Values 68
The Primacy of Godly Character 86
Contemporary Relevance of Paul's Instructions to Slaves 146

SERIES PREFACE

What's unique about the Asia Bible Commentary Series? It is a commentary series written especially for Asian Christians, which incorporates and addresses Asian concerns, cultures, and practices. As Asian scholars – either by nationality, passion, or calling – the authors identify with the biblical text, understand it culturally, and apply its principles in Asian contexts to strengthen the churches in Asia. Missiologists tell us that Christianity has shifted from being a Western majority religion to a South, Southeastern, and Eastern majority religion and that the church is growing at an unprecedented rate in these regions. This series meets the need for evangelical commentaries written specifically for an Asian audience.

This is not to say that Asian churches and Asian Christians don't want to partner with Western Christians and churches or that they spurn Western influences. A house divided cannot stand. The books in this series complement the existing Western commentaries by taking into consideration the cultural nuances familiar to the Eastern world so that the Eastern readership is not inundated with Western clichés and illustrations that they are unable to relate to and which may not be applicable to them.

The mission of this series is "to produce resources that are biblical, pastoral, contextual, missional, and prophetic for pastors, Christian leaders, cross-cultural workers, and students in Asia." While using approved exegetical principles, the writers strive to be culturally relevant, offer practical applications, and provide clear explanations of the texts so that readers can grow in understanding and maturity in Christ, and so that Christian leaders can guide their congregations into maturity. May we be found faithful to this endeavor and may God be glorified!

Andrew B. Spurgeon
General Editor

AUTHORS' PREFACE

An earlier edition of this commentary, written by Paul Trebilco and Simon Rae, was published by the Asia Theological Association and OMF Literature in the Asia Bible Commentary Series in 2006. Paul and Simon are now very grateful to have been given the opportunity by Dr. Andrew Spurgeon, who is the current general editor of this commentary series to revise and update it. Paul and Simon are also very grateful that Deolito Vistar was willing to assist in this revision process. It has been a joy and privilege for the three of us to work together in this way.

The authors are also very grateful to Dr. Andrew Spurgeon for his encouragement and for his editorial suggestions which have helped improve this work. We are also very grateful to Ms. Bubbles Lactaoen for her efficiency and assistance in the final stages of the production of this commentary.

LIST OF ABBREVIATIONS

BOOKS OF THE BIBLE

Old Testament

Gen, Exod, Lev, Num, Deut, Josh, Judg, Ruth, 1–2 Sam, 1–2 Kgs, 1–2 Chr, Ezra, Neh, Esth, Job, Ps/Pss, Prov, Eccl, Song, Isa, Jer, Lam, Ezek, Dan, Hos, Joel, Amos, Obad, Jonah, Mic, Nah, Hab, Zeph, Hag, Zech, Mal

New Testament

Matt, Mark, Luke, John, Acts, Rom, 1–2 Cor, Gal, Eph, Phil, Col, 1–2 Thess, 1–2 Tim, Titus, Phlm, Heb, Jas, 1–2 Pet, 1–2–3 John, Jude, Rev

BIBLE TEXTS AND VERSIONS

Divisions of the canon

NT	New Testament
OT	Old Testament

Ancient texts and versions

LXX	Septuagint
MT	Masoretic Text

Modern versions

KJV	King James Version
NIV	New International Version
NASB	New American Standard Bible
NKJV	New King James Version
NRSV	New Revised Standard Version

Journals, reference works, and series

AB	Anchor Bible
BST	The Bible Speaks Today
CBQ	*Catholic Biblical Quarterly*

ICC	International Critical Commentary
ITC	International Theological Commentary
JBL	*Journal of Biblical Literature*
JETS	*Journal of the Evangelical Theological Society*
JTS	*Journal of Theological Studies*
JSNTSup	Journal for the Study of the New Testament Supplements
NICNT	New International Commentary on the New Testament
NIGTC	New International Greek Testament Commentary
SBL	Society of Biblical Literature
TDNT	*Theological Dictionary of the New Testament*
WBC	Word Biblical Commentary

OUTLINE

1 Timothy 1
- 1:1–2   Greetings
- 1:3–7   Warning against False Teachers
- 1:8–11   The Lawful Use of the Law
- 1:12–17   Paul, an Example of God's Saving Mercy
- 1:18–20   Paul's Charge to Timothy

1 Timothy 2
- 2:1–7   Prayer in Public Worship
- 2:8–15   Men and Women in Worship

1 Timothy 3
- 3:1–7   Qualifications for Overseers
- 3:8–13   Qualifications for Deacons
- 3:14–16   The Church: God's Family

1 Timothy 4
- 4:1–5   Asceticism of the False Teachers
- 4:6–16   Lifestyle of a Christian Leader
  - 4:6–10   Sound Doctrine and Godly Living
  - 4:11–16   Faithfulness in Personal Life and Public Ministry

1 Timothy 5
- 5:1–2   The Congregation
- 5:3–16   The Widows
  - 5:3–8   Caring for Widows
  - 5:9–16   Cautions about Widows
- 5:17–25   The Elders
  - 5:17–18   Caring for Elders
  - 5:19–25   Cautions about Elders

1 Timothy 6
- 6:1–2   Instructions for Slaves
- 6:3–10   False Teachers and Their Love of Money

1 Timothy

6:11–21   Final Charge to Timothy
          6:11–16   A Word to Timothy
          6:17–19   A Word to the Rich
          6:20–21   Final Word to Timothy

INTRODUCTION

First Timothy, 2 Timothy, and Titus are collectively described as "Pastoral Epistles" because they deal with matters related to pastoring a community of believers. These letters are as relevant today as when they were first written.

First Timothy includes matters such as sound doctrines and false teachings, true and false beliefs, encouragement to those who suffer, caring for other Christians, leadership in the church, instructions to rich Christians, the goodness of the created world, and the importance of behavior that reflects Christian beliefs. The Christian community Paul addresses was under pressure because of influences exerted by the religious beliefs and lifestyles of neighboring communities, as well as because of sporadic persecution. Paul's letter shows how Christians can live with both integrity and harmony in a society which includes people with differing religious and cultural beliefs and values.

As someone who was as much at home in the Greek and Roman worlds as he was in the world of Palestinian and Diaspora Judaism, Paul was the ideal candidate to minister to both Jewish and Gentile Christians and to bring reconciliation between these two communities when misunderstandings arose. His ministry was international in scope and multicultural in outlook. As someone who had suffered many hardships, imprisonment, and persecution for the sake of the gospel – even bearing on his body the marks of Christ's suffering (Gal 6:17) – Paul wrote this letter to instruct Timothy, the young pastor and leader of a young faith community, about how to apply the good news of Jesus faithfully and diligently amid challenges and change.

Paul's letter to Timothy speaks with great relevance to many theological and pastoral situations faced by Asian church communities in our own day. Traditional Christian communities in Asia are subjected to the increasingly secular and materialistic influences of modern Westernized lifestyles. Many young churches in Asia are struggling with the challenge of directing and disciplining their members. In many places in Asia, Christian witness is still dangerous and allegiance to a kingdom not of this world is not only misunderstood but often results in oppression by rulers who demand the total allegiance of all their citizens. As such, instructions in 1 Timothy are helpful for the young and vibrant churches in Asia.

1 Timothy

THE AUTHORSHIP OF THE LETTER

For several reasons, some scholars question the Pauline authorship of the Pastoral Epistles (1 Timothy, 2 Timothy, and Titus).[1] First, the historical situation presupposed in the letters does not seem to correspond to the details of Paul's career as related in Acts. If the Pastorals are by Paul, then it seems likely that Paul wrote these letters after he was released from his imprisonment in Rome (Acts 28:16, 30–31) and was continuing his missionary work elsewhere (2 Tim 4:13, 20; Titus 1:5). He probably wrote 1 Timothy and Titus from Macedonia (1 Tim 1:3), before being rearrested and taken to Rome (2 Tim 1:8, 16–17) – where he wrote 2 Timothy. Only the Pastoral Epistles offer evidence that Paul's missionary work extended beyond his ministry as recounted in Acts.

Second, there are significant differences in vocabulary between the Pastorals and the other Pauline epistles, with the Pastorals containing far more words that are not found elsewhere in the New Testament than any other Pauline letters. Unlike Paul's other letters, the Pastorals are also closer in style to Greek literature and distinctive in style in comparison to the Septuagint. But other scholars argue that analysis of vocabulary and style is difficult with comparatively short texts.

Third, many scholars argue that the organizational development of the church, as depicted in the Pastorals, seems to have reached a stage beyond the time when Paul wrote his other letters.

Fourth, there are differences in the theology of the Pastorals compared with Paul's other letters in areas such as Christology (who Jesus is), the way the Christian life is described, and the attitude to tradition.

Other scholars offer counterarguments, defending Paul's authorship of the Pastoral Epistles. They suggest that the differences between the Pastorals and other Pauline letters are due to factors such as different subject matter, the addressees being individuals – who were well-known to Paul – rather than churches, an audience that was more thoroughly hellenized, and the nature of the opponents in view in these letters. They also argue that Paul used a secretary differently to the way he used secretaries in the composition of his other letters. In writing the Pastorals, Paul might have given the secretary a general outline and left much of the detailed content of the letter to the secretary.

---

[1]. All major commentaries discuss this issue. See, in particular, I. H. Marshall, *The Pastoral Epistles*, 2nd edition. ICC (Edinburgh: T&T Clark, 2004), 57–92; see also M. Harding, *What Are They Saying About the Pastoral Epistles* (New York: Paulist Press, 2001), 9–27.

Introduction

Luke, who was familiar with Paul's journeys and his preaching, might have been that secretary.

Some scholars argue that the Pastoral Epistles are pseudonymous letters – that is, that these letters were written by someone other than Paul, who stood in the Pauline tradition and applied this tradition to new problems that arose in Pauline churches in his own day. In other words, the author was expressing what he believed Paul would have said in such a situation. In the ancient world, pseudonymous writing was not considered improper or deceitful, and such writings were common in Judaism. If the Pastorals were in fact pseudonymous, this would have been the author's way of acknowledging his indebtedness to Paul's theology.[2]

In this commentary, the authors will write of the author as Paul, and will see these letters as part of the Pauline corpus, while noting their distinctive voice in comparison with the other Pauline letters.

THE LETTER'S AUDIENCE

The letter is addressed to Timothy (1:2), who was one of Paul's traveling companions, his co-worker, and co-writer of some of Paul's letters.[3] Timothy is often said to be engaged in ministry apart from Paul, as is the case in 1 Timothy.[4]

Paul's command to "stay there in Ephesus" (1:3) makes it clear that Timothy was in Ephesus when Paul wrote.[5] Paul wanted Timothy to remain in Ephesus to counter the "false doctrines" that were being taught by "certain people." The letter portrays Timothy as a key church leader, responsible for the community's spiritual well-being and growth, as well as for the appointment and oversight of elders and deacons (3:1–13; 5:17–22). The letter gives insights into important aspects of the Ephesian church: false teachers and their false doctrines (1:3–7, 19–20; 4:1–5; 6:3–5); the role of women (2:9–15); church leadership (3:1–13; 5:17–22); widows (5:3–17); slaves (1 Tim 6:1–2); and the right attitude to riches (6:9–10, 17–19).

---

2. Further, the author might have incorporated "Pauline fragments" in the letters, which would explain the presence of personal notes from Paul in the text. However, this theory is unlikely since these so-called fragments are couched in the same vocabulary and style as the rest of the letter; if the author had used any such fragments, they have been rewritten, making these impossible to distinguish from the rest of the letter.
3. See Romans 16:21; 2 Corinthians 1:1, 19; Philippians 1:1; 1 Thessalonians 1:1; 2 Thessalonians 1:1; Philemon 1.
4. See Acts 17:14–15; 19:22; 1 Corinthians 4:17; 16:10; Philippians 2:19; 1 Thessalonians 3:2.
5. 2 Timothy 1:18 and 4:12 also mention Ephesus.

1 Timothy

The final greeting – "Grace be with you all" (6:21) – with its plural "you," implies that Paul envisaged his letter being read to all Christians in Ephesus. The instructions about prayer and worship were intended for the whole church, not just for Timothy (2:1–10), while the exhortation to Timothy to "point these things out to the brothers and sisters" (4:6) also suggests that Paul intended that his instructions be made known to all Christians in Ephesus. So although addressed to an individual, 1 Timothy was clearly meant to be "overheard" and obeyed by the whole Christian community in Ephesus.

1 TIMOTHY 1

In 1 Timothy 1, Paul challenges his audience to guard the faith in their local church. The Ephesian church was beset by false teachers whose teachings were contrary to the gospel that Paul had preached. Paul instructs Timothy, as an apostolic representative in Ephesus, to command these teachers to stop teaching false doctrines. Because these false teachers used God's law (the Old Testament) as the basis for their beliefs, Paul also writes about the proper use of the law. He includes a brief personal testimony – calling attention to the true nature of the apostolic gospel – and a charge to Timothy.

Regardless of where a local church is, the apostolic faith is crucial, because without the apostolic faith, without the gospel of Jesus Christ, there would be no church. If a particular church departs from the apostolic faith and embraces a counterfeit gospel, that church will eventually cease to be the church of Jesus Christ. This truth is very important for the church in Asia. In the Philippines, for instance, Christianity has been around for over five hundred years, and the country is often described as a Christian nation even though the majority of the population are not adherents of biblical Christianity. *Kristiyano sa nguso, ngunit hindi sa puso* is a Tagalog saying that means "Christian by lips but not by heart." Perhaps this saying originated with someone who observed that while many people readily professed to be believers in Christ, their lifestyle did not manifest the transformation that Christ and the gospel must bring. Such lip service to Christianity is short-lived, as evidenced by what happens in the Philippines during Holy Week. Thousands of penitent Filipinos lash their bare backs with whips and rods as a sign of anguish for their sins and their intense devotion to Christ. Some go so far as to reenact the extreme suffering of Christ by having themselves nailed on crosses (without dying).[1] After Holy Week, however, several revert to their old lifestyles.

Many groups in Asia, although they identify themselves as "Christian" and use the Bible as the basis for their beliefs, deviate from the historic Christian faith. For example, the *Iglesia ni Cristo* (meaning, "Church of Christ") – a non-Trinitarian group with its headquarters in Quezon City – teaches that

---

1. See Anril Pineda Tiatco and Amihan Bonifacio-Ramolete, "Cutud's Ritual of Nailing on the Cross: Performance of Pain and Suffering," in *Asian Theatre Journal* 25.1 (2008): 58–76. Also, D. Diamante et al., "Crowd Estimation of the Black Nazarene Procession in Manila, Philippines," *Philippine Journal of Science* 150 (2021): 883–93.

Jesus Christ does not share in God's divine identity.[2] Sometime leaders today can make claims for themselves or in relation to the Gospel that are clearly not endorsed by the Scriptures.

A similar problem is evident in Paul's description of the false teachers in Ephesus: "They do not know what they are talking about or what they so confidently affirm" (1:7).

In the context of false teaching, the task of Christian ministry may be compared to the way bank tellers are trained to recognize counterfeit money. Tellers are made to spend countless hours handling currency notes until they become so familiar with genuine notes that they can (generally!) detect counterfeits. The church must help believers to become so familiar with the true gospel that they are not easily deceived by counterfeit teachings.

Paul entrusted Timothy with the task of guarding the apostolic gospel by commanding false teachers to stop spreading false teachings in the Ephesian church. By talking about the miracle of God's grace which saved him even though he was "the worst of sinners" (1:16), Paul showed that there was hope for those in the Ephesian church who had wandered away from the faith. Most of chapter 1 focuses on the importance of guarding the true gospel which was being threatened by the explosion of false teachings in the Ephesian church.

1:1–2 GREETINGS

In this section, Paul identifies himself as the author of the letter and Timothy as its recipient. In addition, he includes a greeting like that found in his other NT letters. An Asian reader would see this introduction as clarifying and establishing relationships. Relationships matter, not least in the church and in ministry. In his opening greeting, Paul situates himself in the context of his relationship to God and Jesus, as well as his relationship to Timothy.

Paul describes himself as an "apostle," someone sent out as an authorized representative of the sender. Since the letter addresses the problem of a deviation from the apostolic gospel, establishing this apostolic authority was crucial. Paul had not appointed himself to this role; nor had he been appointed an apostle by the churches. On the contrary, his apostleship had its origin in the "command" of both God and Jesus Christ (1:1; Gal 1:1). The word "command," which indicates an order, was often used of royal commands which had to be obeyed. Paul saw himself as one under divine orders, appointed as a guardian or trustee of the deposit of faith that he had received by divine

---

2. Anne C. Harper, *Understanding the Iglesia ni Christo* (Eugene, OR: Wipf & Stock, 2017).

revelation (Gal 1:11–12). Similarly, Paul commanded Timothy and Titus to guard the body of sound doctrine that had been entrusted to them (1 Tim 6:20; 2 Tim 1:13–14; 2:1–2; Titus 2:1).

Paul describes God as "our Savior," a title that occurs ten times in the Pastorals, six times with reference to God and four times in relation to Christ. While the OT presents God as Savior (Deut 32:15; Ps 24:5; Isa 17:10), this title was also used of Greek rulers, the Roman emperor, and benefactors of a city, and was even found in mystery religions.[3] Salvation is a key theme in Paul's letter, and the apostle might have used this title here to emphasize that God (or Christ) is the true Savior, while others to whom the title was applied were deceivers. Salvation is found in God and in Christ, not in the emperor or in any other cult of the day.

The description of Christ Jesus as "our hope" is unique in the NT. The false teachers seemed to have taught that the end had already arrived and that "the resurrection has already taken place" (2 Tim 2:18). It might have been in response to this idea that Paul consistently emphasizes the future dimension of the Christian faith. Salvation can be spoken of as a past event accomplished by Christ (1 Tim 1:15; 2 Tim 1:9; Titus 3:5), but there is also a future dimension to this salvation, for which we wait in hope (1 Tim 6:13–19; Titus 1:2; 3:7). Since hope for the fullness of salvation is focused on Christ and his future appearing (Titus 2:13), Christ can simply be called "our hope" (compare Rom 15:13; Col 1:27). For the Christian, hope is not based on what we do or on vague ideas about what God might do, "but simply on the fact of Jesus Christ."[4]

The mention of God as "our Savior" and Christ as "our hope" anticipates major themes of the letter. As in many of Paul's other letters, the greeting introduces key concepts which are developed in the body of the letter. Further, as Yarbrough notes,

> Timothy's challenging assignment at Ephesus (see 1:3) will benefit from the conviction that the apostolic gospel he ministers goes forth under the auspices of God who rescues and Christ who confers a sense of confidence in the future that is so strong that it transforms the present.[5]

---

3. See G. Fohrer and W. Foerster, "σωτήρ," in *TDNT*, Volume 7, edited by G. Friedrich (Grand Rapids: Eerdmans, 1971), 1003–21.
4. C. K. Barrett, *The Pastoral Epistles in the New English Bible, with introduction and commentary*. New Clarendon Bible (Oxford: Clarendon Press, 1963), 39.
5. R. W. Yarbrough, *The Letters to Timothy and Titus*. Pillar New Testament Commentary (Grand Rapids: Eerdmans, 2018), 90.

The letter is addressed to "Timothy" (1:2), a well-known figure in the NT. Timothy was a regular traveling companion of Paul (Acts 16:1–3), a trusted co-worker (Phil 2:22; 1 Thess 3:2), and co-writer of several of Paul's letters (2 Cor 1:1; Phil 1:1; Philemon 1). Paul calls Timothy "my true son in the faith" (1:2). "Son" is an affectionate term, and its use here includes the idea that Paul nurtured Timothy as a Christian (1 Cor 4:15–17) and that Timothy was a true, genuine, or loyal child in the faith (see also Phil 2:22). The emphasis is on faithful service and proven worth and may have been intended as a contrast to the teachers of false doctrine. This way of designating Timothy is a vote of confidence: Timothy was to be listened to because he was a trustworthy and faithful disciple, who had continued in the Christian faith and tradition he had received. Paul's close and affectionate relationship with Timothy is an example worthy of emulation since it illustrates both the kind of nurturing mentor-disciple relationship that helps to form young leaders and the kind of relationship that should exist among church leaders – for Paul was writing to Timothy as a leader who had been entrusted with pastoring the church at Ephesus. The letter also validates Timothy's role as Paul's representative. Despite his youth, Timothy had authority to command, to rebuke, and to teach in the church (1:3; 3:14–15; 4:6, 11–12). The greeting to Timothy, while similar to greetings in other Pauline letters, includes the additional word "mercy," which occurs only in 1 and 2 Timothy. The expression "grace, mercy and peace" (1:2) seems to capture the essence of the Christian faith. "Grace" – which means undeserved favor – describes God's offer of salvation to humanity, which draws them to himself, in Christ, without their having to work for it. This grace is not a one-time offer but is God's ongoing forgiveness and enabling. "Mercy" conveys the idea of compassion, either for the needy or for sinners in need of God's favor; and the idea of mercy is expanded on in 1 Timothy 1:12–16. "Peace" is the common Jewish greeting, "Shalom." While "Shalom" includes peace with God, the term is more extensive and probably includes the idea of peace and stability in the Christian community. In his greeting, Paul acts as a herald of good tidings from God and Christ. These blessings of grace, mercy, and peace will sustain the church as it faces the challenges posed by the false teachers.

Jesus is called "Lord." In the NT, this term ranges in meaning from a respectful "sir" to a "virtual designation of deity."[6] Since "Lord" (Gr. *kurios*)

---

6. G. W. Knight, *The Pastoral Epistles. A Commentary on the Greek Text*. NIGTC (Grand Rapids: Eerdmans, 1992), 68.

is used in the LXX – the Greek translation of the OT – as a substitute for the divine name Yahweh, it refers to Jesus's status as one who shares God's name. Here, "Lord" indicates that Christ Jesus participates in the gracious activity of God (see also 1 Cor 8:6).

Verses 1 and 2 link the activity of God and of Jesus. Paul's apostleship was jointly commanded by God and Christ, and grace, mercy, and peace originate with both God and Christ. This linking of the activity of God and Christ, which is also found elsewhere in the Pastoral Epistles (see 1 Tim 5:21; 6:13; 2 Tim 4:1; Titus 1:4), indicates a developed Christology. Christ shares in the activity of God, in God's title of "Savior" (2 Tim 1:10; Titus 1:4; 2:13; 3:6), and in God's name of "Lord" (1 Tim 1:12; 6:3, 14; 2 Tim 1:8, 18; 4:8).

1:3–7 WARNING AGAINST FALSE TEACHERS

One of the dominant traits of Filipinos is *pakikisama*, a Tagalog word meaning "to accompany" or "to go along with." According to Tomas Andres and Pilar Corazon Andres, *pakikisama* is "the Filipino natural instinct of uniting one's will with the will of others in a gang or peer group [in] the sense of camaraderie."[7] In many ways it is a wonderful trait, and many Filipinos will probably resonate with Paul's command to the Philippian church to "look not to your own interests, but to the interests of others" (Phil 2:4 NRSV). But the challenge is to identify and set boundaries and limits to *pakikisama*, so that we are able to say "no" to our peers if going along with them would compromise our Christian faith and witness. While the NT commands us to live in harmony with all people, it also warns against being conformed to "the pattern of this world" (Rom 12:2).

Paul instructs Timothy to do something which many people would probably find difficult – to confront the false teachers in the church and command them to stop teaching false doctrines (1:3–7). Hard though this is, it must be done, so that the apostolic faith is safeguarded, and the church is shielded from the destructive effects of false teachings.

In almost all Paul's letters, a thanksgiving follows the greeting (Galatians is a notable exception). In 1 Timothy, Paul's thanksgiving is postponed until he gets to verse 12. Further, the content of the thanksgiving relates to Paul's experience and mission rather than to Timothy or the believers in Ephesus. Perhaps the situation in the church at the time was so serious, and the threat

---

7. T. Q. D. Andres and P. C. Lada-Andres, *Making the Filipino Values Work for You* (Makati: St. Paul Publication, 1988), 42.

of the false teachers so alarming and urgent, that Paul decided to delay his usual introductory thanksgiving and, instead, immediately state his purpose in writing – that is, that Timothy must oppose these false teachers (1:3–5) who posed a threat to the church (1:6–7).

The journey to Macedonia (1:3) might have taken place after Paul's stay in Ephesus (Acts 19:1–20) or after Paul's release from prison in Rome (Acts 28). Many scholars favor the latter view since the travel mentioned in 1 Timothy does not seem to correspond to the travels mentioned in Acts and Paul's other letters.

The Roman province of Macedonia, in the northern part of Greece, included Philippi, Thessalonica, and Berea. Ephesus was the principal city of Asia Minor and the seat of the provincial governor. The Christian community in Ephesus had probably been established through the work of Aquila and Priscilla (Acts 18:24–28), the apostle Paul – who had worked in that city for over two years and three months (Acts 19:1–20:31) – and Timothy (1:3).

Paul instructs Timothy to remain in Ephesus and command "certain people" not to teach false doctrines (1:3). The plural ("people") indicates that Paul had more than one person in view; and since these people were teaching, they were probably leaders in the church. There is no indication that those spreading false doctrines were outsiders (compare 2 Cor 11:4, 12–13; Gal 2:4). Since Timothy is told to command them to stop teaching false doctrines, it is likely that they were part of the church. Since teaching was one of the responsibilities of an elder (1 Tim 5:17), Fee suggests that some of the false teachers were elders in the church.[8] Further, the concern about elders in 1 Timothy makes this theory plausible (3:1–7; 5:19–25). We see that there is a serious crisis in the Ephesian church.

"False doctrine" may be defined as doctrine which "does not agree to the sound instruction of our Lord Jesus Christ" (6:3). While the letter touches briefly on these false doctrines, it does not give a detailed description of its contents. While Paul occasionally outlines some facet of these "false doctrines" and then refutes it (4:1–5), his general approach is to instruct Timothy and the church to have nothing to do with the false teachers or their teaching and to reproach the false teachers themselves in strongly negative terms (1:20).[9] With

---

[8]. G. D. Fee, *1 and 2 Timothy, Titus*. Understanding the Bible Commentary Series (Grand Rapids: Baker Books, 2011), 7–9, 40.

[9]. Karris argues that Paul uses much of the language used by popular philosophers to describe their own philosophical opponents. R. J. Karris, "The Background and Significance of the Polemic of the Pastoral Epistles," *JBL* 92 (1973): 549–64.

so few details about the nature of the false teaching, it is difficult to equate it precisely with other movements or trends in the early church.

Although Paul does not specify what the false teaching is, he describes some of its attributes: "myths and endless genealogies," which give rise to "controversial speculations" (1:4). Paul also links "godless myths" with "old wives' tales" (4:7) and, elsewhere in the Pastorals, describes such myths as being opposed to "truth" (2 Tim 4:4). Paul sees myths as untrue, of no value, and as tales that only the gullible believe. It seems likely that these myths have a Jewish background. This view is supported by the fact that Paul's letter to Titus also mentions "Jewish myths" (1:14) and refers to "genealogies and arguments and quarrels about the law" (3:9). These genealogies are not just lists of names but include edifying stories about creation and prominent OT figures such as the patriarchs. The false teachers may have been using speculative interpretations based on OT narratives in support of their false doctrines.

Stott notes that the Pastoral Epistles often refer to a core of doctrine from which the false teachers have deviated.[10] This doctrinal core is referred to in various ways: "the faith" (1 Tim 1:19; 2 Tim 3:8; 4:7; Titus 3:15); "the truth" (1 Tim 2:4; 2 Tim 2:18; Titus 1:1, 14); "sound" doctrine or instruction or teaching (1 Tim 1:10; 2 Tim 1:13; Titus 1:9); "good teaching" (1 Tim 4:6); "our teaching" (1 Tim 6:1); and "the good deposit" (2 Tim 1:14). All teachings must be tested against the teaching of Christ (1 Tim 6:3) and the apostles (1 Tim 1:11; 2 Tim 1:13).

The result of a devotion to myths and genealogies is "controversial speculations," which Paul contrasts with the desired outcome of "advancing God's work" (Gk. *oikonomian theou*), which can also be translated "divine training" (NRSV). The meaning of this phrase is debated. *Oikonomia* is the work done by a steward in managing a household. In this context, the reference could be to God's plan of salvation or to the stewardship which God entrusts to his people to fulfill God's purposes. The former is more likely since the emphasis here seems to be on God's work of salvation. The false teachers' speculative myths and genealogies are thus contrasted with God's great and authentic plan of salvation. As Davies notes, "The orderliness and the comprehensive and complete nature of God's plan suggests that there is no need for speculation."[11]

---

10. J. R. W. Stott, *The Message of 1 Timothy and Titus*. BST (Leicester: Inter-Varsity Press, 1996), 42–43.
11. M. Davies, *The Pastoral Epistles*. Epworth NT Commentaries (London: Epworth, 1996), 5.

"God's work" or this "divine training" is "by faith" (1:4). On the human side, God's work of salvation is apprehended by faith, which probably does not refer to initial faith alone but to faith as the ongoing trust in which the Christian life is lived, as the reference to "sincere faith" also shows (1:5). The contrast here is between faith on the one hand and the elaborate speculations of the false teachers on the other.

Paul states that the true goal of his exhortation is love (1:5). While Timothy is charged with confronting and correcting errors, this charge also has the positive aim of establishing love in the church, in place of the speculations and vain discussions that had resulted from the false teachers' work. The proper result of God's work of salvation must be that believers love one another. Faith and love appear together, as they do elsewhere in the Pastoral Epistles.[12] Believers are repeatedly urged to pursue or practice love (1 Tim 1:14; 2 Tim 1:7; Titus 2:2). Wall notes:

> In Pauline thought, *agapē* [love] is not an abstract rule of life but the principal characteristic of a congregation's life together, formed in the company of the indwelling Spirit (Gal 5:16–26). As such, love for neighbor is a marker of the congregation's love in Christ (Rom 5:5; 8:35; 13:9).[13]

The love which is the goal of Paul's command comes from three sources: the heart, the conscience, and faith (1:5). The heart, which the Bible sees as the center of a person's spiritual and thought life, refers to volition rather than to emotions. A "pure heart" is undivided, and it has been and goes on being cleansed by forgiveness. Without purity in the core of a person's being, they cannot radiate true Christian love.

Through "a good conscience," which functions as an accuser or judge, a person is made aware of the rightness or wrongness before God of an action or attitude, thus enabling honest self-evaluation of actions and providing guidance for future moral action. In the Pastoral Epistles, the conscience can be "good," "clear" (1 Tim 3:9; 2 Tim 1:3), "seared" (1 Tim 4:2), or "corrupted" (Titus 1:15). A "good" conscience is one that is rightly aligned with God; it

---

12. 1 Timothy 1:14; 2:15; 4:12; 6:11; 2 Timothy 1:13; 2:22; 3:10; Titus 2:2. For a study of the interrelationship between faith and love, see R. Saarinen, *The Pastoral Epistles with Philemon & Jude*. Brazos Theological Commentary on the Bible (Grand Rapids: Brazos Press, 2008), 35.
13. R. W. Wall, with R. B. Steele, *1 & 2 Timothy and Titus*. Two Horizons New Testament Commentary (Grand Rapids: Eerdmans, 2012), 66.

is a source of love because it makes a person aware of whether they have been obedient to God.

The "some" people Paul refers to in 1 Timothy 1:6 are those who taught false doctrines (1:3). These people had not only replaced God's instruction with myths, genealogies, and speculation (1:4), they had also wandered away from "a pure heart and a good conscience and a sincere faith" into "meaningless talk," which is idle, useless, and devoid of truth. As Barrett comments, "Nothing grieves our author more than a religion which is mere talk."[14]

The false teachers are described as people who "want to be teachers of the law" (1:7). Given the immediate context (1:8–11), as well as what Paul says in Titus (1:14; 3:9), it is clear that the reference is to the Mosaic law. Paul does not call these people "teachers of the law"; rather, they were aspiring to be authoritative interpreters of Scripture, experts in teaching Jewish law.

Paul also accuses the false teachers of failing to understand the things about which they speak so confidently. Not only is their talk "meaningless" and full of "speculations," they also fail to understand their own doctrinal assertions about the law. They combine error, a lack of authority, and incompetence.

In Asia, too, many factors divert our attention and prevent us from devoting ourselves to sound doctrine, serving in love, and being faithful in discipleship. An example is syncretism – incorporating the practices of other religions along with Christianity. For instance, some Asian Christians may be tempted to visit a Hindu temple and eat the food offered there. While Christians may study and be sympathetic to other religions and practices, they should not incorporate the doctrines and rituals of other religions in the practice of their Christian faith. Fascination with endless details about the rituals and practices of other religions may have the same effect on us as fascination with Jewish myths and endless genealogies had on the original readers of this letter.

In the pastoral care of Christian communities, it is important to be aware of the attraction of teachers who claim to offer "something extra" – something they claim is lacking in the life and witness of orthodox teachers. New believers, eager to learn more, are particularly vulnerable to such teachers. Paul's pastoral response to this problem was to teach the faith, both by word and example, in such a way that the focus was not speculation and endless discussion, but effective witness based on good conduct, a practical and loving attitude to others, and a good conscience (see 4:11–16).

---

14. Barrett, *The Pastoral Epistles*, 42. See also 1 Timothy 1:4, 7; 4:2, 7; 6:4, 20; 2 Timothy 2:16, 23; 3:5, 7; 4:4; Titus 1:10, 14, 16; 3:9.

It is also important that all those appointed to any kind of teaching office in the church – whether as elders, pastors, presbyters, or bishops – are well-instructed, as well as open to the review of their peers so that personal bias, special interests, or eccentric tendencies do not become a barrier to the correct understanding of the Christian faith.

1:8–11 THE LAWFUL USE OF THE LAW

A survey conducted in 2017 shows that the Bible remains a widely read book in the Philippines. Seventy-two percent of the population surveyed indicated that the Bible was their most read book. Christian leaders have gladly welcomed this news. Bishop Noel Pantoja – Chairman of the Philippine Bible Society and General Secretary of the Philippine Council of Evangelical Churches – said that the survey results "reveal [the Filipino people's] desire to know God and make Him known" and show that the Philippines is "a God-fearing nation."[15]

Reading the Bible is important; reading it correctly is even more important. In 1 Timothy 1:8–11, Paul demonstrates the proper use of God's law (more broadly, the Scriptures). He does this because some teachers in the Ephesian church had misused God's law and made it a basis for teaching false doctrines (1:3).

Since the false teachers wanted to be teachers of the law (1:7), it is clear that they were not against the law; nor does Paul imply that they disregarded the law. Rather, it seems likely that the false teachers' preoccupation with myths and genealogies from the OT – which probably involved seeing the OT in a new light – led to their using the law wrongly and missing its true purpose. Paul thus found it necessary to explain the proper function and role of the OT, which was to expose sin (1:9–10). Since the false teachers' use of the OT did not promote God's great plan of salvation (1:4), Paul shows how the OT should be used in accordance with its intended purpose in a way that is consistent with that plan.

Paul begins by stating what was probably the common understanding among his readers: "Now we know that the law is good, if anyone uses it lawfully" (1:8 RSV). This translation brings out the play on words that is evident in the Greek text: law (*nomos*) and lawfully (*nomimos*). Since the law is given by God, it is intrinsically good. It is beneficial if used according to

---

15. J. Torres, "Bible is the most read book among Filipinos," in *Godgossip*, October 29, 2018; http://www.godgossip.org/article/bible-is-most-read-book-among-filipinos (accessed May 3, 2022).

its true nature or in the right way, rather than illegitimately as a source for myths and genealogies (1:4). By "law," Paul probably meant the Mosaic law since the kinds of sins he lists in verses 9 and 10 follow the pattern of the Ten Commandments in Exodus 20:1–17.

Paul does not develop his understanding of the law in these verses. He simply counters the position of the false teachers who wanted to be teachers of the law and for whom law was a source of myths and genealogies. Paul's argument here is not developed as it is in Romans and Galatians; nor does he deal with the issue of justification by faith as opposed to justification by the works of the law.

Paul says that "the law is made not for the righteous" (1:9). But who are these "righteous" (*dikaios*) or "innocent" (NRSV) ones? Paul has already noted that promoting God's work of salvation is "by faith" (1:4). In addition, the goal of Paul's instruction is "love," which comes from "a sincere faith" (1:5). Since this is part of the "sound doctrine that conforms to the gospel" (1:10–11), we can conclude that it is "by such faith and love that a person is a 'righteous person.'"[16] The law, on the other hand, although it speaks out against sin which is "contrary to the sound doctrine" (1:10), cannot make a person righteous.

Paul is saying that the law is not given for the benefit of those who are already seeking to conform to the gospel but, rather, to expose the sins of "lawbreakers and rebels." This is the lawful use of the law that Paul illustrates with nine examples of lawbreaking which the law opposes (1:9b–10), which seem to loosely parallel the Ten Commandments. Similar "sin lists" are also found in Paul's other writings (Rom 1:29–31; 1 Cor 6:9–10; Gal 5:19–21).

---

16. Johnson, *Letters to Paul's Delegates*, 116.

1 Timothy	Ten Commandments
Ungodly	do not keep the commandment to love God exclusively (Exod 20:3)
Sinful	worship idols (Exod 20:4–6)
Unholy	do not keep the commandment concerning God's name (Exod 20:7)
Irreligious	do not keep the commandment concerning the Sabbath (Exod 20:8–11)
Kill their fathers or mothers	do not honor parents (Exod 20:12)
Murderers	do not keep the commandment against murder (Exod 20:13)
Sexually immoral	do not keep the commandment prohibiting adultery (Exod 20:14)
Slave traders (stealers of people)	do not keep the commandment against stealing (Exod 20:15)
Liars and perjurers	do not keep the commandment against bearing false witness (Exod 20:16)

The tenth commandment concerning covetousness is not included in this passage, perhaps because it is a sin of thought and attitude, not of deed.[17]

While this list demonstrates how the law is to function as an ethical guide to warn against sin, note Hanson's view: "There is not a single item in this list that would not have been condemned just as vigorously in most contemporary pagan moral codes."[18]

Paul concludes by saying that the law is also laid down "for whatever else is contrary to the sound doctrine" (1:10). So clearly, this list is not meant to be exhaustive but illustrative (for other such sin lists, see Rom 13:9; Gal 5:21). Paul implies that the "sound doctrine" of the Christian faith has the same

---

17. Freedman argues that the tenth commandment is a summary of the previous nine commandments. So an alternative explanation for why Paul does not include the final commandment is that he might also have seen the tenth commandment as a summary of the previous nine, and so may have chosen not to include it. D. N. Freedman, *The Nine Commandments: Uncovering the Hidden Pattern of Crime and Punishment in the Hebrew Bible* (Anchor Bible Reference Library, New York: Doubleday, 2000).
18. A. T. Hanson, *The Pastoral Epistles*. New Century Bible (Grand Rapids: Eerdmans, 1982), 59.

ethical perspective as the law, provided the latter is rightly understood. Law and the sound teaching of the gospel work together to expose and oppose sin, and neither is inconsistent with the principal concerns of civic morality of the communities in which these believers lived. Indeed, we see in the Pastorals a recurring appeal to what we might call "universal wisdom" or the "contemporary norms" of social behavior – for example in their praise of hospitality, holiness, purity, and restraint.

CUSTOM AND GOSPEL

The Pastorals have sometimes been accused of being "conventional," even "middle class," in their advocacy of the civic values of their own day. This criticism, however, misses an essential point. Paul claims that the law (Torah) rightly understood, the "sound doctrine" of the gospel, and the universal wisdom a community has inherited from the past are all able to help form "a pure heart and a good conscience and a sincere faith" (1 Tim 1:5). Each is to be applied with critical discernment. It is an emphasis of these letters that Christian faith and the best of contemporary ethics can, together, teach the wisdom essential for life in a world that is not bound by fate but is profoundly influenced by the choices people make.

In an Asian context, and particularly in societies that have followed their own traditional religions, the question of "custom" arises. This is the custom represented by the Malay and Indonesian term *adat*. It varies from one tribal or ethnic society to another. Each case represents a sophisticated pattern of responses to the various issues that arise in communal life. *Adat* is seen as a gift from one's ancestors that has their authority. On a more mundane level, people realize that custom is an accumulation of their society's experience over many generations.

Custom regulates who one may marry, by what ceremony, and after what formal negotiations and agreements. Custom regulates all aspects of communal behavior, enunciating rules very similar to those of the European natural law tradition – laws to enhance the flourishing of human life and to limit actions and behaviors that diminish it. Custom regulates social interactions, and the way things are done. Custom helps to ensure that, as Aquinas said of the natural law, "good is to be sought and done, and evil to be avoided."[1]

Questions of "Custom and Gospel" still excite considerable interest in many Asian church contexts. Is the *adat* still binding on Christians?

> Is all of it binding? What, on the other hand, would happen if Christians rejected the *adat* as if it were some pre-Christian irrelevance? Would it matter if everyone adopted a kind of globalized Christian lifestyle in place of old folkways?
>
> Many Indonesian churches, in societies where the *adat* provided an essential social framework, have found it impossible to teach and nurture Christians without affirming at least those aspects of the *adat* that regulate social life. In some Indonesian churches, Christian guidelines are put in place to ensure proper pastoral care for situations involving elopement, betrothal, marriage, annulment, and divorce in the context of *adat* law, supporting both its provisions and its sanctions. Where Christian denominations operating in these societies have removed their converts from the *adat* community, those Christians have frequently failed to grow or been marginalized by their own communities. Their faith and witness are rejected, along with them.[2]
>
> Christian endorsement of *adat* or custom calls for care and discernment. In practice, this is a process rather than the result of a sudden decision. It may begin with Christians taking a hard line on such things as traditional music and dancing – or anything else that seems to have a connection with traditional religion – and then a slow process of reclaiming the social elements of the *adat* as local Christians do their own theological reflections and then reassess these matters.
>
> Paul's exhortation to Timothy – not to be caught up with endless mythologies and genealogies but to surrender himself to the Torah – gives us a paradigm for responding in similar circumstances. We put God's word first, and then *adat* or tradition.
>
> ---
>
> 1. Thomas Aquinas, *Summa Theologiae: Latin Text and English Translation* (London: Blackfriars with Eyre & Spottiswoode, 1964–66), 1:2.94.2.
> 2. These are the field observations of one of the authors, Simon Rae. See S. H. Rae, *Breath Becomes the Wind: Old and New in Karo Religion* (Dunedin: University of Otago Press, 1994), 218.

In verse 10 Paul describes the gospel as "sound doctrine." The word "sound" is often used in relation to a standard from which soundness is derived, and this term is frequently used in the Pastoral Epistles to refer to the content of the Christian faith: "sound doctrine" (1 Tim 1:10; 2 Tim 4:3; Titus 1:9; 2:1); "sound instruction" or "sound teaching" (1 Tim 6:3; 2 Tim 1:13); "sound in faith" (Titus 1:13; 2:2); and "soundness of speech" (Titus 2:8). These terms, derived from imagery related to health and well-being, do not occur elsewhere in the NT. Here, sound doctrine denotes that which is healthy, and therefore correct, as opposed to what is false or sick. As Marshall notes, sound doctrine "is a technical term in the PE [Pastoral Epistles] for the approved, apostolic doctrine."[19] The imagery is generally used with reference to the behavior to which certain teaching leads. "Healthy teaching leads to proper Christian behavior, love and good works; the diseased teaching of the heretics leads to controversies, arrogance, abusiveness, and strife (6:4)."[20]

The sound doctrine is further qualified as teaching "that conforms to the gospel concerning the glory of the blessed God, which he entrusted to me" (1:11). The gospel is the true source for sound teaching. The noun "glory" could modify either "the gospel" – the "glorious gospel" (as in NASB) – or "God" (as in NIV). It is more likely to be the latter – "the glory of the blessed God." The gospel reveals or sets forth God's full glory so that we can see and know God's glory. Sound doctrine must be in accord with the gospel that displays God's glory. Whereas the law can only bring sinfulness to light, the gospel reveals God's glory. In the NT, "blessed" is used of God only here and in 1 Timothy 6:15,[21] which does not mean that people bless God but, rather, that all blessedness comes from God.

Paul, as an apostle, had been entrusted with this gospel that glorifies God. The false teachers wanted to be regarded as authoritative teachers of the law, but Paul's teaching was authoritative because the gospel was entrusted to him by God (1:1). Not only does this gospel glorify God (1:11), it conforms to the ethical teachings of the Mosaic law. Both the gospel and the proper use of the law teach Christians how to live righteous lives. Using the law as a basis for myths and genealogies violates the purpose for which the law was given.

1:12–17 PAUL, AN EXAMPLE OF GOD'S SAVING MERCY

Ang hindi marunong lumingon sa kanyang pinanggalingan ay hindi makakarating sa kanyang paroroonan. This familiar saying in the Philippines, attributed to Dr. Jose Rizal, means that "whoever forgets where they came from may not reach where they wish to go." Rizal is not urging people to dwell on the past but is

---

19. Marshall, *The Pastoral Epistles*, 381.
20. Fee, *1 & 2 Timothy*, 46.
21. Although uncommon in the NT, the term "blessed" was common in Greek literature, with Philo using this word several times. The use of the term here is perhaps derived from Hellenistic Judaism. Johnson says, "the perfect example of the slightly more 'hellenistic' tone that we find in 1 Timothy." Johnson, *Letters to Paul's Delegates*, 112.

encouraging an attitude of awareness, thankfulness, and appreciation for their origins. In this section, Paul magnifies the greatness of God's grace in his life, a grace poured out on Paul even though he was the worst of sinners, a grace that called and appointed Paul to be a messenger of the gospel.

This section follows from the earlier verses which also speak of sin and the gospel entrusted to Paul (1:9–11). Paul argues that since the gospel of overwhelming grace has saved him, a sinner par excellence, it can save any sinner. Beginning with a specific focus on Paul (1:12–14), the passage then illustrates this general truth (1:15–17).

In verse 11 Paul spoke of being entrusted with the gospel. Now he expands on this statement and expresses his thankfulness to Christ for considering him faithful and appointing him to service. Christ strengthened Paul and empowered him to fulfill the tasks to which he had been called. The abundant grace of verse 14 is thus seen as "an empowerment and a transformation. The mercy shown to Paul (1:13, 16) was not simply forgiveness of past behavior, but the gift of power that enables him to live in a new way."[22]

Paul was appointed to serve because the Lord Jesus considered him "trustworthy" (1:12) or "faithful" (NRSV). The Pastoral Epistles call various groups in the church to be faithful or "trustworthy": women (1 Tim 3:11), apostles (4:10), Timothy (4:12), widows (5:16), slaves (6:2), and elders (2 Tim 2:2). *Diakonia* is a general word for service, which Paul also uses for ministry in a special office (Rom 11:13; 1 Cor 16:15; 2 Cor 3:9). While it seems that apostleship is in view in verse 12 (compare 1:1), the use of "service" to describe being an apostle is a reminder that even this most significant office in the early church involved serving rather than being served (compare Mark 10:45). In modern sociological terms, ministry – as well as service in the church in general – is a "function" and not a "status," and remembering this will save believers from many arguments about the office and status of ministers in their own or other churches.

Paul's gratitude (1:12) is that of one who had previously been "a persecutor and a violent man" and who, from the perspective of his new life in Christ, viewed his old life as the life of "a blasphemer" (1:13). When Paul refers to his conversion, he almost invariably mentions his persecution of believers (Acts 22:4–8; 1 Cor 15:9; Gal 1:13). Without implying that sin is condoned, Paul says, "I was shown mercy because I acted in ignorance and unbelief" (1:13). His sin was not high-handed – a sin committed deliberately – but an

---

22. Johnson, *Letters to Paul's Delegates*, 121.

"unwitting" sin, committed in ignorance of Jesus's true significance (compare Num 15:22–31). However, we should not conclude from this verse that if Paul had acted in full knowledge, rather than in ignorance, he would *not* have been forgiven. His explanation of the circumstances in which he received mercy does not mean that Paul denies the role of grace. Paul speaks of the overflowing grace of Christ (1:14; see also 2 Tim 1:9; Titus 3:4–7), who came into the world to save sinners (1:15), not just those who were ignorant of their sin. As Barrett notes, "Paul's ignorance and unbelief, and the example he was to show to later generations, form as it were the context in which his forgiveness took place and became operative, and thus give to it a special significance."[23]

Superabundant or overflowing grace (1:14; compare Rom 5:20; 2 Cor 4:15) brought Paul out of his ignorance and opposition to Christ. Salvation is something given, an act of grace by God through Christ. When Paul speaks of "the grace of our Lord," the word "Lord" refers to Jesus, whom the apostle has already spoken of as "Christ Jesus our Lord" (1:12).

Along with overflowing grace, Paul also received "the faith and love that are in Christ Jesus" (1:14). Since this faith and love are "in Christ Jesus," their source is Christ. Paul possessed these qualities as one who was in union with Christ. His faith toward God and his fidelity in that relationship had been created in him by God; and the same can be said of love. This faith and love are not independent human attitudes or attributes but, rather, are called into being "in Christ." In this way, Paul the persecutor and blasphemer was transformed so that he had a new perspective of faith in place of unbelief and a new attitude of love in place of violence (1:13). In these things, too, Paul is a prototype of all believers. We note also the contrast with the false teachers, who had turned away from faith and love (1:6).

From the particular example of his own experience, from which even the worst of sinners may take hope, Paul now spells out a general truth (1:15–17). He begins with the first of what has been called the "trustworthy sayings." This formula, which Knight calls a "quotation-commendation formula,"[24] is found five times in the Pastoral Epistles but nowhere else in the NT (1 Tim 1:15; 3:1; 4:9; 2 Tim 2:11; Titus 3:8; for a similar formula, see Rev 21:5; 22:6). Each of the statements that follow or precede the phrase "trustworthy saying" concern an important Christian belief or practice. Paul uses this formula to link traditional material – perhaps a creed or liturgy used in the early

---

23. Barrett, *The Pastoral Epistles*, 45.
24. Knight, *The Pastoral Epistles*, 99.

church – with his present situation, while adding emphasis and solemnity to what he says. Here, Paul also stresses that the saying demands a response – wholehearted personal acceptance and application (compare 4:9). He uses this formula to restate a general truth which is illustrated by Paul's own life: "Christ Jesus came into the world to save sinners" (1:15). The Christian life is entirely dependent on God's gracious initiative in sending Christ into the world. This is the "trustworthy" content of the gospel, in contrast to the speculations and meaningless talk of the false teachers (1:4, 6). A person is not saved by speculation and words but by grace.

The expression "came into the world" (1:15), although not common in Paul's writings, appears frequently in John (1:9; 3:19; 11:27; 12:46; 16:28; 18:37) to refer to the incarnation of the preexistent Christ. The Pastorals, too, allude to Christ's preexistence and appearance "in the flesh" (3:16; see also 2 Tim 1:10).

The purpose of Christ's coming was "to save sinners" (1:15). Paul sees people as alienated from God through their own wrongdoing, while salvation involves delivering sinners from their sin and its consequences. This is the good news of the gospel, which Paul, as the "worst" of sinners (compare 1 Cor 15:9; Eph 3:8), had also received. Jesus did for Paul what he came to do for everyone. Paul was delivered from sin to a life of faith and love in the service of Christ (1:12–14). God, who is called "Savior" (1:1), acted to achieve salvation through Jesus. In the Pastoral Epistles, salvation may refer to the accomplished event (2 Tim 1:9; Titus 3:5) or to the future anticipated event (1 Tim 2:15; 4:16; 2 Tim 4:18).

Where does this trustworthy saying come from? Knight suggests that it is a restatement of what Jesus had said about himself (Matt 9:13; Mark 2:17; Luke 5:32; 19:10), along with the Johannine concept of Jesus coming into the world (John 12:46–47).[25]

After the saying about Christ saving sinners, Paul adds "of whom I am the worst" (1:15b; compare Eph 3:8). There is a sense of awareness of his sinfulness before God, combined with the powerful sense of God's unconditional grace despite this sin. Note, too, the present tense: "I *am* the worst" (emphasis added), not "I *was* the worst." As Fee notes, Paul "recognized himself as always having the status of 'sinner redeemed.'"[26]

---

25. Knight, *The Pastoral Epistles*, 101–2; see also Marshall, *The Pastoral Epistles*, 397–99.
26. Fee, *1 & 2 Timothy*, 53.

Paul goes on to show the significance of his own salvation for others (1:16). Christ demonstrated "immense patience" by being merciful to Paul, delaying judgment and giving him an opportunity to repent and receive salvation. Although God's patience with sinners is often mentioned in both Testaments (Ps 86:15; Rom 9:22; 1 Pet 3:20), it is only in 1 Timothy that there is reference to Christ's patience (1:16). Christ, as one who can act in God's stead, is shown as fulfillling the actions of God.

This patience was "immense" because Paul was "the worst of sinners" – someone who had even tried to destroy the church. Paul thus sees himself as an example or prototype of Christ's redemption, demonstrating the overflowing mercy which any sinner can experience. The "lesser to the greater" argument – also used by Jesus in his teaching (see Matt 6:25–33) – is evident here. If Christ showed patience and mercy even to Paul, will he not also do so for all others (compare 1 Tim 2:6)? Christ's patience should prevent anyone from despairing of Christ's mercy. Perhaps Paul also had in mind the false teachers. If Paul, the worst of sinners, could be saved, then the false teachers could also receive grace and be saved. The passage also underlines the authenticity of the gospel Paul preached by showing its transforming power in his own life.

These verses also give a solution to a problem posed earlier by reference to the law's role in exposing sin (1:9–10). There, Paul said nothing about the solution to the problem caused by such sins. Here, Paul gives the solution. By God's grace, Paul was transformed from being the worst of sinners to being an apostle of Christ Jesus. Other "lawbreakers and rebels" (1:9) can also receive mercy and be transformed by grace.

But this offer of mercy and grace is "for those who would believe in him and receive eternal life" (1:16). To "believe" involves both recognition of the person and work of Christ and personal trust in him. The result of such faith is "eternal life" – a transformed life with God and Christ in the future (Titus 1:2; 3:7), as well as joy in the present (1 Tim 4:8; 6:12; 2 Tim 1:9–10).

As he contemplates God's mercy and the salvation Christ brings to undeserving sinners, Paul bursts into praise (1:17). The experience of God's mercy and grace must lead us to worship, and our worship must be rooted in a true apprehension of the gospel of grace. Paul's doxology was probably used by the early Christian community in its liturgy.

"To the King eternal" means that God is the eternal and sovereign King, the ruler in the past, present, and future (for a song declaring God's kingship, see Rev 15:3–4). The terms "immortal" and "invisible" – common in Greek philosophical writings and Jewish literature, and also used in the undisputed

Pauline letters (Rom 1:20, 23) – signify that God is truly God. The phrase "the only God" underlines the monotheism of both Testaments and is an affirmation of great importance, asserting that there is no God but the one true God. "Honor" designates that which rightly belongs to God, and so people should seek to give such honor to God. "Glory" is "the luminous manifestation of God's person, his glorious revelation of himself."[27] In a doxology, it expresses the desire that God's glory continue to be seen and that appropriate praise be given to extol and acknowledge God's glory. "For ever and ever" brings out the concept of eternity. Jewish and NT doxologies often conclude with "Amen."

In this section in which the grace and patience shown in Christ has been emphasized, the doxology speaks of God in transcendent terms, rather than portraying him as involved in the world. The contrast, however, is significant. It is the King of the ages – who is transcendent and who alone is God – who has come into the world in Christ to save sinners. This marvelous act of grace and mercy should lead to praise, honor, and glory being given to God by his people.

1:18–20 PAUL'S CHARGE TO TIMOTHY

Having explained the power of the gospel, as exemplified in his own life (1:12–17), Paul reiterates his charge to Timothy. Paul's "command" to Timothy (1:18) recalls the "command" that Timothy was to give the false teachers (1:3). Paul is not merely reiterating his charge concerning the false teachers but also including the wider instructions of this chapter, perhaps even the whole letter. Central to this charge is the defense and preservation of the true faith, which was now under threat.

Timothy was entrusted with this charge because of his call and enabling. The expression "my son" is the affectionate address of a spiritual father to his spiritual son. "The prophecies once made about you" may refer to the occasion when the elders laid hands on Timothy and prophesied (4:14; Acts 13:1–4). Recalling that significant occasion would undoubtedly have encouraged Timothy to remain strong when confronted by the false teachers so that he could "fight the battle well" (1:18). Writers used military images widely during this period (2 Cor 10:3–6; Eph 6:11–18; 1 Thess 5:8; 2 Tim 2:3–4). Timothy was not to wage warfare by using violence but by "holding on to faith and a good conscience" (1:19). Doing so would prevent Timothy from endangering himself as he opposed the false teachers. Here "faith" does not refer to a body of truth but to the act of trusting God. "A good conscience"

---

27. Knight, *The Pastoral Epistles*, 106.

is the state where a person's own moral self-evaluation assures them that they have been obedient to God. There is a close connection between faith and morality (compare 1:5; 3:9). The fight is against those who abandon a good conscience, shipwreck their faith, and blaspheme (1:19–20).

But a good conscience is not something one inevitably or automatically possesses. Historically, people in the West have argued about whether conscience is a function (something we do, like thinking) or an attribute (something we have, like a mind). Western wisdom holds that if people follow the dictates of conscience they cannot go wrong. It is because of this belief that Western societies place a high value on guarding the "freedom of conscience" – the freedom to act or speak as one's conscience dictates.

But much of this misses the reality we face in making decisions. We are not born with a well-formed conscience, nor are we given a conscience "ready to use" at some point in life. The individual's conscience must be "formed" or developed. This can happen in either of two ways – through programming or through a community of people.

A person's conscience can be "programmed," much as we program a computer, by manipulating inputs and establishing programs to secure predetermined outputs when certain triggers are released. This programming may occur in the home, through education, by deliberate ideological indoctrination, or by persistent social influence and peer pressure. The intention, which may be benevolent or manipulative, is often unconscious. As we saw in the twentieth century, the outcome of this process can be tragic. Mass ideological movements like European fascism, international communism, extreme communalism, and racism have claimed countless victims – both followers who acted "in good conscience" and their victims.

The second way in which conscience can be formed is within a community of people. Some modern sociologists argue that many of our most cherished values, attitudes, and convictions come from the community and the society in which we live. But we know from our own experience that just being "religious" or even belonging to a Christian community is not enough. Far too many people have grown up in places where centuries of ethnic and political strife, often with deep religious convictions, have engendered the moral conviction that murder, and other forms of political violence are legitimate and even necessary actions. Even a "Christian" conscience, formed in such an environment, may not be an infallible guide to good conduct.

What all this means is that we must always be aware that everything we do within our church communities – our attitudes as much as our teaching – shapes and forms the consciences of all who are involved, from the most recently baptized child to the elders and pastors. If people are to have the power of moral self-evaluation – that is, "a good conscience" – this is something that needs to grow out of the inner life of the community of faith, shaped by the ministry of the risen Christ, and empowered by the Holy Spirit. It is not that the community should seek to program its members, for this is manipulative and harmful. Rather, we must be seriously committed to forming communities in which people naturally encounter and take up attitudes and values that enhance human life and further the purposes of God.

The Pastorals, with their emphasis on love and good conduct as the outward expression of faith, were written on the assumption that this is how people are to be formed in discipleship. In Asian societies – where community solidarity is strong and where people often follow the lead of strong people or conform to patterns of behavior called for by powerful leaders – the role of the congregation in forming "a good conscience" and a healthy power of moral self-evaluation in its members is vital.

Paul says that some have "rejected" a good conscience (1:19); clearly, the false teachers are in view here. A good conscience is one that is rightly aligned with God, making a person aware of whether they have been obedient to God (1 Tim 1:5); rejecting a good conscience involves being disobedient to God. The false teachers had rejected a good conscience and, thereby, shipwrecked their faith. To "shipwreck" is literally to break a ship to pieces; it was used as a metaphor for moral or religious disaster and would have been a vivid image of destruction for the listening church. The only specific indication of what might have been involved is blasphemy (1:20). The false teachers might have been wronging God by making false statements about him.

Hymenaeus and Alexander must have been well-known in the Ephesian church (1:20). The phrase "among them" implies that others, too, had shipwrecked their faith. Hymenaeus, along with Philetus, was someone who had claimed that "the resurrection has already taken place" (2 Tim 2:17–18). Both Hymenaeus and Alexander (probably the person mentioned in 2 Tim 4:14) appear to have been church leaders who later became false teachers.

These two individuals had already been "handed over to Satan to be taught not to blaspheme" (1:20; compare 1 Cor 5:3–5, 13). Turning someone over to Satan involved putting a person out of the congregation.

> Whereas congregations would normally have prayed for one another, there were evidently cases where petition would shift

from divine protection to divine discipline (with Satan as God's agent). Sometimes harsh measures are required to wake people up.[28]

The purpose of this discipline was reform – specifically, that they might learn not to blaspheme (compare 1 Cor 5:5). Therefore, there was hope that the false teachers might repent and be restored. Perhaps they might have resolved not to blaspheme when they realized that their beliefs and actions had separated them from God's people and thus also from God.

The mention of blasphemy means that the passage ends on a hopeful note. Paul himself had been a blasphemer (1:13), yet through the overflowing mercy and grace of Christ he was saved and appointed to service. Hymenaeus, Alexander, and others were blasphemers, but since "Christ Jesus came into the world to save sinners" (1:15), these false teachers could, like Paul, be saved and transformed (compare 2 Tim 2:25–26). This is an important principle and has a very real and relevant pastoral application for us. We are often quick to condemn "false teachers." But this passage encourages us to pray for false teachers that they, like Paul, might know (again) the overflowing mercy and grace of Christ and be transformed. Accordingly, we can and should remain hopeful in our attitude to those who are currently teaching "false doctrines" (1:3).

The topic of the false teachers is taken up twice in this chapter (1:4–11, 18–20), forming a literary bracket around the presentation of Paul as an example of the saved sinner (1:12–17). This has the effect of contrasting the sound doctrine of the gospel – exemplified in Paul's teaching and experience – with the false teachers' myths, genealogies, meaningless talk, and wrongful use of the law. This contrast also demonstrates the significance of experience for true Christian faith, for Paul's theology grew out of and was validated by his experience of overwhelming grace. In contrast, the false teachers' theology, led by speculation, shipwrecked their faith.

The theme of apostolic faith (the gospel) thus binds together the whole of 1 Timothy 1. In the Ephesian church, the apostolic faith was under threat from the false teaching being propagated by some church leaders. Paul sent Timothy to the church as an apostolic representative to stop the spread of false teachings. Positively, this involved promoting the true gospel; negatively, Timothy was told to command the false teachers to stop teaching false doctrines. Because the false teachers were misusing the Scriptures, Paul demonstrates the proper

---

28. Yarbrough, *The Letters to Timothy and Titus*, 136.

use of God's word. He also narrates his own personal story of how he came to faith in Christ through the gospel. This was not just to encourage Timothy but to show the false teachers that the gospel is about saving sinners and making them God's children and servants, and to show that if they repented, they, like Paul, would also receive mercy from God.

> ## TRUTH, LOVE, AND SOCIAL SENSIBILITIES
>
> Paul instructs Timothy to confront the false teachers in the Ephesian church and to command them to stop teaching false doctrines. Filipino readers will probably feel somewhat uneasy with this direct, blunt, and bold approach. Many Asian readers will share this unease.
>
> Filipinos have very keen social sensibilities; they are friendly and generally nonconfrontational. This stems from the Filipino values of social and group harmony, where people consider not just their own feelings, perspectives, and benefits but also those of the whole group to which they belong. Also dominant in Filipino culture is the concept of *hiya* (shame). Just as a person does not want to be shamed, they also do not want to bring shame to another. This is connected to the concept of saving face: to save face is to avoid causing *hiya* to someone else as well as to avoid experiencing *hiya* yourself.
>
> These social sensibilities pose a problem when someone clearly needs to be corrected or held accountable for wrongdoing. The Filipinos' acute social sensibilities can be a boon by helping to make sure that the process of correcting a person does not end in losing the person altogether. In other words, if we are not careful, our actions for the sake of the truth may come across as being too legalistic and we may end up alienating the person altogether. The strength of the Filipino approach is to correct without causing undue hurt to the person in the process.
>
> But the weakness of the Filipino approach lies in its tendency to avoid correction altogether to ensure that no offense is caused. Usually, this is not because there is no desire to preserve truth but, rather, because the desire to preserve truth is trumped by fears of causing shame to the person. This problem is sometimes cast as a conflict between truth and love. In many instances, truth loses and love wins.
>
> Any unease over Paul's seemingly blunt and confrontational approach must be tempered by the fact that the false teachers in Ephesus, by spreading false teachings, were causing great damage to the body

of Christ. This was why Paul wrote with a great sense of urgency. Moreover, the reference to the excommunication of Hymenaeus and Alexander suggests that Paul had first used a preliminary and milder means of instructing the false teachers to refrain from teaching false doctrines and return to the truth. When such measures did not work, as a final resort, he excommunicated these two individuals.

When someone is doing something wrong that affects the community, it is important and urgent to take action to rectify the matter. Filipinos need to adopt this broader point of view, instead of just focusing on the dynamics of *hiya* and saving face.

Truth does matter. But what is truth? Truth is not just the truth of the necessity of not causing *hiya* on someone or avoiding *hiya* yourself. Truth is not just the importance of social cohesion and harmony. In 1 Timothy 1, Paul argues on the basis that truth is objective. His focus is gospel truth – the apostolic gospel that came from Jesus himself and that focuses on Jesus. The integrity of that truth is absolutely important. The apostolic gospel must be preserved and protected from any deviation or distortion. Love must not be played off against truth (as is sometimes argued) because, in fact, love and truth are not opposed to each other. Paul insists that Christians must uphold both. He says that the church must be growing in truth and abounding in love.

It is good news to Filipino readers that love does not preclude correction and discipline. Biblical love necessitates both. It is equally good news that truth needs to be preserved and protected against tendencies of neglect or watering down in the name of social harmony and cohesion.

1 TIMOTHY 2

Years ago, when one of the writers was a Bible college student in Manila, he saw a banner promoting an upcoming event at a local church. The banner announced "24-hour praise and worship." Although this may surprise many, especially those in the West, some churches in Asia do conduct long worship services and prayer meetings. Corporate worship, which is an essential part of church life, is Paul's concern in 1 Timothy 2; and church leaders in particular will find this chapter instructive.

Chapter 1 focuses on the purity of doctrine in the church – not just the need for doctrine but also, in the context of the Ephesian church, how the apostolic gospel was being threatened by teachers who were propagating false doctrines. Paul instructs Timothy to command such teachers to stop spreading false teachings and, positively, to return to and uphold the historic faith received from the apostles.

In chapter 2, Paul turns to public worship in the church. This chapter divides naturally into two parts: the role of prayer in public worship (2:1–7) and specific instructions about the roles of men and women in public worship (2:8–15).

2:1–7 PRAYER IN PUBLIC WORSHIP

Since chapters 2 and 3 do not refer directly to false teachers, it has often been thought that there is no connection between chapter 1 and the two chapters that follow. This has led to the view that the letter is primarily a manual of church order. However, as Fee argues, the whole letter is a response to the false teachers.[1] First, the chapter begins with "then" (Gk. *oun*), which suggests that there is a connection between chapters 1 and 2. Second, the instructions in 1 Timothy 2–3 are best understood as a response to the false teachers (as we will show further down). Third, the letter presupposes that the church was already fully functional with regard to its arrangements for worship and collecting money for the poor. What Paul recommends seems to be just some fine-tuning of this order – demeanor in prayer, qualifications for elders, and so on – because of specific problems that had been encountered in the church at Ephesus.

---

1. Fee, *1 and 2 Timothy, Titus*, 5–14.

So how does 1 Timothy 2:1–7 relate to the false teachers? Four times, the passage emphasizes that the gospel is for everyone: first, prayer is to be offered for "all people" (2:1); second, God wants "all people" to be saved (2:4); third, Christ gave himself as a ransom for "all people" (2:6); finally, Paul was a teacher to the Gentiles (2:7) – that is, to all nations. It seems likely then that the false teachers – by emphasizing myths and genealogies (1:4), wandering into meaningless talk (1:6), and in their teaching of the law (1:7) – had advocated that salvation was exclusivist or only for an elite.[2] Paul now counters this view. As Johnson notes, "Nowhere in the NT is there such an inclusive statement of hope concerning all humanity."[3]

Paul begins with "then" (*oun*), indicating a connection with what he said earlier about the false teachers (1:3, 18–20). He "then" urges that prayer be made for everyone (2:1) – and the emphasis on "all people" might have been because of the false teachers' exclusivist view. "First of all" may mean first in a sequence or may indicate that this is what is most important. The four words for prayer – "petitions, prayers, intercession and thanksgiving" – were probably not intended to distinguish strictly between different types of prayer but to emphasize that prayer must be all-embracing. Thanksgiving, as an expression of gratitude to God, emphasizes that requests are made in the context of conscious thankfulness, and Paul has already given us an example of such thanksgiving in 1 Timothy 1:12–17. The church must be a praying community and one that is all-inclusive in its concerns.

The exhortation to pray for "all people" counteracts a narrowness on the part of the false teachers. Elsewhere, Paul places God's care for "all people" in the context of false teachers (2:4, 6; 4:10).[4] Further, each of the four references to God as Savior in the Pastoral letters is in a context that connects God as Savior with *all people*.[5] The false teachers might have believed that only the elite could hope for salvation.

Prayer for civil authorities is specifically commanded (2:2). The lives of all people – including Christians whose concern is to live a godly life and proclaim the gospel – are affected by governing authorities. "Kings" refers to supreme rulers, including the emperor and less important kings of the East,

---

2. See also Budiman, who identifies gnostic and Judaic elements of elitism in the false teaching. R. Budiman, *Tafsiran Alkitab: Surat-surat Pastoral I, II Timotius dan Titus* (Jakarta: BPK Gunung Mulia, 1997), 17.
3. Johnson, *Letters to Paul's Delegates*, 132.
4. See Knight, *The Pastoral Epistles*, 62.
5. See 1 Timothy 2:3–4; 4:10; Titus 2:10–11; 3:2, 4.

while "all those in authority" includes those involved in civil authority (Rom 13:1–7; Titus 3:1; 1 Pet 2:13–17). Clearly, none of these people in authority were Christians. But prayer should not be limited simply to Christian leaders. Jewish communities regularly offered prayers for civil leaders (Ezra 6:10; Jer 29:7).[6] In this way, Jews and Christians could fulfill their duty as those living within a certain political and cultural order, while acknowledging God's hand on earthly rulers (Rom 13:1–7). Gloer and Stepp comment:

> The structure of governments may change, and the titles and names of governing officials will change along with those structures, but the need to pray for those officials remains the same. Indeed, whether Christians agree with those in authority over them or not, those who work in government are God's servants, established by God to achieve good purposes (Rom 13:1–7). Throughout Christian history, believers have prayed for the government they lived under, even when they didn't agree with it, especially when they didn't agree with it.[7]

The call to pray for kings and those in authority would not have been unfamiliar to those familiar with the Hebrew scriptures, for they would have recalled that the Persian ruler Cyrus was called God's "shepherd" and God's "anointed" (messiah) and that God's purposes were accomplished through him (Isa 44:28; 45:1). Similarly, the rulers of our day may also have a role to play as liberators or agents of God's justice, although they may fail to fulfill this role if they are proud and arrogantly defiant of God in their pursuit of their own interests. Hope for the coming of the *Ratu Adil* (Just Ruler) has been a persistent theme in many Asian societies.

Budiman also draws attention to Jeremiah 29:7,[8] where the exiles in Babylon are told, "Seek the welfare of the city where I have sent you into exile and pray to the Lord on its behalf, for in its welfare you will find your welfare" (NRSV). Spiritually, we may sometimes feel exiled even in our own homeland. Praying for those who rule and exercise responsibility over us may help us to realize that we share many concerns and interests with our neighbors, as well as being a way of exercising a priestly ministry of intercession on their behalf.

---

6. See also 1 Maccabees 7:33 and Philo, *In Flaccum*, 49.
7. W. H. Gloer and P. L. Stepp, *Reading Paul's Letters to Individuals. A Literary and Theological Commentary on Paul's Letters to Philemon, Titus, and Timothy*. Reading the New Testament (Macon: Smyth & Helwys, 2013), 155–56.
8. Budiman, *Tafsiran Alkitab*, 18.

While Paul acknowledges earthly leaders as kings and rulers, by praying for these leaders "there is an implicit critique of any claims they might put forward concerning their absolute authority. By placing them in God's hands, their power is clearly subordinated to God's."[9]

The specific purpose of such prayer is "that we may live peaceful and quiet lives in all godliness and holiness" (2:2). While the first-person plural "we" shows that the whole Christian community is in view, Paul probably also had in mind all men and women for whom the church was praying. Paul speaks of a similar ideal of a quiet life in 1 Thessalonians 4:11–12 and 2 Thessalonians 3:12.

How does one understand the desire to "live peaceful and quiet lives"? Some scholars see this as evidence that the church was settling down and seeking peace with its surrounding society after hopes of the imminent return of Christ had faded. These scholars argue that the letter represents the ideal of "Christian citizenship."[10] However, Kidd has shown that the phrase "live peaceful and quiet lives" is an exhortation to devote oneself to God who gives eternal life, rather than focusing on the temporal elements of this world (6:17–19).[11] Further, MacDonald shows that belief in the second coming of Jesus must lead to ethical changes in a person's life.[12]

Fee offers an alternative explanation, linking the call to prayer for those in authority with the situation created by the false teachers.[13] Because of the activities of these teachers, the life of the community had been disrupted (1:4) and the church and its message might have been brought into disrepute (3:7; 5:14; Titus 2:5, 8). Paul was concerned "that God's name and our teaching may not be slandered" (6:1). Verse 2 is not advocating a trouble-free life (see 2 Tim 1:8; 3:12). Rather, Paul was concerned that the activities of the false teachers might result in slander of Christians by outsiders, which would then hinder the mission of the church. Paul urges that prayer be offered for those in authority since such people are responsible for maintaining a stable political and social

---

9. Johnson, *Letters to Paul's Delegates*, 130.
10. See W. G. Kümmel, *Introduction to the New Testament*, revised edition (London: SCM Press, 1975), 384. For further discussion, see R. M. Kidd, *Wealth and Beneficence in the Pastoral Epistles*. SBL Dissertation Series 122 (Atlanta: Scholars Press, 1990), 9–34.
11. See Kidd, *Wealth and Beneficence in the Pastoral Epistles*, 124–58.
12. M. Y. MacDonald, *The Pauline Churches. A Socio-historical Study of Institutionalization in the Pauline and Deutero-Pauline Writings*. Society for New Testament Studies Monograph Series 60 (Cambridge: Cambridge University Press, 1988), 159–234. We should also note that Paul retains a lively hope for the return of Christ in the Letters (see 2 Tim 4:8; Titus 2:13).
13. Fee, *1 and 2 Timothy, Titus*, 63–64.

environment which makes it possible for all people to live peaceful and quiet lives, which also helps the church to continue its mission unhindered. This interpretation is supported by the phrase "in all godliness and holiness" (2:2), which refers to outwardly observable behavior that is acceptable in society and does not bring the Christian community into disrepute.

Why is Paul concerned that the Christian community be accepted by the world around them? Why does he care what outsiders think and say about Christians? Towner has shown that the main reason is mission. He notes, "The manner of life here described has the evaluating eye of the observer in mind . . . and is meant to recommend the gospel to those who look on."[14] The emphasis on salvation in this passage and elsewhere in the Pastoral Epistles supports this view. This principle can be seen at work in some modern mission situations. When compact village communities encounter the gospel for the first time, openness is enhanced and the Christian faith community grows when the values, attitudes, and conduct of believers are respected by the community at large since nonbelievers tend to judge these believers by the community's own standards of behavior.

"Godliness" and "holiness," both key terms in the Pastoral Epistles, were common in the Greco-Roman world and refer to outwardly observable behavior. "Godliness" (*eusebeia*), which can also be translated "piety" or "religion," refers to general behavior that is pleasing to God and expresses the Christian's faith in action. The heart of true godliness is Christ Jesus and his saving work (3:16). "Holiness" (*semnotes*) denotes "a solemn, serious, dignified attitude and behavior, 'the attitude (interior and exterior) of respect with regard to the sacred realities, such as decency, seriousness, gravity.'"[15] The ultimate goal of praying for civil leaders is that Christians would be able to live out their Christian faith as it should be lived, in godliness and holiness.

Among the things that please "God our Savior" (2:3) are the prayers offered by God's people for everyone (2:1), God's people living "peacefully" with outsiders (2:2), and God's people wanting all people to be saved as God himself wants everyone to be saved (2:4) – that is, "to come to a knowledge of the truth" (2:5). The reference to God as "our Savior" is a reminder to readers of their own salvation through God's mercy.

---

14. P. H. Towner, *1–2 Timothy & Titus*. IVP NT Commentary Series (Downers Grove: InterVarsity Press, 1994), 65.
15. W. Mounce, *The Pastoral Epistles*. WBC (Nashville: Thomas Nelson, 2000), 84, quoting Spicq.

PRAYING FOR RULERS

Paul's discussion about praying for our rulers so that we may enjoy peace and good order and so that the gospel may reach as many people as possible will resonate with many Asian readers. Asia's century and a half of social and political change has claimed many victims, and many still live in the aftermath of wars of liberation and struggles against despotic and corrupt regimes or are still trying to deal with the displacement of populations, the care of victims of bombs, landmines, and terrorism, and the problem of homeless people and orphaned children.

But Asian Christians are fiercely loyal to their own nations and peoples. In many cases, these loyalties have been tested and refined in the struggles of political liberation and nation building as colonial regimes were overthrown. The first readers or hearers of the Pastoral Epistles may not have had very strong feelings about their citizenship (and many may not even have been citizens) because they still believed that Christ would return in the immediate future. But most Asian Christians are keenly aware of and deeply appreciative of being citizens of important nations and the inheritors of ancient cultures and social systems. For instance, Thai Christians are as proud of their monarch and nation as any of their fellow citizens. Church leaders in Myanmar regularly send ecumenical visitors off to visit the shrines that symbolize the ancient religious and social forces that have made them, like their Buddhist neighbors, the people they are. Indonesians, both Christians and non-Christians, still carrying the fire of their struggle for freedom, are likely to adopt a "my country, right or wrong" attitude when aspects of their political and social life are criticized by outsiders. Indian Christians echo the slogan, "We are all Indians, let none divide us!" Chinese Christians share their nation's pride in five thousand years of recorded history and the ancient traditions and cultural treasures that have made China a great nation. Many Christians in China – within the state-registered "patriotic" churches as well as within unregistered churches – hold to a very strong sense of nationalism. They pray often for their country, for their government leaders, and for the evangelization of the people of their motherland. A striking example of this nationalism is expressed in the so-called "Canaan Hymns," written by a peasant woman from a house church in Henan and sung in both registered and unregistered churches throughout China. Her hymn "China Belongs to the Most High" reads:

> Even when I have only one drop of blood, one drop of sweat,
> it would be shed upon China. Even when I have only one breath, and
> one ounce of strength, it would be offered to China.
> China ah!
> How many of your children over the oceans are weeping in prayers for you,
> standing by the seashore,
> at all times holding you at heart?
> Listen to the sound of a mother's calling across the ocean. The people
> of China are sons and daughters of God.
> China ah! China!
> Quickly come and find rest. God has found you.
> You are no longer lost while scaling mountains, crossing waters.
> China belongs to the Most High![1]
>
> Similarly, Christians in other Asian contexts are aware that God has called them to discipleship in their own nation, among their own people, for whom they have a natural love and affection.
>
> So the Christian's prayer for rulers is not just a conventional prayer for peace and quiet. It is a prayer that the motherland will flourish and be at peace; that harmony will reign; that the Just Ruler may appear; that the people will be fed and housed and able to live in dignity; and, for some, "that they will be saved from the time of trial" (Matt 6:13).
>
> ---
> 1. C. Starr, *Chinese Theology: Text and Context* (New Haven: Yale University Press, 2016), 266–67.

Paul then states that God "wants all people to be saved" (2:4). A connection is made between God's attitude to all people and the call to pray for all people (2:1). The reminder that God is Savior of all must encourage Christians to pray for all people. The gospel is universal in scope.

In an Asian context, where many churches are ethnic in composition and often made up of people from distinct language groups, it is important to emphasize the universality of God's offer of salvation in Jesus Christ. Our own church is important but so is the church of our neighbor. God, who wants all people to be saved, must surely delight in the rich diversity of Asian churches, from the most ancient churches of India to the most recent new church in Singapore, from the high Anglican and Syrian Orthodox liturgies in India to the free charismatic worship of a house church in Nepal.

Fr. Robert Karris, a modern Franciscan commentator, has drawn attention to the special way in which Paul draws implications for how we should live from the short creedal statements of faith he quotes in the Pastoral Epistles.[16] The statement that God "wants all people to be saved" reminds us of the call to pray for all and the need to develop a sympathetic understanding of traditions and practices which, though foreign to us, may speak to the hearts and minds of others. Because God desires all to be saved, we are to be ecumenical and not sectarian, internationalist while maintaining pride in our own nation and its peoples, open to diversity even when we cannot control it. Above all, we are to transcend the exclusivities of clan, race, caste, education, status, and wealth. If God desires all to be saved, then we must not separate ourselves from the fulfilllment of this task. It was said that the saintly Bishop Azariah of India (1874–1945) encouraged those coming into the church by a profession of faith to add to their vows of baptism and confirmation these words of Paul, "Woe is unto me, if I preach not the gospel!" (1 Cor 9:16 KJV).

Knight argues that the phrase "God . . . wants all people to be saved" means "all kinds of people,"[17] which would express the truth that Gentiles could be saved along with Jews. However, this interpretation evades the obvious and plain meaning of these words.[18] The concern of the text is to emphasize the universal scope of salvation,[19] in contrast to the false teachers who restricted the possibility of salvation to the elite. But Fee also notes that

> to say that God wants (not "wills," and therefore it must come to pass) all people to be saved, implies neither that all (meaning everybody) will be saved (against 3:6; 4:2; or 4:10) nor that God's will is somehow frustrated since all, indeed, are not saved.[20]

God wants everyone "to come to a knowledge of the truth" (2:4b). This stresses the rational aspect of belief and involves both coming to know and

---

16. R. J. Karris, *The Pastoral Epistles*, New Testament Message 17 (Wilmington: Michael Glazier, 1979), 60.
17. Knight, *The Pastoral Epistles*, 119.
18. See Hanson, *The Pastoral Epistles*, 68.
19. See P. H. Towner, *The Letters to Timothy and Titus*. NICNT (Grand Rapids: Eerdmans, 2006), 178.
20. Fee, *1 and 2 Timothy, Titus*, 64.

acknowledging the truth of the gospel; the emphasis is probably on the process involved in coming to knowledge. The phrase "knowledge of the truth," which functions as a technical term for conversion, is used only in the Pastorals and Hebrews (2 Tim 2:25; 3:7; Titus 1:1; Heb 10:26). Paul uses the word *epignosis* (knowledge) rather than the more common word *gnosis*. It is noteworthy that Paul does use the word *gnosis* in a negative sense later in the letter: "Turn away from godless chatter and the opposing ideas of what is falsely called knowledge" (6:20). Here, Paul clearly had the false teachers' "gnosis" in view.

Verse 5 is probably a quotation from an early Christian liturgy, but it is one that fits Paul's present purpose. The basis for the earlier argument that God "wants all people to be saved" is that "there is one God and one mediator," as affirmed by the Jewish creed (Deut 6:4) and Paul (Rom 3:29–30; 1 Cor 8:4). If there is more than one God, then, presumably, one should pray to those other gods for the salvation of some people. This was how pagan polytheism worked. But since there is only one God, there are no other gods for both Jew and non-Jew, and so prayer should be made to the one God for all people. As Barrett notes, "The universal scope of the one way of salvation is grounded in the fact that there is one God."[21]

God's concern for the salvation of all is shown by the provision of one mediator "who gave himself as a ransom for all people" (2:5–6). If the mediator ransoms all people, then clearly the one God wants all people to be saved through that one mediator. A mediator is one who "establishes a relation which would not otherwise exist."[22] The term was used for a go-between who was an arbiter or negotiator in legal disputes and business arrangements.[23] Paul emphasizes the humanity of Jesus Christ, not his maleness – since the word used is *anthrōpos* (human being) rather than *anēr* (a male person) – because it is by his humanness that he identifies with those he represents as mediator. The Pastoral Epistles make several very elevated claims about Christ, including linking him with God's activity, giving him God's name of Lord, ascribing preexistence to him, and stating that he is God (Titus 2:13). But Paul was in no doubt that Jesus Christ is also fully human (Rom 5:12–21; Phil 2:7). Some later gnostics spoke of many angelic intermediaries who were neither

---

21. Barrett, *The Pastoral Epistles*, 51.
22. See A. Oepke, "μεσίτης, μεσιτεύω," in *TDNT*, Volume 4, edited by G. Kittel (Grand Rapids: Eerdmans, 1967), 601.
23. Compare Josephus, *Ant.* 7.8.5; Testament of Daniel 6:2; see also Job 9:32–33.

truly human nor truly divine. Christ is both fully human and fully divine; he is also unique, for there is only "one mediator."

The term *antilutron* (ransom) is only found here in the NT, although *lutron* (which means "price of release") occurs twice (Matt 20:28; Mark 10:45). *Antilutron* can mean a price paid to free captives or "redemption" in the sense of freeing someone from bondage. In the NT, words of the *lutr-* family are used of ransom or redemption from sin (Col 1:14; Titus 2:14) and, positively, of redeeming a people for God (Eph 1:14).

The ransom is "for" all, which can mean "on behalf of" (representation) or "in the place of" (substitution). Knight suggests that since the meaning "on behalf of" fits all three occurrences in this chapter (2:1, 2, 6), it probably has that sense here.[24] Christ died for all as a representative. The text speaks of Christ the mediator, providing through his death, on behalf of humanity, the means of liberation from sin and its consequences, which we could not provide for ourselves. In this context, the emphasis is on the universal significance of Jesus's self-giving: Christ gave himself as a ransom for all other human beings. This underlines again the universal scope of God's will to save. There is also a link back to verse 1 – we are to pray for all people because Christ the one mediator gave himself as a ransom for all people. The saying "gave himself as a ransom for all people" (2:6) closely resembles Jesus's declaration that he came "to give his life as a ransom for many" (Mark 10:45).

Christ's giving of himself was attested to at the proper time (2:6) by the witness of the apostles. Paul, too, was appointed to testify as "a herald and an apostle" and to spread this testimony as "a true and faithful teacher of the Gentiles" (2:7).

Paul's ministry involved three roles: herald, apostle, and teacher. The term "herald" stresses Paul's evangelistic role as an announcer of good news. Some might have challenged Paul's apostleship, arguing that apostleship was limited to the Twelve. We know from Paul's letters that his apostleship was often challenged (1 Cor 9:1–2; 2 Cor 11:5) and that he countered these challenges by insisting that his apostleship was a divine appointment (Gal 1:1; 1 Tim 2:7). Others may have criticized Paul for sharing the gospel with the Gentiles. Kelly suggests that "with their Judaizing tendencies they [the false teachers] may well have been critical of evangelizing non-Jews."[25] Paul appeals to God's

---

24. Knight, *The Pastoral Epistles*, 122.
25. J. N. D. Kelly, *A Commentary on The Pastoral Epistles*. Black's New Testament Commentaries (London: A & C Black, 1963), 65.

call on his life to be "a true and faithful teacher of the Gentiles," affirming that his apostleship and ministry to the Gentiles were by God's direct appointment and insisting, "I am telling the truth, I am not lying" (2:7).[26]

Paul calls himself a "teacher" only here and in 2 Timothy 1:11, although he frequently refers to himself as being engaged in teaching (1 Cor 4:17; 2 Thess 2:15). In Paul's other letters, teachers are distinguished from apostles (1 Cor 12:28–29; Eph 4:11). Perhaps Paul uses the word "teacher" here to emphasize his authority over against the false teachers. The three terms herald, apostle, and teacher together emphasize that Paul was involved in evangelism, exhortation, and instruction, and that he was Christ's authoritative eyewitness and spokesperson, particularly to the Gentiles, which once again emphasizes the universal scope of redemption.

Paul was a teacher of the Gentiles "in faith and truth" (2:7b NRSV). His ministry sought to accomplish what God desires for all people – that is, faith which leads to them being "saved" and truth which leads to them coming to "a knowledge of the truth" (2:4). This cannot be said of the false teachers. Alternatively, the phrase may point to Paul's faithfulness in carrying out his task of being "a true and faithful teacher of the Gentiles" (2:7b NIV).

This section (2:1–7) thus emphasizes that the church, like Paul, must be involved in mission. As Fee notes, mission is

> inherent in the very character of God, who wants all *people* to be saved and to come to a knowledge of the truth, and in the redemptive work of Christ, who gave himself as a ransom for all *people*. It is therefore incumbent on God's people to proclaim that good news.[27]

2:8–15 MEN AND WOMEN IN WORSHIP

As in the West, various Christian denominations in Asia also take differing approaches to this passage, particularly in relation to the status of women in the ordained ministry of the church. One of the writers grew up in the Philippines, where women were (and still are) not permitted to participate in governance and preaching roles in the local church. This same view is espoused by certain denominations in other countries as well.

---

26. For similar statements, see Romans 9:1; 2 Corinthians 11:31; Galatians 1:20.
27. Fee, *1 and 2 Timothy, Titus*, 67, emphasis his.

1 Timothy

When the same writer visited mainland China for the first time in 2011, he was greatly surprised by the overwhelming number of women pastors there. In fact, during a visit to a province in Northeast China, all the pastors he met were women, including the senior pastor of a megachurch in the city of Dalian. He could not help asking himself, "Where are the men?" But he also could not help saying to himself, "Thanks be to God for these women who have heeded God's call upon their lives to serve the church!"

As Paul continues his instructions on prayer (2:1–7), why does he address the issue to which he now turns (2:8–15)? And why does he spend so much time addressing women and speak so briefly to the men in the community? Further, Paul appears to restrict the ministry of women to the extent that they cannot teach or have authority over men. But this seems to contradict passages in Paul's other letters, where equality between men and women is advocated (1 Cor 7:4; 11:11–12; Gal 3:28) and where women are referred to as being active in ministry (Rom 16:1–7, 12; 1 Cor 11:3–16; 14:34–35; Phil 4:2–3; Col 4:15). Why does Paul adopt such an approach toward women? Is this passage to be regarded as containing universally binding and normative teaching? Or did Paul intend this teaching for a particular local situation rather than to all churches in all places and at all times?

To find answers to these questions, we must recognize that Paul had in view the false teachers and the situation they had created in the church. The letter has many references to the false teachers and their false doctrines (1:3–7, 19–20; 6:3–5, 20–21). Paul's instructions may point to the strife caused in the community by the false teachers. When we consider the letter as a whole, there are strong indications that the teaching about women here is also connected with what the false teachers had been doing.

First, Paul warns that "in later times some will abandon the faith and follow deceiving spirits and things taught by demons" (4:1). He describes young widows who had been led astray by false doctrines, and his reference to these widows having "turned away to follow Satan" (5:15) suggests that by following the false teachers these women were following Satan. The false teachers seem to have had a particular appeal to and influence among women: "They are the kind who worm their way into homes and gain control over gullible women" (2 Tim 3:6). This may imply that the false teachers conducted a "special mission"[28] among women. The false teachers were eager for financial

---

28. A. J. Hultgren, "I-II Timothy, Titus," in *I-II Timothy, Titus, II Thessalonians*, by A. J. Hultgren and R. Aus, 9–189. Augsburg Commentary on the NT (Minneapolis: Augsburg, 1984), 67.

gain (6:5; Titus 1:11), and it is likely that these women, some of whom were wealthy (2:9), were offering them financial support.

Second, the false teachers might have attacked the importance of marriage, prompting Paul to counter their arguments by referring to Adam and Eve (2:13–14) as a possible allusion to marriage. Later in the letter, Paul advises younger widows to marry, have children, and take care of their homes (5:14).

Third, younger widows in the church had been "going about from house to house" – probably house church to house church – "saying things they ought not to" (5:13). This suggests that these women had not just been following the false teachers but also spreading their false teachings.

Fourth, Paul was concerned about the church's reputation in society (3:7; 5:14; 6:1; Titus 2:5, 8, 10). If the false teaching encouraged women to take on roles which were not generally acceptable for women in that society, thus endangering the church's reputation, Paul would have been concerned about this. We believe that this was indeed the case.

Fifth, a belief prevalent at the time was that "the resurrection has already taken place" (2 Tim 2:18). The view that believers had already experienced the resurrected state in some spiritual sense might have led the false teachers to proclaim that all gender distinctions had ceased to exist because such distinctions belonged to the old age. This, in turn, might have led to some women in the congregation attempting to usurp leadership and teaching roles for which they were not equipped or trained – this was especially true of wealthy women (whose presence in the community is supported by verse 9) who were freer from the restraints imposed by economic need. Paul might have objected to women teaching in the church at Ephesus because they lacked the proper training, were under the influence of false teachers, and perhaps also because this was contrary to cultural norms at the time.[29]

There were undoubtedly men in the Ephesian church who also followed the false teachers; in fact, all Paul's named opponents are men (1 Tim 1:20; 2 Tim 1:15; 2:17; 4:14), and the propagation of the false teaching was probably what had led to "anger" and "disputing" among the men (2:8). However, it seems likely that women were more easily influenced by the false teachers and that some women were also involved in promoting these teachings. It is against this background that 1 Timothy 2:9–15 is best understood. Hultgren notes,

---

29. See further in Towner, *1–2 Timothy & Titus*, 75–76; P. H. Towner, *The Goal of Our Instruction: The Structure of Theology and Ethics in the Pastoral Epistles*. JSNTSup 34 (Sheffield: JSOT Press, 1989), 38–41, 210–12.

The author apparently thought that great strides in the battle against the heretics could be made, and as many people as possible be kept in the true faith, if at least one large segment (the women) could be excluded from teaching and exercising authority. By doing so, and by insisting that they learn in silence and with submissiveness, the author has effectively reduced the pool of possible heretical teachers.[30]

This suggests that the teaching in 1 Timothy 2:9–15 is situational and related to a particular group of women and was not intended by Paul to be binding for all times and places (although we should note that some commentators argue that it was timeless and universally applicable teaching). This passage must be understood in the context of the overall NT teaching on the role of women in the church, which includes the equality espoused by Galatians 3:28 and the outworking of that principle which led to women exercising leadership in the early church. Both this passage in 1 Timothy and 1 Corinthians 14:33–35 must be understood in relation to the basic principle of Galatians 3:28, not vice versa.[31]

We should also note that the teaching of this passage is consistent with Paul's overall attitude to authority structures in the church, structures which are diverse and based on the context of each church. Those who read or hear these letters are expected to contextualize Paul's teachings with the overall aim of fostering unity and good conduct.[32] Paul had in mind particular problems of discipline and pastoral care in the communities to which he wrote, and he addressed those problems directly.

Modern Asian church communities are all too familiar with a variety of sectarian movements that seek to grow at the expense of established congregations. Very often the strategy of such groups is to identify a segment or segments within the Christian congregation that can be destabilized and then either lured away or used as a bridgehead into the congregation itself. It seems that it is this latter strategy that is being addressed in 1 Timothy. Some of the false teachers were trying to entrap women by teachings that disagreed with the apostles' teachings. Paul instructs Timothy to prevent such false teachers and their students from promoting teachings contrary to sound doctrine.

---

30. Hultgren, "I-II Timothy, Titus," 67–68.
31. See F. F. Bruce, *The Epistle of Paul to the Galatians*. NIGTC (Exeter: Paternoster Press, 1982), 190.
32. Karris, *The Pastoral Epistles*, 62.

The role of women in the church is a key issue for many Asian Christians, Asian theologians, and Asian church leaders. In seeking a biblical basis for dealing with this issue, we must look beyond passages that have a particular contextual reference and review the NT material as a whole. At the same time, a careful study of contextual references to issues of this kind is also valuable. In today's church we need to be alert to all kinds of sectarian infiltration. Not only are there sectarian groups promoting unbalanced, and frequently unhealthy teachings, there are also groups springing up that promote various religious and quasi-religious patterns of life – for instance, New Age cults that draw on folklore and the aspirations of people who feel marginalized in their own religions, as women might have felt in some early Christian communities.

Sadly, proselytism is also a growing feature of the modern church in Asia, as well as elsewhere. Proselytism is the building up of congregations, particular "ministries," or even whole denominations by attracting members from other churches. It is natural that, from time to time, people's convictions change, and they decide to cross one of the major confessional boundaries. But proselytism is the deliberate, intentional dislocation of people – who are happily engaged in witness and ministry where they are – as a policy or strategy for promoting the growth of another congregation or "ministry."

False teachings vary from region to region, especially as people interact with and incorporate religious practices prevalent in the region. Any teaching that goes against the sound doctrines of the apostles' teaching must be banned. Allowing false teachings to have free rein in a community can cause irreversible damage to the life and witness of the church. At the same time, following Paul's example, local churches must actively promote sound doctrine and good conduct.

Paul begins this section (2:8–15) by saying that he wants "the men everywhere to pray, lifting up holy hands without anger or disputing" (2:8). This verse is a bridge between what went before and what follows. The word "therefore" links it to the preceding verses, while the focus on how people should pray is related thematically to the previous section that made it clear that Christians should pray (2:1–7). Verse 8 is also connected to verse 9 by the fact that the latter has no verb and must be read in relation to the "I want" (*boulomai*) of verse 8. In addition, verse 8 addresses men and verses 9–15 address women, thus thematically linking verse 8 with what follows. Public prayer by more than one individual in a church gathering seems to be in view.

In an authoritative command, Paul addresses men – the word used is *anēr* (male) and not *anthrōpos* (man) – as a group. The word "everywhere" could indicate universality, but Paul was probably referring to the house churches in which the Christians were meeting in and around Ephesus, which implies that there was more than one house church in the city at the time. The house church was the fundamental structure of the early church in the NT period (compare Rom 16:3–5; 1 Cor 16:19 [which refers to a house church in Ephesus]; Col 4:15), as it continues to be in some parts of modern Asia. In the late 1980s, one of the writers attended a house church service in a township in Nepal that must have been very like a gathering of the first Christians. The people met for an informal, dignified, very lively, and charismatic service. While there were clearly identified leaders, everyone dressed in the same, everyday style, sat together on the same level, joining in worship that was led by designated church members and in which singing was accompanied by indigenous instruments. Such orderly worship was probably what Paul had in mind as he instructed Timothy.

Prayer is to be offered by "lifting up holy hands without anger or disputing" (2:8). The raising of hands in prayer is found both in the OT (Exod 9:29; 1 Kgs 8:54; Neh 8:6; Pss 28:2; 141:2) and in non-Christian literature. In the NT, however, it is mentioned only here. "Holy hands" represent the inward purity of a person's whole life. The emphasis on avoiding "anger" and "disputing" implies that such attitudes and actions are sins that hinder a person's prayers by creating a barrier between the person and God (Matt 5:23–24; Mark 11:25; 1 Cor 11:17–34). As Hultgren notes, "True worship of God can take place only when those who participate are at peace with others."[33]

Perhaps the false teachers' "unhealthy interest in controversies and quarrels about words" (6:4–5) resulted in arguments and disputes that disrupted prayer. It is likely that this situation prompted Paul to urge men to pray without engaging in such fruitless controversies. As we review the centuries that have passed since these words were written we might be forgiven for concluding that controversy is endemic in religion, not least in Christianity. Disputes seem endless and sometimes tragically violent. While some disputes have been over matters of profound importance, others have been so trivial as to be foolish.

A shipboard traveling companion in Eastern Indonesia told one of the writers that at his ordination in the late 1950s he had been required to make a formal renunciation of the errors of the Remonstrant Brethren – a movement of some significance in the past in the Netherlands, from which the founding missionaries of this Indonesian church had originally come. What significance

---

33. Hultgren, "I-II Timothy, Titus," 66.

this old controversy had for the life and witness of a modern Indonesian Reformed church was not clear to the writer or to his companion.

Asian responses to controversy vary. While Asian Christians are not immune to quarrels over doctrines and practices, there are examples of churches actively seeking to promote unity through diversity. In some countries, various churches broke out of their denominational boundaries to form union churches – for example, the Church of North India (CNI). The beautiful new CNI church built in the architecturally designed city of Chandigarh, in the Indian Punjab, has both a font for infant baptisms and a baptistry for full immersion adult baptisms. Here, one imagines, the congregation has learned to lift up holy hands in worship without anger or quarreling about this particular ancient dispute. Similarly, Baptists and Presbyterians joined hands to form the vibrant Church of Christ in Thailand.

The teaching of the Pastorals is that diversity is positive and must be accepted and affirmed, provided it is based on sound doctrine and promotes good conduct. Deciding which issues actually need to be debated in the interest of sound (but not necessarily uniform) doctrine is a matter of mature spiritual discernment. Many issues do not matter, and hence do not merit debate or discussion.

At yet another level, there is sometimes suspicion or distrust of theology among believers, both in Asia and in the West. Many people maintain that Christian life and doctrine are simple and should not be disrupted by scholarly arguments about matters too complicated to affect the lives of ordinary Christians. Some theology, to be sure, is arrogant and serves the interests of theologians in their ivory towers rather than edifying the church as a whole. But in every generation questions must be raised about the nature and content of the faith the church is teaching, about worship and mission, and about how Scripture is to be applied in modern life situations. Theology should seek to establish and affirm sound doctrine – by asking persistently of the church's teachings, "Is this really the gospel?" – and good conduct – by helping people to grapple with contemporary issues in the light of Scripture and the tradition of faith.

The Reformed (Calvinist) churches have given formal recognition to the theological office (the Teacher) in their church order. Other churches recognize the teaching office of the bishop or the designated theologian. In the Orthodox communion, this latter designation is limited to those who are formally recognized by church authorities as theologians.

Theology is important, but it is a human activity that forms part of the faithful response of fallible Christian people to the love and grace of God in Jesus Christ. Those who engage in theology will raise some questions that people do not want to address or issues that cannot easily be resolved. But theological reflection, when engaged upon in response to a genuine calling and authorization, is part of the healthy mission of the church. A vocation in theology should embody both academic rigor and the personal humility that arises from a realization that all one's work is conditional and subject to assessment and correction. When theologians worship, they too should be able to lift up holy hands in the sanctuary without anger or quarreling.

Paul then addresses the women (2:9). The word "also" connects this verse with verse 8, where the main verb is "pray." Paul first specifies the manner in which women must pray – they must "dress modestly, with decency and propriety" (2:9). He then names particular practices that violated the principles of modesty and decency: elaborately braided hair, jewelry, and ostentatious dress – which required expense, time, and effort. These were the normal attire of courtesans and harlots and those who were insubordinate to their husbands.[34] Women who dressed in extravagant outfits were widely regarded as disreputable, and the note of insubordination connected with such a style of dress might have been the reason for Paul's instruction in verse 11. Pearls were considered even more precious than gold. The OT, extrabiblical Jewish literature, and Greco-Roman literature also criticize women for inappropriate and immodest dress,[35] and the qualities that Paul praises in women are also affirmed in pagan and Jewish literature.

Fee suggests that there is a connection between the modesty that the apostles promote and the freedom of expression that the false teachers advocate.[36] For example, because of false teaching, some women had become "wanton against Christ" (5:11 RSV), were being "swayed by all kinds of evil desires" (2 Tim 3:6), and perhaps wore immodest clothing. In any case, dressing immodestly risked bringing the community itself into disrepute, and so this falls into the category of disruptive behavior that Paul was at pains to avoid.

---

34. Knight, *The Pastoral Epistles*, 135–36.
35. See, for example, Isaiah 3:16–26; in extra-Biblical Jewish literature; see, for example, 1 Enoch 8:1–2; Testament of Reuben 5:1–5; in Greco-Roman literature, see, for example, Juvenal 6.502–503; see also 1 Peter 3:4–5.
36. Fee, *1 and 2 Timothy, Titus*, 71.

Towner suggests that the problem was wealthy women who dressed in a way that demeaned the poor and so disturbed the church.[37]

Some women in the community were wealthy, well able to afford luxuries. Some of them might have owned the houses in which the house churches met and would thus have played a prominent role in these churches. If such women were following the false teachers, the whole house church would have been vulnerable to false teaching through their leadership (compare 2 Tim 3:6–7). This would have been an additional reason for Paul's concern.

A Christian woman's finest adornment is not extravagant attire or expensive jewelry but "good deeds" (2:10). The Pastoral Epistles speak frequently of the kind of "good deeds" required of all categories of Christians: church leaders (Titus 2:7); the wealthy (1 Tim 6:18); widows (1 Tim 5:10); and all believers (Titus 3:8, 14). However, this emphasis on doing good does not suggest that people are saved by their good deeds (2 Tim 1:9; Titus 3:5); rather, such deeds are viewed as the outcome of being saved (Titus 2:14), a sign of genuine faith that is "appropriate for women who profess to worship God" (2:10).

The principles that Paul emphasizes are modesty and propriety. In Paul's culture, this meant avoiding certain types of dress or adornment, not necessarily because these were wrong in themselves but because they were associated with values that were contrary to the gospel and risked bringing disrepute to the Christian community. In the diverse cultures of our world today, the way we apply these principles will vary from place to place and from church to church.

In Asia, with its many colorful traditions and modes of dress, the question of appropriate dress for Sunday worship may arise. In many churches, women choose to wear traditional dress – their "Sunday best" – when attending worship. This is often an affirmation of who they are. For instance, one of the writers has an Indian doctor friend – a Christian convert from a Hindu family – who continues to wear the *tika* mark on her forehead as a cultural symbol "to show," she says, "that I am an Indian woman!" In some traditions, jewelry and heavy gold ornaments are important on festive occasions, such as weddings, which take place in the context of Christian worship. Paul's principles would require conformity to what is perceived by the local community to be good and contextually appropriate conduct. The symbolism of "elaborate hairstyles or gold or pearls" in the context of the Pastoral Epistles was negative and unworthy; the affirmation of cultural identity – one of God's

---

37. Towner, *1–2 Timothy & Titus*, 71.

good gifts – in our style of dress and adornment for worship must be viewed positively. In some Indonesian settings, the refusal of some Christian groups to wear any form of traditional dress or any of the customary traditional ornaments – even for an occasion such as a wedding – has resulted in their being marginalized by their neighbors. In consequence, their gospel witness has also been disregarded by their neighbors.

Gunē, the word translated "woman" (2:11), may also be translated "wife." However, the latter meaning seems unlikely since both here and in verse 9 the definite article is lacking and because the passage is speaking of public worship and prayer rather than about the household. The verb "learn" (2:11) involves learning through instruction, which has a positive implication – a woman's role is not solely in the home, but she is to receive instruction and to learn in public worship, which is the overall context of the passage. This represents a striking departure from the social attitudes of the day, for Jewish women were generally not instructed in the Torah and so would not usually have been able to teach.

Paul says that "a woman should learn in quietness" (2:11). The Greek word used is *hēsuchia*. Although sometimes translated "silence" (KJV, NRSV), *hēsuchia* is better translated quietness, calmness, or tranquility. Paul's call is not for complete silence from women (see 1 Corinthians 11, where he asks women to pray and prophesy in the congregation) but for a willingness to listen and learn "in quietness." Fee thinks that since "quietness" is the first thing mentioned in verse 11 and "quiet" is the last word in verse 12, the emphasis lies on this attitude of quietness.[38] Since Paul was concerned that women in the church, influenced by the false teachers, were engaging in idle, foolish, or malicious talk (5:13; 6:4), he wanted them to learn the sound doctrine that would protect them from false teachings.

A woman must also learn in "full submission" (2:11). Knight thinks that "submission is the norm for the relationship of women to men in authority functions within the church."[39] Chris Marshall, however, notes that Paul does not specify the object of the woman's submission and points out that there is nothing here to indicate that Paul means that women are to submit to men in the congregation.[40] In contrast, when Paul instructs wives, "submit yourselves

---

38. Fee, *1 and 2 Timothy, Titus*, 72.
39. Knight, *The Pastoral Epistles*, 139.
40. C. Marshall. "What did you say, Paul? 'Let A Woman Learn': 1 Timothy 2:8–15 in Context," *Today's Christian* (1989, no. 9), 47.

to your own husbands" (Eph 5:21–22), he uses the same verb "submit," but it is clear that the submission in this case is to husbands. In 1 Timothy, however, Paul was probably referring to women submitting to the teaching they were receiving. The Greek is literally, "Woman, in quietness, let her learn in all submission." Clearly the context reflects a concern with *how* a woman is to learn. Perhaps Paul also had in mind the younger widows who were "going about from house to house" (probably house church to house church) and "saying things they ought not to" (5:13). It was vital that such women learned in "full submission" to sound teaching, which probably means learning sound doctrine in an attitude of quiet receptivity.

The instruction of verse 11 is carried further in verse 12: "I do not permit a woman to teach or to assume authority over a man." False teaching was at the heart of the problem addressed by Paul in this letter. His opening charge involves commanding certain people, who wanted to be teachers of the law, not to teach false doctrines (1:3, 7), and he says that those whose teachings are contrary to "sound doctrine" are "conceited and understand nothing" (6:3–4). As noted before, it is probably because some women were propagating false doctrines that Paul prohibited them from teaching publicly in the house churches of Ephesus. The prohibition is related to the situation. Since these women were active in promoting false teaching, Paul restricted their authority to teach in the church. Fee suggests that by "teaching" Paul means instruction in Scripture.[41]

Paul forbids a woman "to assume authority over a man" (2:12). He uses the rare verb *authentein* (authority), only found here in the NT. The verb's meaning is greatly debated. Knight claims that the word "shows no inherent negative sense of grasping or usurping authority or of exercising it in a harsh or authoritative way, but simply means 'to have or exercise authority.'"[42] He takes this to refer to exercising a leadership role or function in the church, and thus to the office of an overseer or presbyter. Fee, on the other hand, favors the translation of "to domineer,"[43] and Towner notes that it may mean to "usurp or misappropriate authority."[44] Davies suggests that it may mean to "dictate to a man" and notes that men, too, are discouraged from domineering behavior (5:1).[45] In this case, the meaning may be that women should not interrupt

---

41. Fee, *1 and 2 Timothy, Titus*, 73.
42. Knight, *The Pastoral Epistles*, 141.
43. Fee, *1 and 2 Timothy, Titus*, 73.
44. Towner, *1–2 Timothy & Titus*, 77.
45. Davies, *The Pastoral Epistles*, 18.

the church elders by bringing up doctrines taught by the false teachers while these elders were teaching. Chris Marshall suggests, "In any event, it is a particular kind of *manipulative dominance* over men in the Ephesian congregation that is forbidden, not all forms of doctrinal or ecclesiastical authority over males."[46] Marshall sees Paul's prohibition as connected with the manner in which women were advancing the false teaching. We conclude, then, that the main concern of verse 12b relates to a disruptive form of behavior by women, which involved manipulative domineering over men and was connected to spreading false teachings.[47]

Paul concludes the verse by underlining that a woman should "be in quietness" (2:12c, translation mine). Although this phrase is sometimes translated "she is to keep silent" (NRSV), *hēsuchia*, as already noted, means quietness or tranquility rather than silence. This reinforces Paul's point that a woman is to learn in quietness (2:11). It is her general demeanor that is in view here, reinforcing the point that she is not to be involved in foolish or malicious talk.

Paul goes on, "For Adam was formed first, then Eve. And Adam was not the one deceived; it was the woman who was deceived and became a sinner" (2:13–14). Here, Paul turns to the OT to support what he has just said (2:11–12). Clearly, he has Genesis chapters 2 and 3 in view. The verb "to form" is used of the creation of Adam (Gen 2:7–8), and 1 Timothy 2:14 reflects events and terms used in Genesis 3, including the verb "deceived" (Gen 3:13). "Adam was not the one deceived" does not deny Adam's sin or his participation in the fall (compare Rom 5:12; 1 Cor 15:21–22). Rather, it notes that Adam sinned willfully, rather than being deceived (Gen 3:6, 12). The contrast is thus with Eve's deception. Eve is referred to as "the woman" (2:14) because this term occurs repeatedly in Genesis 3 (see verses 1, 2, 4, 6, 12, 13, 15, 16) – while the name "Eve" is used only in Genesis 3:20 – and to make the transition from Eve as a type to women in general. Because of her deception, Eve became a "sinner" or "transgressor" (NRSV) – this word is used to describe overstepping set limits and, in the NT, always relates to transgression against God's law.

Through her deception, Eve became "a sinner." Why does Paul refer to Eve here? Some scholars suggest that the verse shows the consequences that result when the divine order is disturbed. These scholars conclude that since Eve – who is regarded as an archetype of all women – was gullible, women cannot

---

46. Marshall, "What did you say, Paul?," 48; emphasis original.
47. See Fee, *1 and 2 Timothy, Titus*, 73.

be trusted to teach. However, the passage does not state that all women are inherently more gullible than men. Such a fatal flaw would suggest that women should be disqualified from all teaching; yet Paul makes positive mention of women teaching children and younger women (5:10; 2 Tim 1:5; 3:14–15; Titus 2:3–5). It is likely that Paul was simply narrating the historical account of Adam willfully disobeying God's command and Eve being deceived into sinful disobedience.

The emphasis on Eve's deception and transgression is a polemical response to the situation in Ephesus. As noted in the introduction to this section, through following the false teachers – who were themselves following "deceiving spirits and things taught by demons" (4:1) – the younger widows had "already turned away to follow Satan" (5:15). In this, they were like Eve, who was also deceived and became a sinner. Eve is thus an illustration or example of the drastic consequences that follow when people (in this case, women) are deceived. Eve's susceptibility to deception was a warning to the Ephesian women of the danger they faced if they continued to follow the false teachers. Chris Marshall comments that here Paul "is not expounding the inherent meaning of the Creation-Fall narratives, but selecting aspects of the biblical accounts to *illustrate* and *reinforce* his specific ethical demands for the Ephesian situation."[48]

Other Jewish writers of the period thought that it was through Eve that the human race fell (see Sir 25:24; 2 Enoch 31:6; compare 2 Cor 11:3). Several passages in Paul's undisputed letters speak of Adam as the first transgressor and as a representative of all humanity (Rom 5:12–21; 1 Cor 15:21–22, 45–49). Eve is spoken of here because of the specific issue of women following and promoting false teachings in Ephesus. The same Scripture, in this case the account of the fall, spoke in different ways to different faith communities, and was interpreted in the light of their concerns and issues. The Pastorals follow this practice, and we also see this pattern of interpretation in the NT, both in the teaching of Jesus and in the way the Gospel writers use scriptural references from the OT to reinforce the points they are making. Asian readers, particularly those in communities that have not been influenced by Western ideas of literalism, will be very much at home with this approach to Scripture.

Does Paul's appeal to Scripture (2:13–14) mean that he is laying down a timeless principle? This need not be the case. Elsewhere in the NT, teaching for a particular situation is often reinforced by a similar appeal to Scripture – for example, Abraham's faith (Gen 15:6) is upheld as a model for the Christian's

---

48. Marshall. "What did you say, Paul?," 50; emphasis original.

faith (Rom 4:1–5). The reference to the creation narrative (Genesis 1–4) also does not necessarily mean that the teaching must be regarded as timeless. Paul alludes to this same Genesis passage when writing about head coverings (1 Cor 11:7–9), but most people regard this 1 Corinthians 11 passage as speaking to a particular situation and culture rather than as being timeless. We have already noted that the false teachers desired to be teachers of the law and that their myths and genealogies were probably based on the OT (1:4–7). The allusions to the OT in this passage were probably Paul's way of countering those claims. However, since we do not know how exactly the false teachers were using these Genesis passages, we cannot say specifically what Paul's counterarguments are. It seems likely that Paul cited the OT (2:13–14) to make some selective observations on Genesis 2–3, observations which were appropriate to the situation being addressed at Ephesus.

Since Paul mentions Eve's transgression, "the question of salvation from divine wrath becomes an urgent one."[49] Otherwise it might be thought that all women were under God's displeasure. Accordingly, Paul concludes this section by adding that "women will be saved through childbearing – if they continue in faith, love and holiness with propriety" (2:15). In the Greek, this verse begins with the singular "she will be saved," which in this context could refer to Eve (2:13–14). But some translations use the plural – "women will be saved" – since Paul was almost certainly referring back to verse 12, where the singular ("woman") was used but clearly with reference to any woman in general. That Paul shifts from Eve to the women in Ephesus is further supported by his use of the plural "if they continue" in verse 15.[50] Having spoken of deception, Paul now speaks of salvation.

What does "through childbearing" mean? Some have suggested that it refers to the birth of Jesus the Savior through Mary and that this event has undone Eve's transgression. However, it is difficult to believe that the Greek text – literally "through the childbearing" – should be understood, without any additional explanation, as a reference to Christ's birth. Further, the verb used here – *teknogonia* (meaning, "childbearing") – is a general one, related to the verb used later in the letter where Paul tells younger widows to marry and "to have children" (5:14), which refers to childbearing as an act, and not to the

---

49. M. Dibelius and H. Conzelmann, *The Pastoral Epistles*. Hermeneia (Philadelphia: Fortress Press, 1972), 48.
50. For "they" referring to Adam and Eve, see Andrew B. Spurgeon, "1 Timothy 2:13–15: Paul's Retelling of Genesis 2:4–4:1," *JETS* 56, no. 3 (September 2013): 543–56.

child or to the birth. Almost certainly then, Paul had childbirth in view. Again, it has been suggested that by "saved" Paul means physical preservation through childbirth – which is currently under the curse of Genesis 3:16 – rather than spiritual salvation. However, the word "saved" in the Pastoral letters always means redemption from sin rather than deliverance from danger (1:15; 2:4; 4:16), while a different word is used for being "rescued" (*hruomai*; see 2 Tim 3:11; 4:18).

How then can Paul say that "women will be saved through childbearing"? Paul clearly does not mean that women will win salvation through giving birth to children. The Pastoral Epistles clearly state that salvation is through the redemptive work of Christ: "He saved us, not because of righteous things we had done, but because of his mercy" (Titus 3:5). Further, in saying that Christ "gave himself as a ransom for all people" (2:6), Paul must surely be including women as well as men.

What then does it mean that "women will be saved through childbearing"? In this regard, it is noteworthy that the false teachers were forbidding marriage (4:3). Perhaps Paul lays such emphasis on the importance of having children and on family life (5:10; Titus 2:4–5) to counter the false teachers and their disparaging views on marriage, and perhaps also sex. The affirmation of childbearing in 1 Timothy 2:15 is a rejection of the false teachers' negativity about marriage and echoes Paul's affirmation that "everything God created is good, and nothing is to be rejected if it is received with thanksgiving" (4:4). Women's salvation (since only women can give birth to children!) is to be found in – and not apart from – the whole-life context in which God has set them, the most marvelous and remarkable aspect of which is the ability to bring new life into the world.

In addition, Fee thinks that this verse means that a woman's salvation

> is to be found in her being a model, godly woman, known for her good works (v. 10; compare 5:11). And her good deeds, according to 5:11 and 14, include marriage, bearing children . . . and keeping a good home. The reason for his saying that she will be saved is that it follows directly out of his having said "the woman came to be in transgression."[51]

In his understanding of "good works," Paul shared many views of his culture about the appropriate delineation of roles for men and women. He seemed

---

51. Fee, *1 and 2 Timothy, Titus*, 75.

to have felt that it was necessary to share, to some extent at least, in many of the values of his culture in order that the message of the gospel might gain a hearing in that culture. Thus Paul seems to endorse what was, for him, a socially acceptable role for women.

But lest anyone misunderstand and think that he is saying that a woman can save herself or that her salvation depends on "good deeds," Paul adds, "if they continue in faith, love and holiness with propriety" (2:15b). That is, a woman will be saved,

> provided of course that she is already a truly Christian woman . . . This is obviously where her salvation ultimately lies . . . It is assumed that such a woman already has faith, which is activating love and holiness. But the whole context of the letter, and the present argument in particular, has generated this rather unusual way of putting it.[52]

Thus, the "if" (*ean*) clause says that women will be "saved through childbearing" only when certain conditions are met; that is, salvation comes to those who have a true and sincere faith and live a godly life. "Faith" here refers to the way salvation is received and experienced. "Holiness" may refer to the earlier emphasis on modesty and good works (2:9–10). The addition of "with propriety" might have been because immodest dress led to a loss of propriety. Women must "continue" in these things which are expressions of salvation, rather than follow the false teachers or spread false teachings in the congregation. Hultgren concludes that Paul "is concerned that women carry out what he takes to be their divinely given role, attended with the proper virtues, and thereby live the life which issues in salvation. Anything else is a sign of being led astray and its consequent peril."[53]

The teaching here is specifically related to the problem created by the false teaching in the house churches of Ephesus. Paul's main concern was to counter the false teaching in which several women had been involved. Inevitably, in the modern church, this raises again the questions relating more generally to woman's ordination or their official commissioning as teachers in the church. On the issue of ordination, we quote Robert Karris, a modern Catholic biblical theologian, who writes of the passage discussed above:

---

52. Fee, *1 and 2 Timothy, Titus*, 76.
53. Hultgren, "I-II Timothy, Titus," 70.

I see that it has nothing to say against the ordination of women to the priesthood. For the threat of gnostic female teachers in the pulpits and classrooms of the church has clearly passed. And with the passing of that threat, so, too, has passed the validity of the harsh injunctions of verses 11–12.[54]

In fact, most sections of the Christian church have been inconsistent almost to the point of dishonesty in the application of these verses to the question of the role of women in the church. Until quite recently, most churches denied women ordination as elders, presbyters, priests, ministers, or bishops. Yet, from very early times, women have been authorized "teachers" in congregations, religious orders, and, in some cases, even as designated "doctors of the church." There is evidence, promptly swept out of sight, that some women were bishops or exercised episcopal roles in certain situations. Women have made increasingly vigorous and creative contributions to formal theology, and countless Christian leaders have looked back to the women who nurtured them in the faith – perhaps a Sunday school teacher, a religious sister, a missionary, or a schoolteacher.

Many Asian Christian congregations were founded and nurtured by the faithful teaching of women missionaries, who often did the work of the ministry while being denied entry to the ordained ministry and, sometimes, even to the eldership. Now, as women's roles change in Asian societies, the opportunity for women to receive ordination and, consequently, to engage in a wider authorized ministry should be affirmed. In an era when a man may appear before a female judge or petition a female cabinet minister, it can no longer be claimed that women in ordained ministries is socially or culturally inappropriate or offensive. Scriptural teaching directed toward the resolution of problems that no longer threaten the churches should not be allowed to raise doubts and misgivings when the general teaching of the NT – and not least, Paul's undisputed letters – affirms the equal giftedness and status of women and men as they engage in the mission of God.

In concluding this section, a historical illustration seems appropriate and helpful. Yu Lingzhi (1873–1931) was a cross-cultural Chinese missionary, who served with the Southern Methodist Mission in Korea from 1897 to 1903. Her work in Korea was multifaceted: Bible teaching, medical work among female patients and school children, teaching poverty-stricken Korean girls

---

54. Karris, *The Pastoral Epistles*, 70.

with learning disabilities, and translating and compiling textbooks. When Yu Lingzhi returned to China, she established what might be called "the first Chinese faith mission, following the footsteps of Hudson Taylor."[55] She hugely influenced the Chinese holiness movement and emphasized, in the Chinese context, the role of women in missions. Thank God for Yu Lingzhi!

---

55. D. L. Robert, *Gospel Bearers, Gender Barriers: Missionary Women in the Twentieth Century* (Maryknoll: Orbis Books, 2002), 92.

1 TIMOTHY 3

Angelito Agbuya was, for many years, a key leader of a Protestant denomination in the Philippines, serving as a denominational leader and educator. But his most significant role was in the pastorate. He pastored the Angeles City First Church for fifty-two years, until his death in 2018. At his funeral a close friend shared this eulogy: "His godly legacy as pastor and friend will live on among us all." These words echo the message of 1 Timothy 3 concerning church leadership: Church leaders must be people of godly character. Like Pastor Agbuya, godly church leaders bless the church and leave behind a lasting legacy.

As we have seen, 1 Timothy 1 deals with the problem of false teachings in the Ephesian church and the task given to Timothy to instruct the false teachers within the church to desist from teaching false doctrines. In chapter 2, Paul gives instructions about the public worship of the church. Chapter 3 includes numerous instructions about church leadership. It is noteworthy that Paul's focus is the character of church leaders. God does not care only about performance; he cares even more about character – who we are when no one is looking.

This chapter has two main parts – qualifications for overseers (3:1–7) and qualifications for deacons (3:8–15) – followed by a bridge section in which Paul speaks of the church as God's "household" (3:14–16).

3:1–7 QUALIFICATIONS FOR OVERSEERS

If the Pastorals are viewed as a manual of "church order," this chapter could be seen as covering one important facet of this order – the qualifications for various offices. But little is said about the responsibilities of the offices themselves, which makes the "church manual" suggestion unlikely. As we have already argued, it is likely that the various offices in the church were already well established, and that Paul is simply giving guidelines about the kind of person who should fill these offices.

On the other hand, if some of the false teachers were leaders, one can understand the need to make clear the qualifications required for leadership positions in the church. The list of qualifications also functions as an exhortation to those who were already overseers concerning how they should conduct their lives. Paul charged Timothy with ensuring that all overseers were meeting these requirements; those who did not needed to be disciplined or replaced (5:20). Many of the characteristics listed here contrast sharply with what is said about the false teachers. So it is probable that the problem of false teachers prompted Paul to emphasize authority structures and the qualities required of church leaders since such leadership was part of the "orderly system which our writer puts forward as the antidote to false teaching and undesirable behavior."[1]

The passage begins and ends with an emphasis on church leaders being "above reproach" or avoiding "disgrace" before outsiders (3:2, 7), probably because the activities of false teachers had already adversely affected the church's reputation in the community (3:7). This would explain why "the character description here of the overseer has some significant overlap with the desirable character traits of other holders of high office in that culture. In some respects, the church had adopted some of the higher standards of the surrounding culture."[2]

The chapter begins with the formula, "Here is a trustworthy saying" (3:1), which could refer either to what follows (as it does in 1 Timothy 1:15) or to what precedes it (as it does in Titus 3:8). Some argue that since all the other "trustworthy sayings" refer to salvation, the formula here must refer back to the previous verse about women being saved through childbearing (2:15). However, what follows – "Whoever aspires to be an overseer desires a noble task" (3:1b) – has the style and ring of a "saying" – which 1 Timothy 2:15 does not – and gives a positive evaluation of the office of overseer.

The office of overseer is presented as a significant position, the kind of task which a person with the right qualities should aspire to. Paul implies that people need to be encouraged to take on leadership responsibilities in the community. In many ways, the office of a Christian leader was unattractive since it required demanding service. At this stage of the church's development, such an office probably did not confer social status, as it often does today. Towner also notes that the unsound doctrines propagated by the false teachers "may have spawned distrust for leaders and a reluctance to take up the responsibilities such leadership required."[3] The situation is probably quite different in many Asian societies, where the clergy are usually held in high regard. In the Philippines, for instance, it brings great joy and pride to the

---

1. J. L. Houlden, *The Pastoral Epistles*. Pelican New Testament Commentaries (Harmondsworth: Penguin Books, 1976), 76.
2. B. Witherington, *A Socio-Rhetorical Commentary on Titus, 1–2 Timothy and 1–3 John*, Volume 1 of *Letters and Homilies for Hellenized Christians* (Downers Grove: IVP Academic, 2006), 236.
3. Towner, *The Letters to Timothy and Titus*, 249.

whole family – even if not all family members are confessing Christians – if one child decides to go into full-time church ministry. Sometimes, this respect extends to the wider community, with the prayers and counsel of a church leader being sought and valued even by non-Christians.

Paul describes the office of *episcopos* (overseer) as "a noble task" (3:1) – literally, "a good work" (*kalon ergon*), one of the many "good works" that the Pastorals recommend. Because theirs is such a noble task, as well as an important one, overseers should live exemplary lives. The title overseer (*episcopos*) is used in secular Greek in a general sense of a person carrying out a variety of supervisory functions in a civil sphere, as well as in a religious sense. In the Qumran community – a Jewish sect that lived near the Dead Sea – one of the officers had the title *mebaqqer*, similar in meaning to "overseer," and this office involved interpreting the law, as well as preaching, pastoral tasks, and administration.[4] Paul uses "overseer" to refer to a fixed office or position within a community with a definite function of oversight (see Acts 20:28; Phil 1:1; Titus 1:7). The overseer had a certain amount of authority and seemed to have been a significant representative of the community in the outside world (3:7).

Some understand the use of the singular – "the overseer" (3:2) – against the plural "deacons" (3:8–13) and "elders" (4:14) to imply that Paul was advocating a single monarchical ruler (that is, a bishop or an overseer) over other church administrators like elders and deacons. Does the text suggest such a church polity? 1 Timothy 5:17 says, "The elders who direct the affairs of the church well are worthy of double honor, especially those whose work is preaching and teaching." The reference to elders who "direct the affairs of the church" suggests that there may have been a council of elders (4:14) who were responsible for governing the community rather than a single authoritarian ruler. Some elders may have been assigned additional roles such as preaching and teaching. Further, when writing to Titus, Paul seems to use the terms "elder" (Titus 1:5–6) and "overseer" (1:7–9) interchangeably. So the question arises, are the offices of elder and overseer identical?

The answer seems to be that these offices change depending on the needs of the community. For example, in Crete, where Titus ministered, *all* elders taught (Titus 1:9), but in Ephesus, where Timothy served, only some elders taught and preached (1 Tim 5:17).[5] Further, while an overseer had to be "able to teach" (3:2), not all elders had to be teachers (5:17). Therefore, we may

---

4. See 1QS 6:12, 20; CD 9:18–19, 22; 13:6–7.
5. Davies, *The Pastoral Epistles*, 22.

assume that the relationship between elder and overseer was that "elders who taught were called overseers."[6] At the same time, there were other "elders" who were not primarily teachers. Further, we may postulate that there was a group of overseers in Ephesus. If so, the singular "overseer" (3:2) must be understood as a generic reference that refers to a class of people, as it does in Titus 1:5–9.[7]

Other scholars have suggested that the body of elders were ruled by a single elder who was called an overseer.[8] However, this view is less convincing since 1 Timothy 5:17 implies that there was more than one elder engaged in teaching, while 1 Timothy 3:2 says that the overseer must be able to teach.

The issue is further complicated because some English translations render *episcopos* as "bishop." The office of "bishop" has changed and developed greatly since the time of the Pastorals. In Paul's time, however, the office of bishop did not involve just one person presiding over a whole region and having complete authority in all facets of church life. "Overseer" is more helpful, but we must not interpret this too informally or generally since we are dealing with an appointment to a definite office.

CHURCH GOVERNMENT AND LEADERSHIP

Church government in the immediate post-apostolic period was experimental and flexible. The "monarchical" (single ruler) bishop, operating within a hierarchy of church ministries, did not emerge until the size of the church and the crisis in its life-and-death struggle with powerful heresies made a unified command structure essential. With the collapse of the Roman Empire, church leaders in Europe took wide responsibility for dioceses and provinces and their peoples; but for the readers of the Pastorals, all that lay in the future.

---

6. Davies, *The Pastoral Epistles*, 23; see also J. P. Meier, "*Presbyteros* in the Pastoral Epistles," *CBQ* 35 (1973): 323–45.
7. The singular in 3:2 may have been prompted by the singular "whoever" (or "if anyone") in 3:1. Similar generic singulars occur elsewhere in the Epistle: singular "a woman" in 2:11–12 (despite the plural in 2:15) and "a widow" in 5:4 (despite the plural in 5:3).
8. See for example Dibelius and Conzelmann, *The Pastoral Epistles*, 54–57.

In the various structures of church leadership prior to such developments, we can detect both Jewish elements – from the pattern of rule of the synagogue – and Greek elements – borrowed from the familiar patterns of civil government. These elements, as we have seen above, existed together, probably in different combinations in different places. Paul made no attempt to harmonize these elements or to present a tidy, unified structure of church government since this did not seem to be important, certainly not as important as ensuring that the life and witness of church leaders were worthy of their calling.

This flexibility and willingness of the apostles to experiment will be encouraging to Asian church communities, who have inherited a wide variety of patterns of church structure, leadership, and ministry from their missionary pioneers and, in some cases, from more recent ecumenical negotiations for reunion.

No single form of church government – episcopal, presbyterial-synodal, or independent – can claim to be universally valid or normative for every time and place; and even claims to universality must include a willingness to be flexible. For example, the Roman Catholic Church sees itself as a church complete, and yet it has been willing to initiate and enter into theological dialogue and some shared activities with other Christians. Presbyterian churches, by contrast, claim only to be part of the "holy catholic and apostolic church"[1] and simply claim that their system of church government is "agreeable to the word of God."

A new reality, in the years following World War II, has been the emergence of uniting churches that intentionally seek to bring together radically different traditions of church structure and government within one united church. Today there are bishops in the two great Indian united churches who began their ministries as Congregationalists or Presbyterians. Asian churches show a far greater creative flexibility in addressing issues of church order (governance) than churches in the West. The variety found in the Pastorals, and in the NT in general, suggests that effective and respected mission leadership was the priority, not uniformity of structure and practice.

---

1. This is from the Nicene Creed, also called the Niceno-Constantinopolitan Creed, agreed to at the First Council of Constantinople in 381 CE. It can be found at https://www.crcna.org/welcome/beliefs/creeds/nicene-creed.

Since there were already "overseers" in the community when Paul wrote this letter, people would have known what an overseer's role involved. So rather than listing the responsibilities of this office, Paul describes the qualifications and qualities required of an overseer (3:2–7). Dibelius and Conzelmann note the similarity between Paul's list of qualifications and the common stylized lists used in the non-Christian world to describe an ideal leader in a particular area such as the military.[9] If Paul had adapted his list from some secular source, this would explain why some items on his list are not specific to church leaders. Mounce comments, "The qualities are those that all people, Christians and non-Christians, hold as laudable."[10] But, as Towner notes, the list has clearly been "Christianized," particularly in verses 6 and 7 (and perhaps also in verse 3 since gentleness was considered a weakness in a secular leader).[11] Similar lists also appear elsewhere in the Pastorals (Titus 2:2; 3:1–2).

The list focuses on two broad areas: first, personal self-discipline and maturity; second, the ability to relate to others and to teach and care for them.

"Above reproach" implies being "of unimpeachable character."[12] The overseer should have no obvious defect in character or behavior that could be used by anyone, within or outside the church, to discredit him or the community.

The meaning of the expression "faithful to his wife" (see 3:12; 5:9; Titus 1:6) – "married only once" (NRSV) – is debated. The phrase could mean "be married" as opposed to singleness. Some Pacific and Asian societies believe that an unmarried person is not yet fully an adult and so is not mature enough to hold office as a church leader. But it is unlikely that Paul was saying that only a married man could be an overseer since such an interpretation places the emphasis on the word "wife," whereas in Greek the emphasis is on the word "one."

Some have argued that the Greek phrase "one woman man" refers to a monogamous relationship and that Paul was prohibiting polygamy by this statement. But Paul was unlikely to have been thinking of polygamy since such a practice was not common within the early church.

This translation "married only once" (NRSV) might suggest that a widower refused remarriage after the death of his first wife. In Greco-Roman society, a person who had married only once or a widow who had not remarried was

---

9. Dibelius and Conzelmann, *The Pastoral Epistles*, 158–60; see also Mounce, *The Pastoral Epistles*, 166–67.
10. Mounce, *The Pastoral Epistles*, 167.
11. Towner, *1–2 Timothy & Titus*, 83.
12. Witherington, *A Socio-Rhetorical Commentary on Titus, 1–2 Timothy and 1–3 John*, 236.

honored. In the Orthodox Church, non-monastic priests must be married but may marry only once – this is how they read this passage. But since Paul specifically permits remarriage (Rom 7:1–3; 1 Cor 7:9) and encourages younger widows to remarry (5:14), this expression is unlikely to be a prohibition of remarriage. Instead, Paul might have been prescribing that the overseer must not be someone who had divorced his wife and then remarried. However, given exceptions to the rule prohibiting remarriage (Matt 5:32; 19:9; 1 Cor 7:15), this is also not a likely interpretation.

"Faithful to his wife" is most probably a reference to marital fidelity. Paul uses a similar expression to affirm a widow who had been "faithful to her husband" (1 Tim 5:9). Since infidelity was common, and at times even assumed, in the Greco-Roman world, Paul probably wanted to emphasize the importance of marital and sexual fidelity. Further, since Paul has just said that an overseer must be "above reproach," following this statement with a warning against infidelity seems appropriate. In contrast to the false teachers, who had a low view of marriage and family (4:3), Paul's assumption that an overseer had a wife and children (3:4) indicates that Paul was not an ascetic.

In Asian societies, where kinship relationships are important, marriages that conform to the norms of local custom and social regulation are regarded as respectable. Respectability helps to enhance the reputation of the church and its leaders, and hence also their message. When one of the authors of this commentary was welcomed into a Karo clan in North Sumatra, great care was taken that his wife was welcomed into a different clan – since marriage within the same clan is considered a socially despised form of incest – as well as into a clan whose relationship to her husband's clan was appropriate. In terms of *adat* (custom), it was an ideal marriage. The care taken to conform to what the community believed was right and proper gained respect even from people with no interest in the church.

Paul goes on to say that the overseer must be "temperate" (*nēphalios*), which could also be translated "sober," "level-headed," "self-controlled" or "respectable" – virtues that Greco-Roman cultures appreciated, a fact we know from other secular writings of the time.

"Hospitable" is a virtue often emphasized in early Christianity (Rom 12:13; 1 Tim 5:10; Titus 1:8; Heb 13:2; 1 Pet 4:9). While Greco-Roman society was mobile, there were no inns, hotels, guesthouses, or Airbnbs to host travelers. Families hosted visitors, just as Abraham welcomed the three guests (Gen 18:2) and Paul asked the churches in Rome to host Phoebe (Rom 16:1). To ensure the safety of women traveling alone, widows might have hosted them, which was probably one reason Paul challenged widows to be hospitable (5:10). As Bray notes, hospitality in the ancient world "was a much more far-reaching concept than anything that goes by that name today. It meant welcoming people into the home, feeding and lodging them, attending to their needs and sending them on their way rejoicing."[13] However, it did not necessarily mean that these leaders were rich since hospitality involved sharing whatever one had, whether it was little or much.

The overseer should also be "able to teach" or be "an apt teacher" (NRSV) – the one item on the list that refers to a competency. Writing to Titus, Paul says of the elder-overseer, "He must hold firmly to the trustworthy message as it has been taught, so that he can encourage others by sound doctrine and refute those who oppose it" (Titus 1:9; see also 2 Tim 2:24). As far as Ephesus was concerned, it appears that not all elders taught (5:17). Paul probably had the false teachers in mind when he emphasizes that the overseer must be able to teach sound doctrine and refute error.

Paul then describes what an overseer must *not* be (3:3). "Not given to drunkenness" is self-explanatory. In contrast to the false teachers, who tended to be argumentative and quarrelsome (see 6:4; 2 Tim 2:23–24; Titus 3:9–11), the overseer's behavior must not be characterized by violence but by gentleness. To be "gentle" refers to "treating others with patience and tolerance and kindness rather than a domineering disposition,"[14] however exasperating they may be. "Not quarrelsome" means peaceable or uncontentious.

The position of overseer probably involved some financial responsibility, which would have presented opportunities for dishonesty. But the overseer must not be "a lover of money" (3:3; 2 Tim 3:2; Titus 1:7); this again was in contrast with the false teachers who were "teaching things they ought not to teach – and that for the sake of dishonest gain" (Titus 1:11; see also 1 Tim 6:5).

The early church met in homes, and the head of the household in which a particular house church met usually functioned as the house church leader. Since it was assumed that overseers would usually be married and have children, it seems logical that an overseer's ability to manage his own family and household – which would have included ensuring that his children were obedient and well-behaved – was one of the criteria by which to evaluate whether he would be able to oversee God's household, the church (3:5, 15). In the society

---

13. G. Bray, *The Pastoral Epistles*. ITC (London: Bloomsbury T&T Clark, 2019), 184.
14. W. H. Gloer, *1 & 2 Timothy-Titus*. Smyth & Helwys Bible Commentary (Macon: Smyth & Helwys, 2010), 151; compare 2 Corinthians 10:1; Titus 3:2.

of the day, the household was patriarchal, and it was expected that children would always obey their father. As Towner notes, "To expect less from church leaders would have been to risk associating the church with charges of social disruption and political subversion."[15] As someone who managed people, an overseer needed to have some administrative skill and a concern for order. But Paul also makes it clear that managing is not just directing but also involves care: "If anyone does not know how to manage his own family, how can he take care of God's church?" (3:5).

The requirement that an overseer should "not be a recent convert" was because of the danger that this could make him "conceited" (3:6) like the false teachers (6:4; 2 Tim 3:4). Perhaps it was a temptation to appoint people of social rank and influence to the position of overseer, even if they had only recently become Christians. But such rapid advancement could make a new convert grow conceited, resulting in him falling under "the same judgment as the devil" – that is, the same kind of condemnation God pronounced on the devil when he fell.

Paul concludes this section by emphasizing the importance of "a good reputation with outsiders" (3:7; see also 5:14; 6:1; Titus 2:5, 8, 10). As noted earlier, the qualities required of an overseer also conformed to the secular ideal of respectability in Greco-Roman society. But if overseers behaved in ways that caused unbelievers to view the Christian community with suspicion or contempt, these "outsiders" might well have refused to hear the gospel. The life and witness of the Christian community are best served by leaders whose lives exemplify gospel values. Another reason for maintaining a good reputation with outsiders is to avoid falling "into disgrace and into the devil's trap" (3:7). "Disgrace" here seems to refer to general disgrace rather than the disgrace that accompanies moral laxity. For example, the polytheistic Greco-Roman world might have considered Christians strange because they worshiped one God and regarded them with contempt. The devil might aim to "trap" church leaders. Outsiders tend to put the most unfavorable interpretation on any misdeed by members of the Christian community, and the devil is always ready to catch people off guard.

Clearly Paul "is setting a high value on stable and peaceful congregational life and therefore values highly the leadership which will perpetuate it."[16] We have also noted that the idea of good management of both one's own household

---

15. Towner, *1–2 Timothy & Titus*, 88.
16. Houlden, *The Pastoral Epistles*, 74.

and "God's household" is important (3:4, 15). Johnson notes that this helps us to understand the qualities of overseers that are spoken of in these verses:

> They are not the virtues of excitement and dynamism, but of steadiness, sobriety, and sanity. It would be a mistake, however, to conclude that the Pastorals are therefore only interested in a "bourgeois mentality." As Paul said in another discussion of "stewards of households" (*oikonomoi*) such as himself and Apollos, "It is required that those who have been given a trust must prove faithful" (1 Cor 4:2). Fidelity to one spouse, sobriety, and hospitality may seem trivial virtues to those who identify authentic faith with momentary conversion or a single spasm of heroism. But to those who have lived longer and who recognize how the administration of a community can erode even the strongest of characters and the best of intentions, finding a leader who truly is a lover of peace and not a lover of money can be downright exciting.[17]

God's word sets the bar higher for those in positions of leadership. Church leaders lead the congregation not just by what they say but also by the example of their godly life. The godly lifestyle of church leaders strengthens the witness of the church to the wider community. There is a continuing great need today, globally and in Asia, for godly leadership in local churches. May God raise up godly leaders for the church in Asia and beyond.

RELATIONS WITH SOCIETY AND SOCIETY'S VALUES

The Pastorals argue that church communities must strive to maintain a positive relationship with the surrounding community by upholding their doctrines, beliefs, and lifestyles. If this is so, it stands to reason that different qualities may be emphasized in different societies and in different eras of history. For example, a modern feminist Christian – even after taking account of the explanations we have offered in this commentary – would probably find the emphasis of the Pastorals on

---

17. Johnson, *Letters to Paul's Delegates*, 148–49.

male leadership and maintaining patriarchal social norms very difficult to live with.

Today's Christian leaders – both male and female – must respect the new social norms that insist on equal opportunities for men and women, as well as for people of differing ages, ethnic and cultural backgrounds, and social outlooks.

In modern Asia, women sit as judges, exercise national leadership, and participate in the professions just as their male counterparts do. So it would be wrong to continue to insist on either maleness or the married state as prerequisites for positions of leadership or ministry. Equal status of men and women and equal opportunities in employment and leadership are values the modern world has widely affirmed. Christians recognize that these are also values which promote and enhance human life and well-being.

While women and organizations that advocate women's freedom have attained great success in many Asian countries, this does not mean that they fight the same battles as their Western counterparts. Instead, many Asian women try to be sensitive to their culture and context in their fight for freedom. For example, a Javanese woman, while she may be quite as tough-minded as her Western counterpart, may choose to operate quite differently, respecting her culture's distaste for strident and confrontational approaches and adopting its preference for bringing about change without destroying or diminishing the respect in which others hope to be held.

Modern Chinese women, in China as well as overseas, have found new and liberating opportunities to participate more fully as equals in society, the professions, the business world, and the world of learning. Even in a normally patriarchal world, these women are making decisions for their families while also maintaining traditional roles of supporting husband, children, and the extended family.

If a congregation is to play a meaningful role in the society in which it is placed and win a hearing for the good news within that society, it must be seen to be at least as upright and as observant of the values of civil society – provided of course that such values are those affirmed by the gospel. For many people in Asia's rapidly changing societies, getting the balance right is as difficult as dancing on a moving carpet.

On the other hand, great damage may be done when church leaders fail to maintain these high standards. For example, lapses in sexual discipline by church workers or mismanagement of finances by church leaders can destroy the credibility of the church and compromise the integrity of the gospel message that is preached. Moral failures of this kind by people in leadership positions can also damage the faith of young Christians. It is of such people that Jesus said, "It would be better for them to have a large millstone hung around their neck and to be drowned in the depths of the sea" (Matt 18:6).

Some may believe that endorsing the values of one's own society – even when these values are affirmed by the gospel and promote good conduct – is conformist and not distinctly Christian. But embracing such values is really a foundation. Only when this foundation is secure may we move on to the acts of love and compassion that are no longer matters of law and morality, but the life of Christ made real in the community of believers. The Chinese say, "Saints and even the immortals begin as ordinary people."[1] Our acts of heroic sanctity and self-sacrifice must begin with careful attention to developing, in the most down-to-earth terms, a good life that commends and adorns the gospel.

In critically adopting the values and norms expected of any important leader in society, the early church was continuing the long "wisdom tradition" which saw Israel adopting ethical teaching material from both neighboring countries and a kind of international treasury of wisdom. Much of this universal wisdom of the ancient world is embodied in the Hebrew Scriptures, and thus also in the Christian Bible. Jesus was, among other things, a teacher of wisdom, and he did not hesitate to use proverbial sayings and teaching images that had their origin in the wisdom tradition of Israel and its neighbors.

Later traditions such as the system of natural law – which is based on human insight and knowledge and is a rational attempt to employ the best contemporary understanding in solving moral and ethical problems – has continued this critical engagement with the best of human wisdom and understanding. In Asian situations, customary law, critiqued by the gospel, also makes the wisdom tradition available as a social and ethical resource.

This has great significance for Asian Christians. Western Christian teachers are often unaware of the degree to which their theological and ethical systems are built on the human wisdom of the cultures and societies in which they, or their forebears, lived. These same theologians are often quick to criticize the attempts of Asian scholars to explore the resources of Asian philosophies, and ancient and modern Asian wisdom, to guide their determination of issues facing Asian Christian communities.

Could it not be that the ancient philosophies of India and China, and the customs and traditions of many other Asian societies, contain the elements of the universal wisdom that may help Christians erect at

> least the foundations of a code of personal discipline that is appropriate to their own social context? Doing so will enhance the church's ability to communicate a living and life-changing gospel.
>
> ---
>
> 1. Wu Ching-tzu (1701–1754), *The Scholars*, E.T. by Hsien-yi and Gladys Yang (Peking: Foreign Languages Press, 3rd ed., 1973), 1.

3:8–13 QUALIFICATIONS FOR DEACONS

Paul now introduces the office of deacon (3:8). Again, his list presents qualifications, not duties since the office of deacon was probably an accepted part of the structure of offices in the early church and did not need to be defined with respect to its scope. This does, however, make it hard for us to determine what tasks a deacon fulfillled. As in the case of overseers, the qualities required of deacons must be viewed against the background of the false teachers. It is because of the failings of false teachers (1:7), which had caused a "leadership crisis,"[18] that Paul found it necessary to give detailed guidance about the qualities needed for faithful leadership.

There are both similarities and differences in the lists of qualifications for overseers and deacons. The similarities include not drinking in excess (3:3, 8), not being a lover of money (3:3, 8), being "above reproach" or not having anything "against them" (3:2, 10), and managing their own household well (3:4, 12). In some cases, the wording is almost identical; in others, the same concept is expressed using slightly different language.

Some qualifications specified for the overseer are not included in the list of requirements for deacons. First, nothing is said about deacons being able to teach (compare 3:2), suggesting that deacons were in a subordinate role to overseers, which is also implied by the fact that qualifications for overseers are mentioned first. While it is possible that deacons were elders who did not undertake preaching and teaching, there is insufficient evidence to be certain about this. Timothy, for instance, who is called a "deacon" (4:6), was called on to teach; and Stephen and his companions, who were elected to serve tables, later responded to the call to preach (Acts 6:1–10; 7:1–60).

---

18. Johnson, *Letters to Paul's Delegates*, 156.

Second, nothing is said about deacons being gentle rather than violent (compare 3:3), which suggests that deacons might not usually have exercised oversight in circumstances that were likely to provoke violent or aggressive reactions.

Third, nothing is said about deacons not being new converts, nor is any mention made of their reputation among outsiders (3:6–7). Perhaps those who exercised a ministry of service were less likely to be puffed up with conceit; and since they had less influence, perhaps what outsiders thought of them was less significant.

Fourth, nothing is said about hospitality (3:2), which suggests that deacons did not act as representatives of the community in the same way that overseers probably did.

Finally, the requirement that deacons must be "sincere" (3:8) or "not double-tongued" (NRSV) is not mentioned in relation to overseers.

"Deacon" (*diakonos*) is used here as a specialized technical term for those who had a serving office in the church.[19] This term – also used in the Greco-Roman world for people who undertook certain tasks for religious associations – was widely used in the NT of apostles and other leaders, who are often referred to as a "servant" or "minister" (Rom 16:1; 1 Cor 3:5; Eph 6:21; Col 1:23; 1 Thess 3:2). Jesus's teaching that he was a servant and that his disciples were to imitate him (Mark 10:45; Luke 22:26–27) led to the apostles referring to various services – including collecting money for the poor – as "ministry" (*diakonia*) – sometimes translated "contribution" (Rom 15:31) or "service" (2 Cor 8:4). Those who served in this way were called "ministers" (*diakonos*). Thus "deacon" both designates an office and describes what the person who holds this office does. Since Paul uses the term to describe his own and his fellow workers' ministries, "deacons" should probably be regarded as leaders. In the context of 1 Timothy, however, "deacons" seem to refer to a second tier of leaders. The plural usage suggests that there were several deacons in the church at a given time.

As with *episcopos*, "deacon" (Gk. *diakonos*) has an established meaning in many churches. It is a church position next to an "elder" and higher than ordinary members. Huizenga suggests that "server" or "assistant" may be reasonable translations for *diakonos*.[20] But since servers and assistants could suggest

---

19. See in general Mounce, *The Pastoral Epistles*, 197–98.
20. A. B. Huizenga, *1–2 Timothy, Titus*. Wisdom Commentary, Volume 53 (Collegeville: Liturgical Press, 2016), 35.

a subordinate position in modern churches, the term "deacon" may be retained as a technical term for this church office.

In the early church, deacons were often entrusted with handling the church's money and granting relief to the poor (Acts 6:1–7). However, we should not restrict the role of deacons in the Pastorals to such activities. The requirement that they must not pursue "dishonest gain" (3:8) is the only indication here that the deacons played a role in business affairs and finances, and a similar statement about money was also made with reference to the overseer (3:3). So all we can say with certainty is that deacons during this period did not seem to have taught or exercised oversight as overseers did and that they were involved in some form of service to and management of the community.

The phrase "in the same way" (*hōsautōs*, an adverb) usually connects two sentences or thoughts. It occurs in verse 8 to connect what Paul says in this section about the deacons (3:8–10) with what Paul has already said about the overseers (3:1–7). In other words, there are special characteristics or qualifications required of overseers as well as of deacons.

Just as overseers must be "above reproach" (3:2), deacons must be "worthy of respect" (3:8). Deacons must be "sincere," which may also be translated "not double-tongued" (NRSV). To be double-tongued means saying one thing to one person and a different thing to someone else, showing that a person's word is not trustworthy. As in the case of overseers, sobriety was also required of deacons (3:3, 8). The warning against "pursuing dishonest gain" – like the caution against being "a lover of money" (3:3) – suggests that the deacons, like overseers, had some financial responsibility.

Paul says that deacons must "keep hold of the deep truths of the faith with a clear conscience" (3:9). This requirement is the only distinctly Christian element in the list and was probably intended as a contrast with the false teachers who had failed to hold on "to faith and a good conscience," resulting in a "shipwreck" of their faith (1:19). The term "deep truths" is "mystery" in Greek (as in 3:16), emphasizing that these fundamental realities of the gospel must be revealed by God since they are hidden from human reason (see Mark 4:11; 1 Cor 2:7; 4:1; Eph 1:9; Col 1:26). "With a clear conscience" means that the genuineness of their faith must be evident in their godly life – correct doctrine must be combined with a pure life, lived in accordance with the ethical demands of the faith (1:5; 2 Tim 2:22).

Deacons must "first be tested" (3:10), just as an overseer was tested in relation to several matters (3:4–7), and 1 Timothy 5:22 suggests that, at least for elders, such testing was to take place over a reasonable period of time.

Deacons are to be examined with reference to the qualities already specified (3:8–9), and since most of these qualities are clearly observable, it would have been clear to the community how a would-be deacon fared. But we are not told whether this testing was done by examining a person's general conduct and understanding of the faith or whether a deacon underwent a period of probation; nor are we told who would carry out the testing, though some scholars suggest that the whole congregation had a say in the appointment of deacons. That deacons are to be tested is hardly surprising, given the problem of false teachers in the church as well as the likelihood of charges being brought against some elders (5:19–20).

In the Greek, verse 11 – "in the same way, the women" – simply has "women," without the article "the." The NRSV translates this, "women likewise must be serious, not slanderers, but temperate, faithful in all things." The reference could be to all women in the community, to the wives of deacons, to a separate and independent group of women, or to women who were part of the group of "deacons." Which view is most likely?

In 1 Timothy 3:8–13, Paul specifies qualifications for "deacons," then for "women," and then for "deacons" again. The character traits required of the "women" are almost identical to those required of "deacons" (3:8–10)[21] and "overseers" (3:1–7).[22]

Paul's mention of "women" here is unlikely to refer to all the women in the community since these women seem to be connected in some way with the "deacons" (3:8–10, 12–13). There seems to be no reason why Paul would speak about women in general in the midst of a discussion about deacons. Since Paul does not use either a possessive ("their wives") or a relative pronoun or adjective with "women," it is also unlikely that these women were wives of the deacons.[23] Additionally, since Paul says nothing about requirements for the wives of overseers,[24] it is unlikely that he would have singled out deacons' wives, especially given that the overseer's role seems to have been more significant than that of a deacon.

---

21. Bailey notes that the only requirement given for deacons but absent in verse 11 is "not greedy for gain." K. E. Bailey, "Women in the New Testament: A Middle Eastern Cultural View," *Evangelical Review of Theology* 22 (1998): 211–12.
22. In his letter to Titus, Paul includes similar characteristics that are to be cultivated by older men and women in the community (2:2–3).
23. A view favored, for example, by Hanson, *The Pastoral Epistles*, 80–81.
24. See J. H. Stiefel, "Women Deacons in 1 Timothy: A Linguistic and Literary Look at 'Women Likewise . . .'," *New Testament Studies* 41 (1995): 446, 452, 455.

1 Timothy 3

The whole passage (3:1–13) is structurally connected by the repeated phrase, "in the same way" (3:8, 11). This phrase seems to signal that, in verse 11, Paul begins discussion about a *third* group that is related to the previous two groups – overseers and deacons. So these "women" could refer to a group who served in the church as "women deacons," as distinct from male deacons. The Greek term "deaconess" had not yet been coined; instead, "deacon" (*diakonon*) is used of Phoebe from the church in Cenchreae (Rom 16:1). Therefore, a reference to "women" in a list about deacons would have been sufficient to indicate that Paul was speaking of women deacons, and their inclusion within this section on "deacons" could imply an equivalent status to male deacons. In summary, the authors of this commentary favor the view that the "women" were not a separate group but were included within the group of "deacons," as women who ministered along with men as deacons.[25] Stiefel notes that "the inclusion of the women in the topic of [*diakonoi*] . . . speak[s] strongly for their status as ministers as part of the group of [*diakonoi*]."[26] The structure of verses 1–13, by which the women are integrated into the discussion, supports this view.

But why are "the women" singled out in verse 11? In the previous chapter, too, Paul addressed women as a group (2:9–15), so it does not seem strange that women deacons – who we are suggesting do *not* form a separate group but belong *within* the order of deacons – are addressed separately.[27] Given what Paul has said about women being silent (2:9–11), however, the question may arise as to why he does not forbid women from being fully part of the order of deacons. Stiefel comments:

> The behaviours that attract notice to women in chapters 2 and 5 may not be so apparent among the women deacons. Neither they, nor the male deacons, are teaching in the congregation; that function is reserved for the [*episcopos*]. Nor are they functioning as a separate group of women, as the widows have been. The situation may thus indeed provoke unease [for Paul] yet not prohibition or redress. Thus the convoluted verse with its multivalent signals images the ambivalent situation of the women

---

25. In support of this view, see for example, Stiefel, "Women Deacons in 1 Timothy," 442, 455–56; Marshall, *The Pastoral Epistles*, 492–95.
26. Stiefel, "Women Deacons in 1 Timothy," 454.
27. See Stiefel, "Women Deacons in 1 Timothy," 455–56.

described. It is probably their status within the diaconal order that shields the women deacons.[28]

We conclude, then, that these women were involved in a diaconal ministry and were part of the one group of "deacons" along with men.

In order to fulfill their particular role as women deacons, these women were required to demonstrate certain characteristics. These characteristics are virtually identical to those of the male deacons: "worthy of respect" (3:8, 11); "sincere" or "not double-tongued" (3:8 NRSV) may be equivalent to not being "malicious talkers" (3:11); "not indulging in much wine" (3:8) probably conveys the same meaning as "temperate" (3:11); and holding fast to the "deep truths of the faith" (3:9) may be broadly equivalent to "trustworthy [or faithful] in everything" (3:11). These qualities stand in sharp contrast to the characteristics of the women who had been influenced by the false teachers (see 5:11–15; 2 Tim 3:6–7). Fee notes, "Their being mentioned, therefore, probably reflects the negative influence of the false teachers on the women of the church."[29]

Paul then returns to the male deacons, almost as an afterthought (3:12). As in the case of overseers, marital fidelity and good management of their own household are also required of deacons (3:2, 4–5). As Mounce notes, "The home is a microcosm of the church, and the qualities necessary for service in the church will be evident in the home."[30] The emphasis on good management suggests that deacons were involved in some form of managerial or governance work in the church.

We see here the same stress on stability, reliability, and respectability of character that we saw about overseers. Davies helpfully comments that these instructions "share with Hellenistic moral exhortation an admiration for sober, sincere, and moderate men. Such characters would not use their authority for aggressive and domineering behavior, and would be free from the vices of rashness, stupidity, greed or ascetic extremes."[31]

Since the failings of the false teachers had brought church leadership into disrepute, Paul might have been trying to restore confidence in these offices. He concludes this section with words of encouragement about the rewards in store for "those who have served well" (3:13; see also 5:17). The term

---

28. Stiefel, "Women Deacons in 1 Timothy," 456.
29. Fee, *1 and 2 Timothy, Titus*, 89.
30. Mounce, *The Pastoral Epistles*, 205.
31. Davies, *The Pastoral Epistles*, 27.

"standing" (*bathmos*), which refers to a step, can also mean rank or degree. Through serving well, a leader would gain an "excellent standing" or reputation in the community. Those who served well would also gain "great assurance" (*parrēsia*) – "great boldness" (NRSV) – which could mean confidence in speaking in the community or confidence in approaching God (see Eph 3:12; 1 John 2:28). The latter meaning is more likely, given that this confidence is in the sphere of "their faith" – that is, a person's trust in Christ – rather than "the faith" – which is the message about Christ.

Modern Asian churches have inherited from their missionary founders a great variety of church structures and systems of administration and governance, each with its own set of officials or leaders. There are ancient and modern episcopal churches in which, long ago, the overseer evolved into a bishop who, today, usually works with a synod that is representative of all sections of the church. Such churches usually maintain a threefold structure of clerical leadership: bishop, priest (presbyter), and deacon.

Some other churches maintain a pattern of ministry and leadership that evolved during and after the Reformation. This form of governance is a not quite coherent amalgamation of what was understood to be the rule of the Jewish synagogue – a council of elders with a designated teaching elder – and the pre-Reformation European pattern of Christian ministry – a "minister of word and sacrament" who presided on all sacramental and liturgical occasions, was the teacher of the congregation, and, along with the elders, was the overseer of the congregation's life. Terms such as "elder" (*presbyter*), deacon, and minister are used in these churches to designate functions and roles that are significantly different from those maintained in the episcopal tradition, while the office of overseer or "bishop" (*episkopos*) has been committed to a body of people (the Presbytery) who exercise oversight of a region.

There are also independent churches, sometimes standing alone, sometimes within loose federations. In these churches, the congregations select and empower pastors, elders, and deacons to carry out the spiritual ministries of teaching, preaching, overseeing, and serving. Some of these independent churches are also evolving and adapting in the area of church governance. For instance, some Baptist groups in the Philippines formerly had just one pastor and a board of deacons in leadership, but no elders; in other words, there was just one elder who was the pastor. But some of these groups now have elders in leadership – a council of elders, where the pastor is the teaching and preaching elder – in addition to a board of deacons.

In all these diverse structures, what is essential is that each is, to use Presbyterian terminology, "agreeable to the word of God." The Pastorals affirm diversity and flexibility in structure, office, and governance of the church – as evident from the differences between the situations in Ephesus (1 and 2 Timothy) and Crete (Titus) – provided that sound doctrine and good conduct are preserved and promoted. It is clear from the Pastorals, read in the light of other NT writings and in the context of what we know of the development of the early church, that evolution and development to meet the demands of changing situations were already underway in Paul's time.

Over the centuries, enormous energy has been devoted to debating matters of church order, and the universal church is still divided by nonrecognition of ministries, division between traditions, and the problem of intolerance between those whose faith is deeply rooted in continuity and tradition on the one hand and those who find Christ in the excitement and freshness of change and renewal on the other.

No modern system of church government is reflected exactly in the NT, nor are the Pastorals concerned with defining the precise roles and functions of the various church offices. This flexibility should be an encouragement to Asian church communities to continue seeking patterns of church government that best secure and promote sound doctrine, good conduct, and a healthy and vigorous congregational life and mission.

The modern ecumenical movement has been fruitful in Asia, with churches of different traditions bringing together different patterns of leadership and governance. Social change in Asia has created opportunities for women to hold office as church or ministry leaders and for unmarried men and women to be nominated to positions of responsibility once reserved for the "adult" heads of households.

A careful reading of the Pastorals encourages us to put much greater emphasis on the quality, character, and suitability of those called or elected to office in the church, while holding on much more loosely than any of us has been accustomed to issues of order that seem to constantly divide and weaken the church.

3:14–16 THE CHURCH: GOD'S FAMILY

This brief section functions as a bridge that follows Paul's instructions about prayer and ministry (chapters 2–3) and is followed by the apostle's words about false teachers, ministry, and practical directions for the Christian life (chapters 4–6). In this bridge, Paul highlights the true function of the church and, through a hymn about Christ and the story of salvation, gives the theological underpinnings for the teachings that precede and follow this section. As Barrett notes, although Paul has borrowed from non-Christian lists of virtues and qualifications in the preceding section, this section shows that "the foundation of his exhortation is specifically Christian, and Christocentric."[32] In the same vein, Frances Young emphasizes that while material is borrowed from non-Christian lists, there is a sufficiently strong emphasis on specifically spiritual and Christian virtues – such as faith, love, and fortitude (required of both women and men) – and on the Spirit's gifts of power, love, and self-discipline to prevent us assuming that the Pastorals are simply adopting patriarchal or Hellenistic virtues.[33] Asian churches that seek to draw wisdom from traditional sources must allow the gospel to critique the values of their culture and traditions to ensure that what is taught by local congregations is authentic, rising above an "I'm alright, you're alright" attitude that loses the treasure of the good news in a comfortable sea of indifferentism – that is, a mindset that believes that differences of religious beliefs are not important or that all religions are equally valid.

Paul explains the context for his letter (3:14–15). If he was "delayed," his letter would instruct Timothy about "how people ought to conduct themselves" in the church. Although these instructions were for Timothy ("you" is singular in verse 14), since Timothy was to teach these things in the church (4:11; 6:2b), Paul was, in effect, addressing the whole church. "These instructions" probably included Paul's charge to Timothy (1:18) – which is related to the material in chapters 2 and 3 about appropriate conduct in God's house – as well as the instructions that follow in chapters 4 to 6. This verse (3:14) also redirects attention to Timothy, to whom the instructions in the following chapters are addressed.

Paul writes so that Timothy and the church may know how Christians ought to live as members of God's household (3:15). This verse is a general summary of the contents of the letter. Fee suggests that "with verse 15 the real urgencies of the letter come into focus. The church itself is at stake."[34] It is crucial that people know how to conduct themselves because they are "the

---

32. Barrett, *The Pastoral Epistles*, 63.
33. F. Young, *The Theology of the Pastoral Letters* (Cambridge: Cambridge University Press, 1994), 37–38.
34. Fee, *1 and 2 Timothy, Titus*, 91.

church of the living God," entrusted with the truth, in a context where the conduct of the false teachers had led to abandonment of that truth (6:5).

The church is spoken of as an *oikos* eight times in the Pastorals. *Oikos* can be translated house (the building) or household (the community who live in the building). The translation of *oikos* as house may seem preferable, given that the terms that follow – "pillar" and "foundation" – are related to buildings. The church is thus depicted as the sacred place where the living God dwells with his people (see 1 Cor 3:16; Eph 2:21–22). Earlier in the letter, however, *oikos* certainly means household (3:4–5, 12), and this seems the most appropriate meaning in verse 15 since the conduct in view in chapter 3 relates to members of God's family and can, therefore, be understood to relate to God's "household." The reference is thus to "a divinely ordered social structure."[35] Paul's focus is not just the question of behavior in God's house – which might be understood as meaning "when the church gathers" – but, rather, what kind of conduct or lifestyle is appropriate for those who are members of God's household. The instructions about conduct given in the letter are standards for God's household, and the teaching given here provides directions for relationships among God's people.

The word "church" can be used of the local congregation (1 Cor 14:19; Gal 1:22) or the church at large (1 Cor 12:28; Col 1:18, 24). As "the church of the living God," the church belongs to God. The word "living" here emphasizes that it is God alone – and not the gods of the nations – who created all things (1 Chr 16:26) and is the source of life (Rom 4:17b). Bassler notes that the phrase "church of the living God," which is found only in the Pastorals, "suggests an active deity working in and through the community."[36] Since God is working through the community, we need to be responsive to his leading.

Having spoken about those who exercise leadership in the church (overseers and male and female deacons), Paul goes on to say more about the nature of the church – a place where God's people gather, just as Israel gathered around the tabernacle in the wilderness and in the temple in Jerusalem. The church is God's temple.[37] As God dwelled in the sanctuary of Israel, now, by the Spirit, God dwells in the new temple, the church.

---

35. J. M. Bassler, *1 Timothy, 2 Timothy, Titus*. Abingdon New Testament Commentaries (Nashville: Abingdon Press, 1996), 73.
36. Bassler, *1 Timothy, 2 Timothy, Titus*, 74.
37. See 1 Corinthians 3:16–17 and 2 Corinthians 6:16; see also Fee, *1 and 2 Timothy, Titus*, 92.

The church is "the pillar and foundation of the truth" (3:15). The word *stylos* means "pillar" or "column" and is used of the pillars in Solomon's temple. Although *hedraiōma* can be translated "foundation, ground, mainstay, support, buttress, fortress, or bulwark (a shelter or protection)" – which are physical components of a building – Paul uses the term figuratively to refer to "members" of a community.[38] "Truth" is used here of the content of Christianity. The church is to uphold the truth of the gospel and, thereby, safeguard true teaching. As Hultgren notes, "The truth does not rest upon the church, as though the church can never err, but the church is ever seeking to uphold the truth."[39] The church is thus seen as the servant of God's truth. Paul probably had in mind the false teachers who had abandoned the truth (4:1–5; 6:5; 2 Tim 2:18; 3:8; 4:4). The church should be a strong and stable structure, supporting the truth of the gospel and standing firm in the midst of conflicting claims or attacks by false teachers. Knight summarizes verse 15 in this way:

> Timothy and the church will conduct their lives appropriately if they remember that they are the home built and owned by God and indwelt by him as the living one, and also remember that they are called on to undergird and hold aloft God's truth in word and deed.[40]

Paul bases his call for godly behavior on the nature of God's church. It is because the church is the household of the living God and the pillar and foundation of the truth that people must live in the way that Paul prescribed.

Paul then elaborates on the greatness of this "truth" from which the church's godliness derives and of which the church is to be the pillar and foundation. This truth is manifested in the revelation of Christ.

The term "mystery" (3:16) is used with reference to the good news of Christ. Paul calls this a "mystery" because God's plan for salvation, which had previously been kept secret, was revealed in the appearance of Jesus Christ. *Eusebeia* – translated "godliness" – usually refers to "the wholeness of Christian existence as the integration of faith and behavior."[41] But in this verse, godliness is "thought of in a more objective way as the content or basis of Christianity."[42]

---

38. The Qumran community, for example, speaks of members laying "a foundation of truth for Israel" (*Rules of the Community*, 5:6).
39. Hultgren, "I-II Timothy, Titus," 77.
40. Knight, *The Pastoral Epistles*, 181–82.
41. Towner, *The Letters to Timothy and Titus*, 277.
42. Fee, *1 and 2 Timothy, Titus*, 92.

The verse goes on to explain that "the mystery" or the gospel is revealed and known in Jesus Christ. The mystery is "great" in the sense that it is sublime or important. Paul then spells out the content of this "mystery" in what has been called the "high-point of the whole letter."[43]

The content of the Christian mystery is given in six clauses that describe key moments in Christ's ministry and the continuing impact of that ministry (3:16b). It is likely that Paul was quoting a section of a creed or hymn used by the early church. Several factors support this view. First, although the NIV omits the word "who" (to facilitate easy reading), the sentence in Greek begins with "who" (*os*) – a feature of Greek poetry (see Phil 2:6; Col 1:15 in the Greek NT). Second, the six lines of the verse are almost identical in form and rhythm, which point to its being a hymn or creed of some sort. Third, the contents of the verse seem to be liturgical. So it seems likely that this verse (3:16b) is a quotation from a creed or a hymn, probably one that the Ephesian Christians were already familiar with. We can imagine a community gathered for worship, proclaiming the story of salvation by reciting this hymn or creed.[44] In an Asian Christian context, and indeed for many Christians around the world, repetition of the story of salvation is not simply a matter of recitation or completing an element in a liturgy but is also a way to remember God's work in redeeming them.

By prayer, religious songs, and rituals, people enter into the story of their salvation in a reality that transcends space-time. By repeating and remembering the salvation story, they may find wholeness, or salvation. This is as true of the rituals of a local traditional religion as it is of the great *wayang* dramas of Java and Bali.

What can we say about the structure of the hymn? Some have suggested that the clauses are arranged chronologically, but this is unlikely since "taken up in glory" – which almost certainly refers to the ascension – comes after "preached among the nations." The most obvious structural feature is the contrast between pairs of lines, whereby the hymn is divided into three couplets or stanzas: first, "appeared in the flesh," paired by "vindicated by the Spirit"; second, "seen by angels," coupled with "preached among the nations"; and third, "believed on in the world," which is paired with "taken up in glory."

---

43. Hultgren, "I-II Timothy, Titus," 77, quoting Jeremias.
44. On the importance of hymns or songs in worship, see 1 Corinthians 14:26; Ephesians 5:18–20; Colossians 3:16–17.

The contrasts are between the flesh and the Spirit, angels and the nations, and the world and glory. We see the repetition of the antithesis between the earthly and the heavenly (although in the second couplet the order is heavenly and then earthly). The passage thus presents Christ "at the two contrasting and complementary levels of 'flesh' and 'spirit,' heaven and earth."[45] We also see a progression or theological direction in the six clauses: the first couplet concentrates on Christ's work accomplished; the second on Christ's work made known; the third on Christ's work acknowledged. Overall, the emphasis is on Christ's triumph and the effects of that triumph. The six clauses tell the story of salvation (clauses one, two, and six) and also describe the response to that story (clauses three, four, and five). We now consider each of these clauses in turn (noting that there is some disagreement about the meanings of clauses two, three, and six).

In the first clause – "he appeared in the flesh" – the verb is passive and is better translated "he was revealed in flesh" (NRSV). Hence Christ is said to be "revealed" by another, that is, by God. That Christ is revealed implies that he existed previously but was unknown, a reference to Christ's preexistence (see also 2 Tim 1:9). Since "in the flesh" means that he became a real human being, his appearing or revelation was by way of the incarnation. As Fee notes, "In Christ, God himself has appeared 'in flesh.'"[46]

Christ was "vindicated by the Spirit." This vindication took place *en pneumati*, literally "in spirit" ("by the Spirit" in NIV). Should this be translated "by the Spirit" (a reference to the Holy Spirit) or "by the spirit" (a reference to Jesus's spirit)? Parallels in Romans 1:4 and 8:11 seem to suggest that vindication by the Holy Spirit through resurrection is meant. Although Jesus was crucified, God vindicated him and declared him righteous when he raised Jesus from the dead through the Holy Spirit. However, since the contrast in the couplet is with Christ who appeared "in the flesh," it is more likely that "by the spirit" is meant. In this case, vindication occurred at the point when Christ entered the spiritual or heavenly realm. The clause thus speaks of Christ's vindication in resurrection and exaltation (Acts 2:23–24; 10:39–40), God's vindication of Jesus's claim to be Messiah and Son of God,[47] and Christ's victory over evil powers.

---

45. Houlden, *The Pastoral Epistles*, 85.
46. Fee, *1 and 2 Timothy, Titus*, 93.
47. See Knight, *The Pastoral Epistles*, 184.

Christ was seen by "angels" (*angelos*) – the basic meaning of this word is messenger, and Paul's use of *angelos* may refer either to heavenly angelic messengers or to earthly human messengers. If the reference here is to heavenly messengers, Paul probably had in mind Jesus's ascension, glorification, and the angels' subsequent worship of him. But if the reference is to human messengers, then it seems likely that Paul had in mind the apostolic witnesses to Jesus's resurrection – the verb "was seen" (*horaō*) is also used to describe resurrection appearances in the NT (see Acts 9:17; 1 Cor 15:5–8). Christ's death, resurrection, and exaltation did not impact humans alone but was a cosmic event affecting even creation (Rom 8:18–25) and angels (1 Pet 1:12) – and Paul might have had in mind the appearance of the risen Christ before angelic powers when he speaks of Christ being "seen by angels."

Christ is then said to be "preached among the nations." The preaching is done by the apostolic church, and the scope of the preaching is universal. In the NT, the word *ethnē*, when used in contrast to "Jews," means "Gentiles" (Rom 3:29). But in other instances, *ethnē* may refer to nations, people groups, or humanity as a whole, as evident in the Great Commission (Matt 28:18–20). Given that verse 16 does not contrast Jews and Gentiles, and since the phrase that follows refers to "the world," Paul is almost certainly referring to the entire humanity as the recipients of the gospel being preached.

The last two clauses present the response to Christ "in the world" and then describe a further stage in the story of salvation where Christ is "taken up in glory." That Christ was "believed on in the world" refers to people's response to the Lord Jesus's preaching before his ascension and the apostles' preaching after the ascension. The universality of the gospel is again emphasized (2:4–6), and the importance of Christian proclamation is presupposed.

Christ was "taken up in glory." Glory indicates "brightness, splendor, or radiance and denotes in particular the glory, majesty and sublimity of God."[48] To enter glory is thus to enter God's presence. The emphasis is on Christ's triumph and his sharing in the heavenly glory of God. The clause seems to refer to the ascension since the verb "taken up" (*analambanō*) is used elsewhere of Christ's ascension (Luke 9:51; Acts 1:2, 11, 22). But the phrase implies not just that Christ ascended but also that he reigns with the Father in glory. Further, as Bray notes, "It is from his throne in heaven that the king rules over his people on earth, and it is from there that he will come to judge the world at the end

---

48. Knight, *The Pastoral Epistles*, 186.

of time."⁴⁹ Clause six is the doxological conclusion and glorious climax of the story which began in clause one with the "in the flesh" of the incarnation.

Elsewhere in the letter, Paul deals with organizational matters such as qualifications for leadership, but here, as he expresses the great mystery of the Christian faith, his thoughts soar – and they soar highest when he quotes the language of the community at worship. We see that the great mystery of the faith has to do with Christ's incarnation and glorious exaltation but also, significantly, with the church's ongoing witness to Christ. The hymn thus grounds the life of the household of God in the experience of the revelation of Jesus Christ, rather than in "speculations" or the dictates of the law (see 1:4–11). "The 'mystery of godliness' for this community is a living person, the resurrected Lord Jesus."⁵⁰

Knight sums up the meaning of the hymn:

> It is this great mystery of godliness that the church confesses, that the church, as the pillar and support of the truth, holds aloft, and that shapes the church's conduct before the living God. The preceding (and following) instructions have as their theological basis this great truth concerning the cosmic Christ who is the Lord and Savior of his church.⁵¹

Christ's universal triumph, spoken of in the hymn, provides the theological underpinnings for the instructions in the letter. According to Bassler, the main reason Paul cites the hymn here "is to underscore the connection between doctrine (represented here by the hymnic fragment) and behavior. The behavior defined by the letter's instructions properly reflects the theological truth preserved, proclaimed, and protected by the church and summarized in verse 16."⁵² Further, Paul will return to a censure of the false teachers in the next chapter (4:1–5), and the hymn reiterates the essential truths of the gospel as centered on Jesus Christ, his work, and the apostolic and angelic witness to these truths. We know that a doctrine is biblical and true when it centers on who Jesus is, what he has accomplished for his people, and how God has exalted Christ above all earthly and heavenly beings.

---

49. Bray, *The Pastoral Epistles*, 208.
50. Johnson, *Letters to Paul's Delegates*, 157.
51. Knight, *The Pastoral Epistles*, 186.
52. Bassler, *1 Timothy, 2 Timothy, Titus*, 77.

THE PRIMACY OF GODLY CHARACTER

The qualifications for elders and deacons listed in 1 Timothy 3 make it obvious that what is looked for in those who minister in God's kingdom is not primarily their education, skills, or achievements, but their godly character. Of the many qualifications listed in this passage and elsewhere in the NT, only one relates to skill (that is, an elder or deacon must be able to teach others) and just one relates to experience (that is, the person must not be a recent convert). The rest of the nearly twenty qualifications pertain to godly character.

The importance and primacy of godly character cannot be emphasized enough. Pastors who desire to strengthen, deepen, and broaden the work of God's kingdom in Asia must take godly character seriously. As Paul himself tells Timothy, "Watch your life and doctrine closely. Persevere in them, because if you do, you will save both yourself and your hearers" (4:16). Godly pastors, missionaries, and Bible teachers are a blessing to the people they minister to, and their godly influence and legacy will make a difference in the mission field. Such people are committed to their calling and exemplify the character of Jesus in their ministry. They serve and lead not just by what they say but also by how they live. They not only give direction and make decisions but also model a life which is transformed by the gospel and the Holy Spirit. However great their abilities or educational achievements, pastors who engages in illicit relationships can hardly challenge their congregations to live a life of purity and godliness. But the pastor who is faithful to his wife and loves his family models love, purity, and faithfulness for his congregation. The church leader who lives simply and gives generously models what it means to live by faith and be free from the love of money.

The church belongs to God, and God wants his church to be led by men and women of godly, Christlike character. Talents and skills are important, but godly character is primary.

1 TIMOTHY 4

Christians are a tiny minority in Japan, comprising less than one percent of the population. As such a tiny minority, what challenges might the Japanese church face? How do they cope with these challenges? Here's what Katsuki Hirano, a Presbyterian pastor in Tokyo, says:

> The smallness of the church does not matter for us. What is important is how we obey and how we follow Jesus, honestly and faithfully. Our responsibility is to preach the word of God faithfully. After that, God will do something, although we cannot predict that. We cannot manage the size of the churches, but God will do something through our preaching.[1]

Pastor Hirano's comment echoes what Paul says to Timothy in chapter 4 of his letter. Paul exhorts Timothy to focus on being "a good minister of Christ Jesus" and gives specific guidance on how to do this. The chapter has two parts: first, Paul describes the false teachers in Ephesus and their false asceticism (4:1–5), and then he prescribes how Christian leaders should live (4:6–16).

4:1–5 ASCETICISM OF THE FALSE TEACHERS

Paul has spoken about conduct at worship (2:1–15), the qualifications of overseers and deacons (3:1–13), and the church and its confession (3:14–16). In chapter 4, he speaks about problems and duties of those involved in ministry. He begins with a warning against the false teachers and a brief description about some of their false doctrines. This is one of the few passages in the Pastorals in which Paul gives a theological rebuttal of the false teachers (see also 1 Tim 1:8–11; 6:5–10; Titus 1:15). As Bassler notes, these verses (4:1–5) "temper the preceding celebration of worldwide faith (3:14–16) with the sober reminder of apostasy."[2]

Having spoken of the truth with which the church has been entrusted and the triumph of Christ (3:15–16), Paul goes on to state that some will renounce "the faith" (4:1). Since "the faith" refers to the content of the faith,

---

1. Katsuki Hirano "Don't be afraid to become a minority," *Faith and Leadership*, February 11, 2013, https://faithandleadership.com/katsuki-hirano-dont-be-afraid-become-minority (accessed April 18, 2022).
2. Bassler, *1 Timothy, 2 Timothy, Titus*, 78.

Paul is speaking of doctrinal error. The church should not be caught unaware by this departure from the faith because the Spirit had spoken about this possibility previously. The present tense of the verb "says" indicates that the Spirit's speaking has present and ongoing significance. Even though the Spirit has spoken in the past, "says" indicates that what the Spirit said is a constantly present authority (see Rev 2:7, 11). We do not know the details of how, when, or where the Spirit gave this message. Perhaps the Spirit had spoken through a prophet in the church; alternatively, Paul might have been claiming that the Spirit was the source for the apostle's own words (compare 1 Cor 7:40). The prophecy – "some will abandon the faith" – is expressed in the future tense as is characteristic of prophecy.

The Spirit says that people will renounce the faith "in later times" (4:1). Although the passage does not explicitly state that the prophecy has now been fulfillled, it is evident that Paul thought so since he goes on to address the present situation based on the prophecy, gives a detailed rebuttal of the false teachings (4:3–5), and urges Timothy to instruct the church in this regard (4:6). Paul has already stated that he wrote this letter so that if he was "delayed," believers would know how to "conduct themselves in God's household" (3:14–15). It seems that Paul is now addressing those who had departed from this household of faith (4:1–5). Clearly, Paul regarded the false teachers as a present danger and "the later times" as referring to his present situation.[3] The present situation of people falling away from the faith was clear evidence that they were living in the later times. Other NT writers also regard the Christian era – inaugurated by Jesus's life, death, and resurrection – as the "last days" (see Acts 2:17; 1 Cor 10:11; Heb 1:2).

It is said that some people will "abandon the faith" (4:1), which denotes separating themselves from the living God after previously having turned toward him. Since the false teachers are referred to in verse 2, the "some" who will fall away (4:1) does not refer to these teachers but to members of God's household (3:15) who had been led astray by the false teachers. This is one of several indications that the false teachers had gained a considerable following among the believers in Ephesus (see also 1:6–7; 4:1–3; 6:21; 2 Tim 2:17–18; 3:6).

The ultimate cause of the apostasy (that is, departing from their faith) was that people "follow deceiving spirits and things taught by demons" (4:1). Just

---

3. See also 2 Timothy 3:1; on the appearance of transgressors in the last days, see Matthew 24:12; Mark 13:22; 2 Thessalonians 2:3, 11–12; 2 Peter 3:3–7; Jude 17–18.

as Paul discerned the work of Satan behind his opponents in Corinth (2 Cor 4:4; 11:3, 13–15), he recognized that deceitful spirits were working through the false teachers in Ephesus.

These false teachings were mediated by the false teachers, whom Paul calls "hypocritical liars" (4:2). They were "liars" because they contradicted the truth of God as it is found in the gospel. They were "hypocritical" because, as Marshall suggests, "they may have deliberately pretended to be Christian teachers and to be speaking the truth in order to deceive people."[4]

That the consciences of these teachers were "seared as with a hot iron" (4:2) could mean that the false teachers' consciences had become desensitized and were no longer functioning properly because these teachers had deliberately ignored their consciences. Hence, these people sinned deliberately and consciously.

As noted earlier, a believer's conscience must be "formed"; it is not provided perfect and ready to use. The formation of a healthy, functioning conscience is fostered by regular and disciplined use of means of grace such as prayer, worship, fellowship with mature believers, and the careful study of Scripture. Through practicing such disciplines, believers become sensitive to the truths of the faith and increasingly able to discern truth and deviation in the way faith is expressed and taught. Conversely, those who are careless in these matters may end up with seared or deadened consciences that are no longer reliable. Such people may attempt to assert their own views over against the faith affirmed by the Christian community and even stand over against the community in the promotion of a new "gospel." They may insist on the validity of their personal interpretation of Scripture, contrary to the rule of faith – that is, the summary of doctrine that was a standard of faith in the early church. Sadly, church history is littered with examples of tragic divisions in the body of Christ, caused by individual teachers drawing away groups of believers – not because they were trying to protect some vital truth of the faith but to assert some egocentric or self-serving emphasis of their own. While it may seem unconventional, a peer review of those who feel called to put themselves forward for ministry and teaching in the church is one way in which the community itself can safeguard its fellowship and the gospel it preaches.

Paul then goes on to describe the false teaching in more detail (4:3). Contrary to the apostles' teachings, the false teachers were forbidding marriage and demanding abstinence from certain kinds of foods. The false teachers

---

4. Marshall, *The Pastoral Epistles*, 540.

seemed to have been teaching that marriage was inherently wrong. In response to some Christians in Corinth, who also looked down on sex and marriage, Paul commended singleness but also affirmed that marriage was not wrong (1 Cor 7:1–7, 25–38).

The false teaching Paul was combating also involved abstinence from "certain foods." While the word translated "food" (*brōma*) can mean food in general, it is also used to refer to meat (Rom 14:21; 1 Cor 8:13), which might have been in view here. The plural "foods" probably refers to certain types of food. Paul addresses the question of abstinence from food in his other letters too (see Rom 14:1–23; 1 Cor 10:23–33; Col 2:16, 21).

Why were the false teachers promoting this kind of asceticism or severe self-discipline? What influences might have led them to adopt such views? It appears that the false teachers believed that the resurrection had already occurred in some spiritual sense (2 Tim 2:18). This belief represents an over-realized eschatology, which did not merely claim that the new age had begun but that it had arrived in its fullness and promoted the idea that believers were to live a resurrected or spiritual life that avoided all human and physical relationships and pleasure. Those who espoused this teaching could either become ascetic or libertine (people who use their liberty or freedom to sin) and thus either ignore the things of the material world or regard them as belonging to the old age. Perhaps the belief was that for those who had "arrived," for whom the resurrection had already occurred, marriage was unspiritual and fitting only for the old order. It seems likely that the false teachers' rejection of marriage was connected to this over-realized eschatology.

The false teachers might have believed that the resurrection had already occurred (2 Tim 2:18) because they viewed the material world as tainted, or even evil, and therefore an impediment to salvation. Given that Paul emphasizes that creation is good (4:4), this seems likely. A negative view of the physical world probably led the false teachers to affirm that resurrection could only be spiritual – and that such spiritual resurrection had already occurred – and to a rejection of marriage, which was clearly part of the material order.

Paul was dealing with Christians rejecting marriage and, given that some denominations promote celibacy, his teachings have relevance for the church today. While Paul accepted and even promoted celibacy as a means of single-minded dedication in the service of God (1 Cor 7:25–35), he opposed the idea of imposing celibacy on a person as opposed to celibacy as a conscious choice. Paul upheld the sanctity of marriage and instructed overseers and deacons to be faithful to their wives (3:2, 12). Celibacy can present its own share of pastoral problems. If celibate clergy are not disciplined, this may lead to immorality, just as married clergy, if they are not careful, may be tempted to indulge in immorality. In Asian societies, which place a high value on family, celibacy could create suspicion or even give the family a bad name. Celibacy is a calling that must be entered into carefully and prayerfully, having sought the advice and support of family and spiritual leaders.

Why did the false teachers demand abstinence from "certain foods"? There are two possible answers. First, as in the case of forbidding marriage, belief that the resurrection had already occurred might have led to the view that since the material world belonged to the old age, contact with it should be curtailed. The connected belief that physical matter was evil or tainted would have led to the same result.

Second, there seems to have been a Jewish dimension to the false teaching about foods. The false teachers might have been invoking Jewish food laws and insisting that these laws, or parts of it, still applied to Christians (Titus 1:10–15). This might have been the basis for their demand for abstinence from certain foods or an additional reason to do so, along with the view that since the resurrection had already occurred, matter was evil.

Laws about abstinence from marriage and from certain foods were found in later Gnosticism – a heretical movement of the second century AD. However, since the main features of a developed Gnosticism are not found in the Pastorals, we should not regard the false teachers as gnostics. The closest parallel to the false teaching spoken of in this passage is the teaching of Paul's opponents in Colossae (see Col 2:16–23).

In response to the reports of false teachers who "forbid people to marry and order them to abstain from certain foods," Paul reminds Timothy that these things were "created [by God] to be received with thanksgiving by those who believe and who know the truth" (4:3) and that "everything God created is good" (4:4).

In responding to the false teachers' views about abstinence from certain foods, Paul focuses first on the fact that these foods were created by God to nourish humanity, drawing on passages in Genesis to support his argument (Gen 1:29; 2:9, 16; 3:2; 9:3). To abstain from food is thus directly contrary to God's actions, for God created the food, and receiving it with thanksgiving – rather than abstention – is the appropriate response by human beings.

Food is to be received "with thanksgiving" (4:3). A benediction or thanksgiving always accompanied meals in Judaism, and Jesus and the early Christians blessed God before a meal (see Matt 15:36; John 6:11; Acts 27:35; 1 Cor

10:30). Such prayers of thanksgiving at meals acknowledge God's prior creative action and express gratitude to the Creator for his gift of food.

But it is only "those who believe and who know the truth" (4:3b) who can appropriately receive and give thanks for God's good gifts. The false teachers at Ephesus had rejected and opposed the truth (1:19; 2 Tim 3:8; Titus 1:14). Instead of giving thanks and gratefully enjoying God's gift of food, they demanded abstinence from it.

Paul then puts forward another argument against the false teachers' asceticism – not only did God create food to be received with thanksgiving, "everything God created is good" (4:4). Note that Paul does not say that "everything" is good but that everything "God created" is good, which refers to things in their original created state. This is an important qualifier since much of God's good creation has been distorted by human sinfulness.

That "everything God created is good" means that "nothing is to be rejected if it is received with thanksgiving" (4:4). This is another affirmation by Paul that God is the creator not just of food but of everything, and that everything God created is good and intended to be used and enjoyed by human beings (see also 5:23; 6:17; Titus 1:15). As Fee notes, "The very fact that God created something has inherent in it the fact of its goodness."[5] Clearly marriage, as well as food, is now in view;[6] Paul grounds the acceptability of marriage in the goodness of all that God has created. But he also goes further and affirms that all God's creation is good. This implies that nothing is to be rejected in the way the false teachers were rejecting marriage and certain foods. Such teachings are false because they deny that everything God created is good. By affirming that nothing is to be rejected if it can be received with thanksgiving, Paul implies that Jewish food laws are a thing of the past.

Paul's all-encompassing statement about the goodness of creation seems to echo God's repeated affirmation that each component of creation is "good" (Gen 1:4, 10, 12, 18, 21, 25, 31). Through echoing one of the key features of the Genesis 1 creation story, Paul probably intended to remind his readers of the whole creation narrative. Since God created food, demanding abstinence from some foods is wrong. Since God specifically commanded humanity to "be fruitful and increase in number" (Gen 1:28) and then pronounced all creation "very good" (Gen 1:31), it is wrong to forbid marriage. As Davies notes "Although the practice of forbidding marriage is not formally refuted, the

---

5. Fee, *1 and 2 Timothy, Titus*, 100.
6. See Johnson, *Letters to Paul's Delegates*, 163–65.

assertion of the goodness of God's creation and the echoes of Genesis 1, which also enjoins marriage and bearing children, implies the error of such teaching."[7] Belief in the goodness of God's creation leaves no room for asceticism.

Paul reaffirms that everything created by God is to be "received with thanksgiving." The appropriate response to what God has created is not abstention but reception with thanksgiving. The repeated emphasis on thanksgiving reminds the reader that creation is God's and that it is good. But why does Paul lay such a strong emphasis on "thanksgiving"? Bassler notes that the false teachers' ascetic views probably impacted their attitude to the whole issue of meals and worship. She writes: "The negative view of the material world implied by this asceticism would have vitiated the Christian practice of grace before meals and possibly the Eucharist as well."[8] Given that the Eucharist was probably part of a full meal, if some Christians followed food laws and others did not, this would undoubtedly have caused problems for the community. Paul's emphasis on receiving food with thanksgiving might also have been a defense of the Eucharist.

Asian Christian communities and recent converts from other religions may have questions about the food laws, especially the dietary restrictions of the OT. The most obvious case is eating pork, which – although too expensive to be a daily or regular item of diet – is often a central feature of many traditional feasts and celebrations. One of the authors of this commentary was required to purchase and present a live pig for his adoption ceremony in North Sumatra, for the traditional (*adat*) ceremony. In such communities, and where Christians live alongside or among Muslim people, pastoral questions are often raised about eating pork.

In traditional communities, a more pressing concern may be the question of blood. In many Asian communities outside the spheres of Muslim and Buddhist influence, it is customary to use the blood of a slaughtered chicken or pig to make a rich sauce, which is then used to garnish the main dish. New Christians in these communities seem to quickly become aware of the prohibition of this practice in Israel – perhaps because people accustomed to being governed by their own customary laws tend to be naturally interested in such cultic rules. Pastoral questions about "eating blood" and "eating something in its own blood" are often raised with reference to particular OT passages (Gen

---

7. Davies, *The Pastoral Epistles*, 32.
8. Bassler, *1 Timothy, 2 Timothy, Titus*, 81.

9:4; Lev 3:17; Deut 12:16), not as idle queries but as issues of conscience for these new believers.

An adequate pastoral response must consider these issues along several dimensions. At one level, we must remember that there was a practical dimension to many of Israel's food laws – people in the ancient world knew that certain foods were likely to carry diseases and, as is also customary in some Asian societies, prohibited their use by appealing to divine or supernatural sanctions. Pork and blood clearly fall into this category.

But the prohibition of blood in the Torah is linked to a far more significant issue. Blood is seen as the site or source of the life-principle that is God's gift – not only to humans (Gen 2:7) but to all created beings (Gen 9:4; Lev 17:10–14; Deut 12:23). This life-principle – *nephesh* in Hebrew – is not to be consumed but must be returned to God by being poured out on the ground. A modern pastoral response to an inquiry about "eating blood" would need to go beyond a simple literalism and address the issues that the Torah was seeking to safeguard. Today, we no longer see *nephesh* or the life-principle located particularly in blood but have a more unified sense of the integrity of the whole being – the "living being" of Genesis 2:7. Reverence for the life-principle and the integrity of every part of God's creation is taken up today, appropriately, in environmental theology and in the practice of good stewardship. The cultic rules – that is, rituals – in the Torah can be respected as part of the holiness code of the people of God, appropriate for their time and situation as they sought to honor God and his gifts in their daily lives. The teaching of the Pastorals, with its emphasis on the goodness of all creation, helps us to form a response appropriate for our time and for differing situations.

The call to receive with thanksgiving also reminds us that not all things are good and, in some contexts, should not be "received" at all. In the mid-1970s, an Indonesian student asked, "Is it permissible to go out to 'get a pleasure'?" – a phrase of that time that represented a widespread attitude in some Christian circles that visiting a prostitute was simply a pleasant and harmless experience. Replying "Can you say a prayer before you go?" left the inquirer in a more thoughtful frame of mind than a stern "Of course it isn't!" might have done. As Paul's words to the Corinthians make it clear (1 Cor 6:15–16), visiting a prostitute can never be "received with thanksgiving."

At the same time, reverence for God's gift of life – which we share with all creation – calls us to move beyond a theology of pietism to join with all who struggle to safeguard the integrity of creation and protect the environment in the face of today's global economic order. Global warming, climate change, and degradation of natural resources are pressing issues of our times. Christian communities and organizations can join and support local and international initiatives to reduce carbon emissions, protect forests and wetlands, and protect natural biodiversity.[9]

All creation is "consecrated by the word of God and prayer" (4:5). What does it mean for all creation to be "consecrated" or "made holy" or "sanctified"? In the OT, the verb "consecrate" is used in relation to people (Exod 29:21; 1 Sam 7:1) and things (Judg 17:3). In the NT, God sanctifies people (Rom 15:16; 1 Cor 1:2; 1 Thess 5:23), the church is made "holy" by Christ (Eph 5:26), and, in the Lord's Prayer, we pray that God's name be "hallowed" (Matt 6:9; Luke 11:2). Procksch notes, "By sanctification [priests, people, holy places, and vessels] are separated from what is profane and set in a consecrated state."[10] It is important to note that elsewhere in the NT, with a few exceptions (see Matt 23:17, 19; 1 Tim 4:5), only *people* are said to be sanctified. But in 1 Timothy 4:5, the statement about sanctification clearly refers to "everything God created" (4:4a), which includes the whole creation. All creation is thus said to be "consecrated" or set apart in a consecrated state by God. Hence God's good gifts of creation should not be "rejected" but received with thankfulness because all creation "is consecrated by the word of God and prayer."

This sanctification occurs through "the word of God and prayer" (4:5). But what does Paul mean here by "the word of God"? Several suggestions have been made. First, the phrase could refer to excerpts from Scripture that were used in prayers before meals – for instance, the use of Psalm 24:1 in such a "grace before meals." However, this seems unlikely since Paul speaks of "everything God created" (4:4) being consecrated, not just what we receive at meals.

Second, Fee notes that in the Pastorals "the word of God" generally refers to the gospel message (2 Tim 2:9; Titus 1:3; 2:5).[11] In 1 Timothy 4:5, the expression could emphasize that the hearers had come to know that, in Christ, they were no longer bound by the OT food laws.

Third, Knight notes that "the word of God" can be used of a statement or message from God.[12] In this context, the phrase is "an abbreviated way of

---

9. For an excellent section on "With Christ in the Care of Creation," see S. Yeoman, *Is Anyone in Charge Here? A Christian Evaluation of the Idea of Human Domination Over Creation* (Eugene: Pickwick Publications, 2019), 228–301.
10. O. Procksch, "ἁγιάζω," in *TDNT*, Volume 1, edited by G. Kittel (Grand Rapids: Eerdmans, 1964), 111.
11. Fee, *1 and 2 Timothy, Titus*, 100–1.
12. Knight, *The Pastoral Epistles*, 192.

recalling those truths that God has communicated, namely that every created thing was made by him and is therefore good."[13] The most important occasion when God communicated this truth was at creation. Given the reference to God's creative activity in verse 3 and the echo of Genesis 1 in verse 4, it is likely that this echo continues here in verse 5. So "the word of God" probably refers to the word that God spoke in Genesis 1, which may be seen as including all that God says in bringing forth creation and approving of it (see Ps 33:6; Wis 9:1; John 1:1–3). The meaning of this phrase would then be that God has "consecrated" or "sanctified" creation by calling it forth, by speaking to creation (Gen 1:29–30), and by pronouncing it very good (Gen 1:31). Through these actions, God has sanctified all that he created. Therefore, the false teachers were wrong to forbid marriage and certain foods.

When doing the work of evangelism in traditional Asian communities, an understanding of the biblical doctrine of creation has frequently proved vital. It is in understanding the gift of creation that many people find salvation – deliverance from fatalism, from the power of spirits and supernatural beings, from the practitioners of the old religions, and from workers of magic. If such supernatural powers exist, they are part of creation, subject to the power of God and no longer to be feared, attended to, or even actively opposed. A mature understanding of creation helps to liberate people from a misdirected rejection of God's gifts that are meant to be received with thanksgiving.

Finally, Paul refers to "prayer" in relation to consecration (4:5). The prayer of thanksgiving (4:3–4) plays a role in consecration, for in such prayer we acknowledge that what we receive is God's gift, created good and consecrated by God. In this section (4:1–5), in response to the false teachers who forbade marriage and demanded abstinence from certain foods, Paul affirms three things: first, the intrinsic value and goodness of God's creation, which echoes God's own affirmation in Genesis 1; second, that God's good creation is to be "received with thanksgiving" as a gift from the Creator; and third, that all creation is holy since it is "consecrated" by God's word.

In an ecologically aware age, what does this passage teach us about the right attitude to the earth? Since everything was created by God, we cannot deal with the inanimate world simply as "stuff." The earth does not consist of disposable matter; rather, it is holy by virtue of being created and sanctified by God.

---

13. Knight, *The Pastoral Epistles*, 192.

In some Asian nations, people's understanding of creation is not very far removed from the Bible's teaching regarding the sacredness of creation. For instance, most Filipinos believe that the earth and everything in it was created by a deity. Traditionally, Filipinos believed in spirits inhabiting the earth and parts of the earth such as rivers, caves, trees, and mountains. Since this belief reinforces their recognition of the sacredness of the created order, it does not require a big leap in their thinking for Filipinos to embrace the biblical teaching about the sanctity of creation.

Although Paul does not go on to reflect further about the matter, what we have deduced about the text's meaning argues against the exploitation of the earth. That food and other facets of creation are to be "received with thanksgiving" must mean that exploitation of the earth is unacceptable. Knight notes that the repeated emphasis on thanksgiving reminds the reader that "it is thankful acceptance of God's good gifts that is being defended (compare 6:6–10), not an autonomous materialism or hedonism."[14] The unstated corollary of the view that created gifts must be received with thanksgiving is that if something *cannot* be accepted in an attitude of thanksgiving, then it should not be accepted at all. In other words, without the qualification about receiving with thanksgiving, the view that everything created by God is good and that nothing is to be rejected could lead to rampant exploitation and self-indulgence. The qualification – "if it is received with thanksgiving" – sets a boundary for the sort of interaction with creation that is acceptable in God's sight. Paul is also affirming that it is not humanity's *right* to receive God's creation and that a facet of creation can only be received when it is "received with thanksgiving." This means that we should always be mindful that what we are receiving is not our own property but a gift, a part of God's good creation. The continual awareness of the giftedness of creation serves as a deterrent to exploitation of the earth. If the earth is sanctified by God's word, holy and set apart by God, then it should not be abused by humanity. To abuse the earth is to abuse something that is holy to and for God.

The passage does speak of the use of creation by humanity. For instance, humans must have food and must receive it "with thanksgiving," knowing that God sanctified his creation. Human beings are responsible custodians of the earth, not the ultimate rulers over creation. While we may use and enjoy creation, we may not exploit it or destroy it.

---

14. Knight, *The Pastoral Epistles*, 192.

In the Asian church today, the false teachers and false teachings that confront Christians in various national settings may not be the asceticism that the Ephesian church faced. In certain Asian countries where wealth has become easy to come by, the pursuit of riches may constitute the biggest challenge to the church. In certain other countries, a perennial problem is what is called "folk Christianity" – a religion without true faith in Christ. This is true in the Philippines, where millions claim to be Christians, yet evidently do not know the Christian gospel. As we mentioned earlier, in Tagalog, it is sometimes said, *Kristiyano sa nguso, hindi sa puso* – meaning "Christian only by lips, not by heart." In other words, a person can claim to be a follower of Christ without leading the transformed life that the Bible describes. Just as Timothy needed to know the nature of the false teachings that threatened the Ephesian congregation, and just as he was called upon to inform and equip the church about the true gospel and warn them about false teachings, leaders of Asian churches must both equip their congregations with the true gospel and inform and warn them about false teachings that threaten the church today.

4:6–16 LIFESTYLE OF A CHRISTIAN LEADER

Having discussed the qualifications of overseers and deacons (1 Timothy 3) and dealt with some of the false doctrines being propagated by the false teachers (4:1–5), Paul now addresses Timothy directly (4:6–16). But Paul's exhortation to Timothy applies to all church leaders, including those whose qualifications Paul discussed in the previous chapter. In the Pastorals, as well as in ethical writings of the period, desired behavior is often spoken of through contrasting personal examples (see 1:18–20; 6:3–16; Titus 1:5–16). Paul's portrait of a church leader in this section (4:6–16) forms a strong contrast to and provides a foil for what has previously been said about the false teachers (4:1–5). This section answers the question, "How should a leader live and act when faced with false teaching?" The passage "creates a portrait of a good teacher who would provide a model for others, in his speech, in his lifestyle and in his progress,"[15] and Paul urges Timothy to model this kind of leadership.

This section, which shows the importance of the faith and practice of its leaders for the health of a church, emphasizes two things: first, teaching sound doctrine and encouraging godly living (4:6–10); second, faithfulness in personal life and public ministry (4:11–16).

---

15. Davies, *The Pastoral Epistles*, 37.

1 Timothy 4

4:6–10 Sound Doctrine and Godly Living

Paul tells Timothy to "point these things out to the brothers and sisters" (4:6a). "These things" probably refer not just to the previous section (4:1–5) but also to the whole letter. While the passage is directed to Timothy, Paul clearly had the whole church in mind as well since he tells Timothy to place these instructions before "the brothers and sisters." In the Pastorals, passing on apostolic teaching is seen as a crucial function of leadership. The community of Christians are to be "brothers and sisters," thus forming a surrogate family, something that has proved to be a great strength in evangelism and church planting in Asian societies that are founded on strong kinship structures. The Christian affirmation and strengthening of traditional kinship ties help to overcome the "alien feel" of the new faith, which opponents of the gospel often cite as a reason for resisting Christian teaching. At the same time, the Christian fellowship is perceived as a new and more inclusive extended family and support group, especially by Christians facing rapid social or political changes in their society. Karonese Christians in North Sumatra begin any kind of formal address with the greeting, *Senina-senina ras turang ibas Tuhanta Yesus Christus* (meaning, "Brothers and sisters in our Lord Jesus Christ"), affirming their oneness in Christ.

By being faithful in passing on sound doctrine, Timothy would be "a good minister" (*diakonos*) of Christ, unlike the "hypocritical liars" who propagated false doctrines (4:2). While Paul uses the term *diakonos* for the specific office of "deacon" (3:8, 12), the term is often used in the NT in the nontechnical sense of "attendants" or "servants" (Matt 22:13; 1 Cor 3:5), which is probably its meaning here. Thus, rather than saying that Timothy fulfills the office of "deacon," Paul is speaking more generally about ministerial service in the church. The title *diakonos* is a reminder that a leader is a servant among brothers and sisters, not a master ruling over his subjects. Although Timothy is being addressed, clearly what is said is relevant to leaders in general. As a good servant, Timothy was an example for the overseers and deacons in the local community.

To be able to instruct others, a person must have been "nourished on the truths of the faith" and "good teaching" (4:6c). If Timothy was faithful in teaching, this would be evidence that he himself had been nourished on good teaching. "Nourished" is a metaphor drawn from child rearing. The use of the present participle (literally, "being nourished") emphasizes that leaders need continuing nourishment. As Kelly notes, the present tense "suggests that feeding upon the truths of the gospel must be Timothy's daily task."[16] Stott notes, "Behind the ministry of public teaching there lies the discipline of private study. All the best teachers have themselves remained students. They teach well because they learn well. So before we can effectively instruct others in the truth we must have 'really digested' it ourselves."[17]

The source of nourishment is "the truths of the faith and of the good teaching" (4:6). There is a connection here between being a "good" (*kalos*) minister and being nourished on "good" (*kalē*) teaching. Being a good minister or servant depends on the goodness of what one has learned. This "good teaching" probably refers to the teaching of Jesus and the apostles (6:3; 2 Tim 1:13). "Good teaching" is emphasized in contrast to false teachings that were spreading in Ephesus (4:1). "The truths of the faith," which refers to the content of the faith, forms a parallel to "the good teaching." Paul ends the verse by saying that Timothy does in fact continue to follow good teaching. As Bassler notes, "The Greek word used here [*parakolouthein*] suggests not merely obedience, but careful attentiveness that yields understanding."[18]

Verse 6 establishes a pattern that is followed in the section as a whole: the minister is called to communicate the truth to others (4:6a, 6b) and to obey the truth (4:6c).

Having outlined what a good minister should do and what good teaching consists of, Paul now describes what a good leader must avoid. To avoid going astray as the false teachers had done, good leaders must have nothing to do with "godless myths and old wives' tales" (4:7). "Godless myths" may concern stories of gods and goddesses coming to earth and seducing humans, since such myths were common in the ancient world. However, given that, in the Pastorals, Paul speaks of "Jewish myths" (Titus 1:14) and uses the word "myth" in the context of a discussion of the Jewish law (1:4–11), "godless myths" probably refers to Jewish myths based on OT material. Fee, noting the connection between myths and genealogies in 1 Timothy 1:4, suggests that myths here may refer to traditions about people's origins since the word "myth" can have this meaning in Hellenistic and Jewish sources.[19] "Myths" would thus be contrasted negatively with historical stories. The myths are described as "godless" or "profane" (NRSV), which means that they are separated

---

16. Kelly, *A Commentary on The Pastoral Epistles*, 98.
17. Stott, *The Message of 1 Timothy and Titus*, 116.
18. Bassler, *1 Timothy, 2 Timothy, Titus*, 83.
19. Fee, *1 and 2 Timothy, Titus*, 41.

from what is holy. As Barrett notes, "They may be full of the word 'God,' but they are godless, because they do not rest upon the Christian revelation of God in Jesus Christ."[20] "Old wives' tales" is a common expression and implies that the teaching is unreliable gossip, as opposed to "truths of the faith" (4:6). Budiman uses a well-known Indonesian expression, *isapan jempol saja* – "mere thumb-sucking" – which has the sense of something someone made up, which is hence worthless.[21] Although we are not told what the contents of these tales are, it is clear that Timothy – as well as any other leader – was expected to repudiate such error.

Instead of paying attention to these tales, Paul advises Timothy, "train yourself to be godly" (4:7b). He uses an image drawn from athletics (see also 1 Cor 9:25; 2 Tim 2:5; 4:7–8) "to capture the sense of hard and steady practice required in the religious and ethical sphere, as in sport."[22] The emphasis on the value of godly training might have been to counterbalance the false teachers' asceticism; the false teachers advocated wrong forms of physical self-discipline, but there is a form of self-discipline which is of great value, which should be practiced by those who want to be godly leaders.

The meaning of the word "godly" (*eusebeia*) is debated. This word is never used by Paul except in the Pastorals, where it is a key term and is found ten times. The Greek word means "reverence for the gods" who guaranteed the stability of society. But what does this term mean here? Some see it as meaning "all for God's honor." Others argue that it represents an adoption of the values and morals of society and so stands for common ground with paganism. However, given its use in the Pastorals (see 2:2; 3:16), "godly" probably refers to both the content of the faith and its visible expression in correct behavior.

Paul instructs Timothy to "train" (*gumnazō*) himself in godliness. Although Paul repudiates the false teachers' asceticism (4:1–5), he acknowledges the need for "training" in the Christian minister's life – not athletic training but spiritual discipline which has godliness as its goal. Budiman, referring to 1 Corinthians 9:25–27, also draws attention to the need for bodily self-discipline (*latihan badani*) if the Christian teacher is not to risk disqualification after having preached the gospel to others.[23]

---

20. Barrett, *The Pastoral Epistles*, 69.
21. Budiman, *Tafsiran Alkitab*, 38.
22. Davies, *The Pastoral Epistles*, 34–35.
23. Budiman, *Tafsiran Alkitab*, 38–39.

Paul says that "physical training is of some value, but godliness has value for all things, holding promise for both the present life and the life to come" (4:8). Readers would have been familiar with the rigorous training that was necessary for athletes who hoped to compete in the games which were popular throughout the Greco-Roman world. But while physical bodily training is of some value, such value is limited to this age since bodily training does not bring spiritual life. However, Paul's comment that "physical training is of some value" does not mean that he advocates some form of asceticism; rather, he is probably referring simply to physical training in general.

But "godliness" (*eusebeia*) is far better than physical training (4:8). Here "godliness" seems to refer to spiritual devotion to God. It has "value for all things," both physical and spiritual, because it holds promise "for both the present life and the life to come," whereas the asceticism advocated by the false teachers is useful only for the present. As Johnson notes, asceticism "is exactly like physical training for the Olympic Games. It is an entirely this-worldly endeavor and does not pertain to the essence of faith, which is a response to the living God."[24] By contrast, those who give themselves to godliness can look for blessings in both the present and the future. The "promise" of life is "the promise of life that is in Christ Jesus" (2 Tim 1:1) – that is, life in union with Christ, which is salvation. Those who live godly lives will have life in the coming age, life with God in eternity. This is the future dimension in Paul's eschatology (see 1:16). There is continuity between life now and the life that is coming.

Therefore, this "life" – which primarily means eternal life, the life of the future – is a present reality experienced now, and also the hope of eternal life to come (see also 1:16; 6:12; Titus 1:2; 3:7). This is the characteristic tension of the "now and not yet" in the NT: Life is entered into here and now, but it is life that will only be fully realized in the age to come. In the contrast between "godless myths" and "godliness," godliness is far preferable because it has to do with life in both the present and the future.

But this life is not something a person owns or earns. Godliness holds the "promise" of life. It is not that the reward of "godliness" is eternal life. Rather, "godliness" possesses the promise of eternal life which God has made available through Jesus Christ (2 Tim 1:10). The one who promises is God – "we have put our hope in the living God" (4:10). In the present, godly leaders must

---

24. Johnson, *Letters to Paul's Delegates*, 171.

"labor and strive," thus exercising godliness (4:7), because they have set their hope on the living God who has promised life.

Paul then repeats the phrase that he uses in this letter to underline the significance of a statement: "This is a trustworthy saying that deserves full acceptance" (4:9). His reference is to verse 8b, which affirms that godliness has value for all things because it holds the promise of life for the present time and for the time to come.

Paul "labors and strives" because of the value of godliness, for godliness brings the promise of life both now and in the future. Part of the training in godliness (4:7b) is the spiritual toil and struggle that Paul refers to in verse 10. Since Paul uses the present tense, this verse could be translated "we are toiling and struggling," which draws attention to ongoing effort and exertion, which involves spiritual struggle and exercise and expresses the idea of "making every possible effort."[25]

Christians in Asia are often reminded by their cultural context that the spiritual life is a difficult journey, a hard struggle. When one of the writers visited Central Java, he went to see the great Borobudur stupa, which depicts on ascending terraces the different stages of life in Buddhist terms. A guide explained to a group of visitors of mixed religious backgrounds why the steps were so high: "This does not mean that our ancestors had longer legs than we do, it is to remind us that life is not easy." The old Benedictine motto *Ora et labora* (pray and work) is popular among the Batak Christians of North Sumatra and vividly expresses the dual focus of this energetic and outgoing Christian community.

Paul explains that the reason for the toil and struggle for godliness is "because we have put our hope in the living God, who is the Savior of all people, and especially of those who believe" (4:10b). It was hope in this God that gave Paul the confidence to keep on laboring and striving in his own ministry. Our hope rests in God because he alone, as the Savior of all who believe in him, can give life. As "the living God," who is the source of life, God can be relied on to fulfill the promise of life (4:8). Hope is also appropriate for those who look forward to the life to come.

Another reason for confidence in God is that he is "the Savior of all people, and especially of those who believe." Again, there is emphasis on the universal offer of salvation (see 2:3–6; 3:16). What does "especially [*malista*] of those who believe" mean? It cannot mean that there is salvation of some sort for those

---

25. Towner, *1–2 Timothy & Titus*, 108.

who do not believe. Skeat argues convincingly that the Greek term *malista* (especially) is better translated "to be precise" or "in other words"[26] and thus provides further definition. Wall notes, "The plain sense of this core belief is that God has offered salvation to everyone, but not everyone has embraced it, since divine grace does not coerce an unwilling acceptance of the gospel."[27] Accordingly, we could translate this, "God is Savior of all people, that is (to be precise), of believers." On this reading, the clear reiteration of God being Savior of all people does not mean that Paul advocates universalism. Rather, he is saying that God wants all people to be saved and that God, while he is potentially the Savior of all people, is actually the Savior only of those who believe.

Alternatively, some argue that "Savior" here has the more general sense of preserver and giver of life, rather than the specific sense of bringing salvation. If this is the case, then "especially of those who believe" would emphasize that God is Savior in a spiritual sense for believers. But this reading of Savior does not seem appropriate, given the earlier mention of the promise of life – that is, salvation – in both the present and the future.

Another possible way of interpreting verse 10b, though less likely than that proposed by Skeat, is to see it as a statement in which Paul holds in tension two facets of his faith: God desires all people to be saved (2:3–6); but only believers know God as Savior now, and so he is especially their Savior. Thus, Paul holds in tension the universality of God's grace for all (compare Rom 5:18–19; 1 Cor 15:22–28) and the particular response of faith by those who accept God's grace for themselves. But Skeat's view that *malista* means "to be precise" is preferred to this view.

Thus, in verses 7b–10, Paul says that since we have set our hope on the living God who saves, we should strive to live "godly" lives, which in turn will mean we will have "life," since godliness holds the promise of true and eternal life.

4:11–16 Faithfulness in Personal Life and Public Ministry

In contrast to the more generalized statements of the previous section (4:6–10), this section (4:11–16) is a personal directive to Timothy "to be courageous, active and diligent in the task of teaching, ignoring his disadvantage of youth

---

26. T. C. Skeat, "'Especially the Parchments': A Note on 2 Tim 4.13," *JETS* 30 (1979): 173–77.
27. Wall, *1 & 2 Timothy and Titus*, 123.

and relying on the power of the Spirit."[28] Paul's words to Timothy continue to be relevant for individual Christian leaders as they guide and direct the church.

Paul begins by saying, "Command and teach these things" (4:11). Since what follows are specific instructions to Timothy (4:12–16), "these things" probably refers to Paul's teaching about godly living (4:7–10), which was intended for the whole church and not just for leaders. Timothy must both "command" – or "insist on" (NRSV) – and "teach" these things; in other words, the teacher must aim for obedience to his teaching.

Although Paul instructed Timothy to "command" certain things (4:11), he must have known that this might lead to resistance because Timothy was young (4:12; see also 1 Cor 16:11). In Greco-Roman society, men below the age of forty were often considered young, "elders" were highly regarded, and it was contrary to custom for younger people to have authority over their elders. So Timothy could have found himself in a difficult position. Since the congregation would also have heard the letter, Paul's instructions would have served as a word to them about how they should treat Timothy. In similar fashion, the second-century bishop Ignatius warned the church at Magnesia in Asia Minor "not to presume on the youth of the bishop, but to render him all respect."[29]

Similar cultural perceptions related to age and seniority are a contemporary concern in many churches in Asia and the Pacific, sometimes resulting in misunderstandings in ecumenical and interchurch gatherings. In many of these societies, an unmarried male is considered a youth regardless of his age and, however mature he may be, his words often carry no weight. Conversely, a thirty-five-year-old unmarried male may expect to be accepted as a youth representative at an ecumenical gathering but find that younger people are unwilling to accept him because they feel that he represents their parents' generation. Some churches do not allow single men, however qualified they may be, to be ordained because, culturally, a man is not regarded as an adult until he marries. In some Chinese churches in Southeast Asia, senior leaders may deliberately delay ordaining young pastors – even though these young men are qualified and married – simply because they want to protect themselves from the challenges of a younger generation with new ideas. The teaching of the Pastorals, and the case of Timothy himself, makes it clear that those called by God to leadership offices in the church must be respected regardless of age, even

---

28. Marshall, *The Pastoral Epistles*, 557.
29. Ignatius, *Letter to the Magnesians*, 3:1.

if their appointment challenges local cultural perceptions. In today's church, and given the rapidly changing dynamics of Asian society, age should no longer be a barrier to a young person serving as an elder, a presbyter, or a bishop.

Paul instructs Timothy to "set an example for the believers in speech, in conduct, in love, in faith, in purity" (4:12b). Faced with opposition from those who looked down on him, Timothy was to be an example of maturity in life and conduct by exemplifying what he taught. In this way, he would be able to win the respect of the community. Church leaders do not gain respect by the arbitrary or aggressive use of authority but by the quality and example of their lives. The NT regularly describes leaders as examples or models (1 Cor 4:6; 11:1; Phil 3:17; 1 Thess 1:6; 2 Thess 3:7, 9; 1 Pet 5:3). As Fee notes, "That the people of God are to learn Christian ethics by modeling after the apostolic example is a thoroughgoing, and crucial, Pauline concept."[30] In this passage, Paul urges Timothy to be a good model, both in his personal life (4:12) and in his ministry (4:13–14), and reminds him that doing so would benefit both Timothy and his congregation (4:15–16).

A lack of credibility has contributed to the dramatic decline in Christian churches in many parts of the world during the latter half of the twentieth century. Other reasons for this decline include the increasing educational and cultural sophistication that has sometimes led to people thinking that faith and belief in God are not essential. Moral failures of the clergy and an overall suspicion of authority have also contributed to this decline. Finally, the widening gap between the church's claims and its inability to fulfill those claims has resulted in a growing sense of disillusionment and alienation, even among Christians.

The long-term damage sustained in many Western churches will take generations of patient and faithful ministry to rectify. In many parts of Asia, however, the church is growing rapidly, and old barriers of denominationalism and clerical domination are being shaken. In this more hopeful situation, it is imperative that we attend carefully to the words addressed to Timothy. Whatever our sphere of leadership, the best gift we can offer the church is a steady, consistent example of "walking the walk" as leaders who minister in the power of the Spirit and are prepared to go the distance.

In the spirit of verse 12, "Don't let anyone look down on you because you are young," we have witnessed, in recent years, one of the greatest shifts in the history of world Christianity: The younger churches of Asia, Africa,

---

30. Fee, *1 and 2 Timothy, Titus*, 107.

and Oceania are now intentionally taking up the mantle of ecumenical and missional leadership in the global church. We are seeing many missionaries from Asia, Africa, and Latin America crossing national borders, even going to the homelands of the missionaries who first brought them the gospel. These are exciting times for global missions, and we can see God building his church in new frontiers.

Godly living is defined in terms of speech, conduct, love, faith, and purity (4:12b). It is characteristic of the Pastorals that "speech" is mentioned first, for there is much in the letters about teaching. The second feature, "conduct" or way of life is also stressed in the Pastorals, particularly in relation to good works. Fee notes the contrast with the false teachers here.[31] Since Timothy is to be an example regarding speech, he must not be involved in arguments and dissension. He is to be an example in relation to conduct, in contrast to the deception of the false teachers (4:2); an example in "love," in contrast to the false teachers' envy and slander (6:4); an example in "faith," unlike the false teachers who had abandoned the faith (1:6, 19); and, finally, an example in "purity," in contrast to the asceticism of his opponents (4:1–5). "Purity" here may refer specifically to chastity or to purity and integrity of motive.

If he exhibited these characteristics, Timothy would be "an example" of spiritual maturity to the brothers and sisters. In many places, the authority enjoyed by teachers and leaders in a community depends on their integrity and conduct. If Timothy's life and character reflected the truth of the gospel, people would listen to him; and the same is true of the village elders and teachers, the town and city pastors, and the bishops and leaders of our day.

Paul then turns to matters concerning public worship and ministry (4:13–14). Timothy, as Paul's representative, was instructed to devote himself "to the public reading of Scripture, to preaching and to teaching" (4:13). In Greek, each of these terms is preceded by the definite article ("the"), which suggests that the public reading of Scripture, preaching, and teaching were recognized elements in worship. Although the first element (in Greek) is literally "give attention to the reading," this clearly refers to public reading of Scripture since what follow are two public activities involving Scripture. The task here would have involved the selection of passages to read – from the OT and perhaps some early Christian writings (see Col 4:16; 1 Thess 5:27; Rev 1:3) – since, as far as we know, lectionaries had not yet been written. The importance of reading the Scriptures regularly during worship is also in view here.

---

31. Fee, *1 and 2 Timothy, Titus*, 107.

Timothy was also to give attention "to preaching and to teaching" (4:13). The word translated "preaching" (*paraklēsis*) can be used of giving encouragement (Rom 15:4) but can also describe an exposition of Scripture (Acts 13:15). Here, where it is mentioned together with the reading of Scripture, "preaching" clearly means an exposition of Scripture in public worship, summoning people to respond to the Scripture which had been read. In this context, "teaching" may refer to teaching about Scripture or more general catechetical instruction in the faith. Teaching has a prominent place in the Pastorals (3:2; 5:17; Titus 1:9), and the reading, preaching, and exposition of Scripture are presented as the way to counteract false teaching (2 Tim 3:14–17). Paul thus "urges a public ministry that reads the Scriptures to the gathered Christians, exhorts them to respond appropriately, and teaches them its principles."[32]

Following the example of the early church, the churches of today must give central place to the public reading and exposition of Scripture in their public worship. Thanks to decades of work in Bible translation, the Bible can now be read in the vernacular in many parts of the world, including Asia. However, the continuing challenge in many rural areas in Asia is the lack of preachers and teachers who have been trained in the craft of Bible interpretation and preaching. Churches from urban centers can provide help by linking up with needy rural churches, providing resources and Bibles in the vernacular, and helping such churches to identify and equip lay leaders from among their congregations.

The fact that Paul does not mention the Eucharist does not mean that conducting the Eucharist was not one of the duties of a church leader. In verse 13, Paul concentrates on activities based on the use of Scripture,[33] but he does not lay down a pattern for worship. We know that public worship involved much more than is specified here; it often included prayer (1 Cor 11:2–5; 1 Tim 2:1–8), singing (Eph 5:19; Col 3:16), prophesying (1 Cor 14:1–5; 1 Thess 5:19–22), and the Lord's Supper (1 Cor 11:17–34). So Paul's mention of reading, preaching, and teaching was probably intended to list a leader's duties in worship that related specifically to the use of Scripture, particularly in response to the false teachers.

Paul goes on to say, "Do not neglect your gift" (4:14a). In the context of verse 13, Paul was probably referring to Timothy's "gift" for ministry as a preacher and a teacher. Timothy's special position as an authoritative teacher, in

---

32. Knight, *The Pastoral Epistles*, 208.
33. See Marshall, *The Pastoral Epistles*, 563.

spite of his youth, was due to this gift. Thus, in carrying out the tasks entrusted to him, Timothy was not to rely on his own ability but on the Spirit's empowering and equipping. This word "gift" (Gk. *charisma*) generally refers to a gift given by the Spirit, by God's grace, to individuals (Rom 12:6; 1 Cor 12:4). This gift, and ultimately the Spirit who had given it, would enable Timothy to fulfill the call to be faithful in his personal life (4:12) and public ministry (4:13). Timothy's life and ministry were the outworking of God's special gift to him. Timothy is told not to "neglect" this gift, which suggests that a gift is neither permanent nor static but must be used and developed (compare 2 Tim 1:6). Fiore notes, "The gift of God, like faith . . . needs practical exercise to come to full expression in the recipient."[34]

The gift was given to Timothy "through prophecy when the body of elders laid their hands" on him (4:14b). The reference to the body or council of elders would have reminded hearers that Timothy's standing had already been acknowledged by the leaders of the community in Ephesus. The laying on of hands in the NT church (5:22; 2 Tim 1:6) was modeled on OT precedents. Moses commissioned Joshua as his successor and gave him authority through the laying on of hands (Num 27:18–23; Deut 34:9). Rabbinic Judaism had a rite whereby a rabbi would pass on his authority to a student at the end of a course of study by laying hands on him, and it is possible that this rite of ordination was adopted by the early church and referred to here by Paul. However, the date of this custom of rabbinic ordination is probably later, and rabbinic texts relating to ordination do not mention the Spirit whose activity is implied here. Further, Lohse does not see the laying on of hands as described in the NT as involving the commissioning of a disciple (as in rabbinic texts) but, rather, as a rite of authorization.[35] Since Timothy is never called a presbyter, we should probably not think of him as being ordained to the presbyterate. Bassler suggests that the most immediate background to the rite described here "was probably the baptismal laying on of hands after the candidate's immersion (see Acts 8:14–17; 19:1–6), for the transmission of the Holy Spirit (or the Spirit's gifts) was central to both."[36] Fee suggests that the closest analogy is to be found in Acts 13:1–3, where the Spirit speaks through

---

34. Fiore, *The Pastoral Epistles*, 96.
35. Lohse, as discussed by Hanson, *The Pastoral Epistles*, 94.
36. Bassler, *1 Timothy, 2 Timothy, Titus*, 87.

prophets (4:1–2), which leads to the prophets and teachers laying on their hands in some form of consecration.[37]

Prophets in the NT church seem to have been involved in identifying those whom God had called and set apart for a particular task (Acts 13:1–3). The "prophecy" about Timothy may have been given by an elder or prophet in the community. Thereafter, the "body of elders" probably laid hands on Timothy as a formal act of ordination or appointment, both in confirmation of his call and as a means of spiritual strengthening for Timothy to carry out his ministry.

This appeal to an official authorization demonstrates that Paul – even though he was a pioneer at a time when there were no established forms and structures to fall back on – did not appeal to his own authority, as though Timothy was his personal representative, but to the collective discernment of the council of elders who, guided by the Spirit, had set apart Timothy to teach and lead in the church. A danger in the rapidly growing churches in former "missionary" lands – where older, more established churches are declining – is the tendency of individuals to seize the initiative without wider authorization, thereby fragmenting the church further and damaging the credibility of its witness. Although "going it alone" is a perilous path to take or advocate, it is one that charismatic individuals often seem keen to follow. The false teachers themselves may have begun to err when they started asserting their authority and their increasingly unorthodox views. On the other hand, a strong model of shared servant-leadership in parish, presbytery, or synod is healthy and provides accountability, mutual support, and fellowship.

Paul urges, "be diligent in these matters; give yourself wholly to them" (4:15a). "These matters" may refer to the whole letter or to what Paul has said since verse 6. "Be diligent" picks up the earlier athletic metaphor which emphasizes diligent training and effort (4:7–10; 2 Tim 2:3–6). "Give yourself wholly to them" is literally "be in them," which means being absorbed in the sense of total involvement and intensity. It is, as Towner expresses using a modern idiom, to "live and breathe" these things.[38]

In these final verses (4:15b–16), Paul returns to the theme of being an example to believers (4:12). Timothy was to devote himself to these things "so that everyone may see your progress" (4:15b) and thereby recognize Timothy's authority. In 2 Timothy 2:16, Paul warned that the "godless chatter" of the false teachers would lead to people becoming "more and more ungodly." The

---

37. Fee, *1 and 2 Timothy, Titus*, 108.
38. Towner, *1–2 Timothy & Titus*, 112.

word for "more and more" (*prokopsousin*) is related to the word Paul uses here for "progress" (*prokopē*). Whereas the false teachers exhibited progressive impiety, Timothy was to be a faithful minister, whose life would demonstrate to people what true progress in the faith looked like.

Paul warns Timothy, "Watch your life and doctrine closely" (4:16a). Timothy was to be an example by ensuring that his life and teaching were in accordance with the truth and that he did not go astray (see 1 Cor 9:24–27). In contrast to the false teachers, Paul urges Timothy to guard his own life (see 4:7) and teaching (see 4:6) with great care, and to "persevere in them" or, perhaps better, "remain steady in both"[39] his life and his teaching. Verse 16a, which emphasizes the importance of both character and teaching, is an apt summary of this section which has focused on these two matters. As Marshall notes, "The personal life and the work of the church leader are closely related and cannot be separated from one another."[40]

The reason for Paul's insistence that Timothy guard both his life and his teaching was because salvation was at stake: "you will save both yourself and your hearers" (4:16b). By their false teaching, teachers risk not only their own salvation but that of others; but by sound doctrine, teachers may "save" their hearers. How can this be? The verb "save" here could mean to keep from harm, preserve, or rescue, in which case this verse could mean that the teacher could "save" hearers in the sense of rescuing or preserving them from theological error. However, since other occurrences of the verb "save" in the Pastorals are clearly soteriological – that is, related to salvation – this explanation seems unlikely.

Fee sees the reference to saving hearers as an example of language that "may not be theologically precise"[41] and compares this verse to 1 Corinthians 7:16 (see also Rom 11:14; 1 Cor 9:22). Paul is not saying that a person can actually achieve salvation for another. Rather, the emphasis here is that salvation involves perseverance and holding on to the faith. Fee notes, "Timothy's task in Ephesus is to model and teach the gospel in such a fashion that it will lead the church to perseverance in faith and love and hence to final, eschatological salvation."[42] God is the ultimate source of salvation, but God may save using human agents as his means of salvation, "and it is thus that one who uses

---

39. Johnson, *Letters to Paul's Delegates*, 165.
40. Marshall, *The Pastoral Epistles*, 558.
41. Fee, *1 and 2 Timothy, Titus*, 109.
42. Fee, *1 and 2 Timothy, Titus*, 109.

and applies these means can very properly be said to save both himself and others."[43] As Barrett notes, "God alone saves; yet his salvation may take effect through faithful preaching and teaching, and this is a truth no minister dare forget."[44] Both teaching and living out the teaching as an example have saving significance because they make clear the salvation which God gives (4:10). Both this section (4:11–16) and the previous one (4:6–10) end by expressing a concern for salvation.

---

43. Knight, *The Pastoral Epistles*, 212.
44. Barrett, *The Pastoral Epistles*, 73.

1 TIMOTHY 5

In recent decades, there has been a growing tendency for people to view local churches as service providers and themselves as customers or clients. So someone who wants to worship God can pick a church, go there at the scheduled time, and the church will provide a "service." This, however, is not a biblical concept of the church.

The Bible frequently uses the metaphor of family to describe the church. Paul defines the church as "God's household" (3:15). His purpose in writing 1 Timothy was to instruct Timothy and the church in Ephesus about appropriate behavior in God's household. In earlier chapters, Paul discussed matters relating to proper order in the church. Now he focuses on the church as God's spiritual family. What does conduct in God's family look like? How should people within this family relate to one another? These are the questions Paul addresses in chapter 5. He begins by telling Timothy how to deal with men and women who belong to different age groups (5:1–2) and then focuses specifically on two groups: widows (5:3–16) and elders (5:17–25). Although Paul addresses Timothy, since the "you" in Paul's final greeting – "grace be with you" (6:21) – is plural, the letter was clearly intended to be heard by everyone in the church.

5:1–2 THE CONGREGATION

In the previous section, Paul told Timothy to "command and teach" (4:11) various things and to devote himself to "the public reading of Scripture" (4:13). Now he focuses on the relational guidelines that a leader must follow in carrying out these tasks.

In the first century AD – as in many parts of modern Asia – society was clearly demarcated along the lines of age and gender, with well-defined social norms about the young respecting those who were older and the exercise of a respectful reserve between men and women. Since Christian leaders were regarded as models, not just for those within the church but even for outsiders (3:7), it was important that they observed these social norms pertaining to respectful relationships.

Paul begins by discussing how Timothy should relate to older men: "Do not rebuke an older man harshly but exhort him as if he were your father" (5:1). The verb "exhort" means to urge, admonish, or encourage; and this exhorting must be done without harshness, with sensitivity and gentleness. The word used for an "older man" (*presbuteros*) – just like the term "elder" today – may designate age or an office. Here, however, it clearly refers to age. In exhorting or appealing to older men, Timothy was to show the same respect that he would show his own father. Even if a "rebuke" was required – as it might have been if there were older men among Timothy's opponents – this was to be done respectfully and with gentleness.

Timothy must "treat younger men as brothers." As Yarbrough notes, "'Younger men' deserve Timothy's gracious regard as if they were his brothers, which they are, inasmuch as God's household, the church, is a family (3:4–5, 15)."[1] Their common bond as "brothers" in Christ is the most important factor in such relationships.

Paul then discusses how Timothy, as a young church leader, should relate to women in the congregation. The command to treat "older women as mothers, and younger women as sisters" emphasizes the importance of respect. Even married men are to treat older women in the church as mothers and younger women as sisters. In Christ, we belong to God's family, and so women in the church must be treated with the same regard and respect one would give to one's mother or sister.

"With absolute purity" probably qualifies relationships with younger women, rather than with all four groups. While the Greek term "purity" can mean purity in general, it may also refer more specifically to chastity, that is, sexual purity. Timothy must avoid all inappropriate behavior and act with utmost propriety in his dealings with these young women.

The dominant idea here is that the church is a family and that believers, regardless of age or gender, are to be regarded as members of God's family. Therefore, believers must relate to everyone else in the church as they would to members of their own biological family.

Extrabiblical materials dealing with communal living – such as the Dead Sea Scrolls that talk about the Qumran community – contain similar advice concerning interpersonal relationships based on age. But Knight notes two distinctions between such texts and 1 Timothy 5.[2] First, the extrabiblical documents only speak of giving honor to an older leader and not to a younger leader instructing an elder. Second, the extrabiblical materials do not require *leaders* to treat younger people as brothers and sisters or as sons and daughters.

---

1. Yarbrough, *The Letters to Timothy and Titus*, 259.
2. Knight, *The Pastoral Epistles*, 215.

Treating fellow believers as brothers and sisters or as sons and daughters reflects the close bonds that exist within the church family.

In 1953, about 90 percent of soldiers in a mainly Karonese battalion of the Indonesian army sought baptism. Second Lieutenant Martin Peranginangin, the battalion's military chaplain, was entrusted with the task of preparing these soldiers and their families for baptism. Since this group included many high-ranking officers, the Lieutenant was initially hesitant. But his task was made easier by a group of officers' wives, who opened their homes for instruction so that it appeared as if the teaching was being done by senior officers, although in fact it was Lieutenant Peranginangin who did the teaching. Because of this sensitivity to a culture that respected elders, Lieutenant Peranginangin was able to prepare a total of 914 people for baptism.[3]

5:3–16 THE WIDOWS

Having spoken, in general terms, about relating to various age groups, Paul now addresses concerns relating to two specific groups within the community: widows (5:3–16) and elders who served as community leaders (5:17–25).

The increasing number of widows is a grave problem in many parts of Asia. In 2019, there were reportedly 46 million widows in India alone,[4] many of them needy. Responding to the plight of widows – who continue to be one of the most vulnerable groups in society – the Family Commission of the Kerala Catholic Bishops Council launched several initiatives.[5] First, they established a forum to provide emotional support for these women and to assist widows from low-income groups by providing them with information about their entitlement to government benefits. Second, they launched a matrimonial website to help younger widows to find suitable husbands.

The passage on widows has two sections: the obligations of family members to care for widows (5:3–8, 16) and guidelines for enrollment of widows to be cared for by the church (5:9–15). This passage thus supports the view

---

3. See S. Rae, *Breath Becomes the Wind: Old and New in Karo Religion*, 144–47.
4. R. Chandran, "Widows of Suicide Farmers to Get Land Titles in Indian State," *Reuters*, June 21, 2019, https://www.reuters.com/article/us-india-landrights-women-idUSKCN1TM14R (accessed April 18, 2022). See also Raja Dave, "Widowhood: The Problems and Challenges Faced by Widows in India," *International Journal of Advanced Research in Commerce, Management & Social Sciences* 3.4 (2020): 34–36.
5. S. Vellaram, "Kerala Church Starts Matrimonial Site to Help Widows, Middle Aged Men Find Life Partners," *The News Minute*, November 19, 2019, https://www.thenewsminute.com/article/kerala-church-starts-matrimonial-site-help-widows-middle-aged-men-find-life-partners-112566 (accessed April 18, 2022).

that a "list of widows" was already in existence at the time (see 5:9). The only other evidence for a special class of widows in the early church is provided by Ignatius and Polycarp.[6] Thus, there were widows who were "really in need" (5:3) and were enrolled on "the lists of widows," as well as women who were widows but were not members of this special class.

Widows were a particularly vulnerable group in the ancient world. Even if her husband had been wealthy, a widow might have been destitute if no provision had been made for her in his will and the property had thus passed to their children.

The passage addresses two issues. First, it seems that there were too many widows on the "list" for the church to support them all. This meant that cases of real need were going unattended, while people who could be supported by their own families were receiving support from the church. Second, the behavior of some of the younger widows who were being supported by the church was proving problematic.

How is this section related to the letter as a whole? Paul gives more space in this letter to widows than to any other group, which suggests that the activities of these women were of great concern to Paul. Fee believes that this section has a prominent place in the letter and comments that the letter has been "moving toward" these instructions on widows and elders all along.[7] He notes that the first section concerns identifying and caring for "widows who are really in need" (5:3) – that is, older widows who had no one to care for them – while the second section deals with "the reprehensible activities of some younger ones"[8] and explains why such widows should not be enrolled in the widows' list but, rather, be encouraged to remarry. Fee also notes that the description of the "widows who are really in need" without someone to care for them (5:5–7, 9–10) stands in sharp contrast to the activities of the younger widows, with their wealth and ungodly behavior.[9] Fee thinks that the real problem was that some of the younger widows had been spreading false

---

6. Ignatius, *Letter to the Smyrnaeans*, 13:1; Polycarp, *Letter to the Philippians*, 4:3. Dibelius and Conzelmann think that "the origin of this class should probably be dated during the period of the consolidation of the churches in the world." Dibelius and Conzelmann, *The Pastoral Epistles*, 74. In these passages the reference is not to a fully organized ministering order of widows but, rather, to the existence of a recognizable group whose care is a concern for the local church.
7. Fee, *1 and 2 Timothy, Titus*, 114.
8. Fee, *1 and 2 Timothy, Titus*, 114.
9. Just as Paul contrasted Timothy, a true teacher, with the false teachers (4:6–16; 6:6–14), here he contrasts the needy and godly widows with the wealthy young widows who were on the side of the false teachers.

teachings, "saying things they ought not to" (5:13), thereby bringing the gospel into disrepute (5:14). These women had "already turned away to follow Satan" (5:15; compare 2:14). They were "gullible women, who are loaded down with sins and are swayed by all kinds of evil desires, always learning but never able to come to a knowledge of the truth" (2 Tim 3:6–7). The real problem with the younger widows was not their age but their involvement with false teaching.[10]

5:3–8 Caring for Widows

Paul begins this section by saying "give proper recognition to those widows who are really in need" (5:3). This verse sets the tone for what follows. While widows must be cared for, discernment must be used in determining who really needs help. Since Timothy is being addressed, the instructions are in the singular, but Paul's use of the plural in verses 4 and 7 ("these should learn" and "so that no one may be open to blame") and his explicit reference to the church (5:16b) make it clear that the whole church is in view.

The instruction to "give proper recognition" to widows repeats the concern for widows found in both the OT and the NT.[11] Paul then goes on to define the kind of widow who is "really in need" of the church's assistance (5:5). His focus here is not on exhorting the church to care for widows (it seems they were already doing this) but on giving guidelines about which widows qualify for such care.

The use of "honor" (NRSV) – "recognition" in NIV – here was probably influenced by the fifth commandment: "Honor your father and your mother" (Exod 20:12; Deut 5:16). As Marshall notes, "In the context of the congregation as a family, believers are to treat widows like other parents."[12] While honor implies respect, here it also includes material provision, implied in verses 4–8 and made explicit in verse 16 (which sums up the section); material provision is also included in the related noun "double honor" (5:17).[13]

Paul speaks of "widows who are really in need" (5:3), also translated "really widows" (NRSV). Here, the word "really" may also mean "indeed" or "genuine." Paul does not imply that other widows do not need help or support. But he is speaking here about widows who have not just lost their husbands but have

---

10. See Fee, *1 and 2 Timothy, Titus*, 70, 114–15.
11. See, for example, Exodus 22:22–23; Deuteronomy 10:18; 14:29; 24:19–22; Psalms 68:5; 94:6; 146:9. In the NT, see Acts 6:1–6; 9:39–41; James 1:27.
12. Marshall, *The Pastoral Epistles*, 582.
13. See Knight, *The Pastoral Epistles*, 216. Dibelius and Conzelmann dispute this. *The Pastoral Epistles*, 73. In 1 Timothy 6:1, the related noun simply means "respect."

been "left all alone," with no relatives who can help them. It is such widows who qualify for material and financial support from the local church.

While recognizing the local church's responsibility to support widows, Paul makes it clear that family members have an obligation to care for those in their extended family who are widows: "But if a widow has children or grandchildren, these should learn first of all to put their religion into practice by caring for their own family" (5:4; see also 5:8). The word translated "grandchildren" can include other descendants as well – perhaps grandnieces and grandnephews. In Asian cultures, "family" is usually defined broadly enough to include not just siblings and direct descendants but also more distant relatives. Before believers devote themselves to other works of love, they must fulfill their religious duty to care for their own extended family, so that the limited resources of the local church can be channelled to those who have no family support (5:16). Knight remarks, "This exhortation is apparently given to overcome reluctance or indifference to the task and responsibility and to remind children that this duty is not to be turned over to the church or to someone or something else."[14]

Believers must "put their religion into practice" (5:4) – "first learn their religious duty" (NRSV) – within their own family. The term "religious duty" – which is related to the word translated "godliness" – means to "live or act piously."[15] To fulfill responsibilities within the family is to act in a godly way; this "religious duty" clearly involves human relationships, as well as our relationship with God. So, for example, the filial piety that lies at the heart of Chinese family life and responsibility is not merely affirmed as good but is a required part of a person's Christian discipleship.[16] Children and grandchildren are to put their faith into practice by repaying the care they have received from their parents. The verb "repaying" is in the present tense, which indicates that they are to keep on giving back. Such repayment, which is required by the fifth of the Ten Commandments, is "pleasing to God."

Fulfillling our obligation to repay those who have helped or nurtured us is not only culturally appropriate, but also one of the core requirements for a healthy attitude to life. A young Karonese poet, writing during the early years

---

14. Knight, *The Pastoral Epistles*, 217.
15. Hanson notes the verb is often used "of reverence towards parents as a religious duty, but not often with any other direct object except 'God' or 'the gods.'" Hanson, *The Pastoral Epistles*, 97.
16. Note, however, that while filial piety is appropriate, filial worship is not.

of Indonesia's independence when many Christians were struggling with the issues of living responsibly in a changed world, put it bluntly:

nggeluh labo mindo-mindo
tapi nggalar utang,

which means,

> life is not about asking and asking [for something for ourselves]
> but paying back what we owe.

Paul makes a noteworthy connection between a person's faith and their family life. As Fee comments, "As with the overseers and deacons (3:4–5, 12), so with the community as a whole; genuine Christian behavior begins at home with their own family."[17]

Paul then resumes his discussion about widows who are "really in need." Such a widow is one who is "left all alone" (5:5) – not just without a husband but also with no children or other family members to care for her – in contrast to a widow who does have children or grandchildren (5:4). She must have placed her hope in God, depended on his help for her present and future needs, and patiently trusted in God's special care for widows (see Deut 10:18; Pss 68:5; 146:9). The context suggests that God meets the needs of such widows through the care of the church.[18]

The widow's hope is expressed through her continuing (present tense) in prayer to God night and day (5:5). The same two Greek words (*deēsis* and *proseuchē*) used by Paul in 1 Timothy 2:1 to describe the prayer life of the church – there translated "petitions" and "prayers" – are also used in relation to the widow who continues to "pray" and to "ask" God for help. Paul's use of the phrase "night and day," rather than "day and night," probably reflects the Jewish understanding that the day begins after sunset. Continual prayer is clearly meant (compare Anna in Luke 2:37), and such a commitment to prayer shows that the widow is dependent on God alone and "demonstrates her lack of earthly helpers."[19] Hence, she deserves help from the local church.

Paul then contrasts the godly widow – who lives for God (5:5) and serves others (5:10) – with "the widow who lives for pleasure" (5:6). No details are given about such a widow's life of pleasure, but the verb used here means "to live luxuriously" and implies that this widow lives only for herself. Since the

---

17. Fee, *1 and 2 Timothy, Titus*, 116.
18. Knight, *The Pastoral Epistles*, 219.
19. Marshall, *The Pastoral Epistles*, 587–88.

verb ("lives for pleasure") implies living well, this widow was not destitute. The problem is not wealth but the misuse of wealth for pleasure. Although such a widow may believe that she is not merely alive but is living it up, in reality, she is "dead even while she lives" (5:6) – that is, she is spiritually dead. For Paul, "life that is truly life" is eternal life (6:19). This self-indulgent widow is not one of the widows who is "really in need" (5:3, 5) and should not be given material assistance by the church.

Paul says, "Give the people these instructions, so that no one may be open to blame" (5:7). The teaching in this section is to be passed on to the church. Whom did Paul have in mind when he wrote, "so that no one may be open to blame"? While Paul might have been thinking of the self-indulgent widow (5:6),[20] it seems more likely that he had in mind the families of needy widows. This latter view is supported by the fact that the family's obligation to provide for needy relatives (5:4) is restated by Paul in the negative form: "anyone who does not provide for their relatives" (5:8). If the families of needy widows fulfilled their obligations toward their needy relatives, they would not "be open to blame" either among the community of the church or among outsiders.

These verses (5:4–8) form a chiastic (mirror) structure:

a words to the relatives (v. 4)
    b words to the widows (v. 5)
        b' judgment on disobedient widows (v. 6)
    a' judgment on disobedient relatives (vv. 7–8)[21]

The specific sin in view is not providing for the needs of the members of one's own family. The word translated "especially" (5:8) is better translated "namely";[22] this means that the meaning of "relatives" is spelled out more clearly by using the term "their own household" or "family members" (NRSV), which would have referred to relatives who lived in the same house. This would be broader than the "nuclear family" of many Western countries. The general principle of care given in verse 4 is repeated in verse 8 in more forceful terms: "Anyone who does not provide for their relatives, and especially for their own household, has denied the faith and is worse than an unbeliever." This

---

20. Fee argues for this. Fee, *1 and 2 Timothy, Titus*, 117.
21. Modified from Fee, *1 and 2 Timothy, Titus*, 117–18.
22. See Marshall, *The Pastoral Epistles*, 590.

strong warning suggests that some people in the church at Ephesus had been neglecting this responsibility.

Failing to provide for one's relatives has two implications. First, the person is deemed to have "denied the faith" – meaning that there has been a failure to live up to the standard of living by faith by trusting God and doing good works. Fiore notes, "Once again one's conduct of life and faith stance are intimately related, such that abandoning Christian duty is tantamount to abandoning the faith itself. . . . The apostates show the emptiness of their faith claims by their deeds."[23] Clearly, the unity of belief and action is presupposed.[24]

Second, the person is considered "worse than an unbeliever." Knight comments,

> Paul regards unbelievers as having "the word of the law written on their hearts," and therefore even unbelievers are known to "do instinctively the things of the Law" (Rom 2:14, 15; compare also 1 Cor 5:1). Thus for a professed believer who has God's law ("honor your father and your mother") to fail to do what even many unbelievers instinctively do warrants the verdict that he is "worse than an unbeliever."[25]

Fee also notes that this fits with the letter's concern that Christian behavior "should be circumspect before the outsider and therefore at least be ethically equal to theirs."[26] Unbelievers take care of widows. "To *do* less is therefore to *be* less than an unbeliever."[27]

The distinction Paul makes between widows who truly need the church's help and those who do not is useful and relevant in many contexts in Asia. In the Philippines, for instance, where there is no universal pension scheme, not every elderly person receives a pension. Many widows (and other elderly folk) struggle financially because they do not have any kind of income. Church leaders need to know whether there are widows (or others) in their congregations who fall into this category so that they can explore ways in which the local church can help. Helping does not always or necessarily mean handing out money, especially if a local church does not have sufficient funds. As Paul's

---

23. Fiore, *The Pastoral Epistles*, 104.
24. "This presupposition illuminates the style of heresy polemic: dogmatic and moral reproaches are combined." Dibelius and Conzelmann, *The Pastoral Epistles*, 74.
25. Knight, *The Pastoral Epistles*, 221.
26. Fee, *1 and 2 Timothy, Titus*, 118.
27. Fee, *1 and 2 Timothy, Titus*, 118; italics original.

letter suggests, if such a widow has children or grandchildren (or other relatives such as siblings, nieces, or nephews), church leaders could encourage these family members to fulfill their obligations toward their widowed mother (or grandmother, or sister, or aunt). If a widow has no surviving family, then the church family must do whatever it can to help her.

This section (5:3–8) stresses the responsibilities of children to care for their parents and members of the wider family to care for widows. As Towner notes, "For both the widow and the family of the widow, these instructions express the need to keep one's confession of the faith and one's conduct in harmony. . . . Spirituality was to have practical, respectable and observable results."[28] The close harmony between this teaching and the cultural ethic of many Asian societies should caution us against the frequent, but mistaken, assertion that Christianity is a "Western religion."

5:9–16 Cautions About Widows

In this section, Paul outlines the responsibilities of the church to needy widows. Paul specifies the qualities and qualifications of widows who may be enrolled on "the list of widows" (5:9–10), explains why younger widows should not be put on this list (5:11–15), and concludes with a statement that shows the importance of both families and the local church being involved in the care of widows (5:16).

Paul discusses widows being "put on the list of widows" (5:9). The verb translated "put on the list" (*katalego*) – also used of those who were enlisted in the army – means to select, to enlist, or to enroll and points to the existence of a list of "enrolled" widows. However, this does not necessarily mean that there was an official "order of widows" at this time, with its members being expected to perform a list of duties (see 5:10), while the church, in return, would care for them. Such a formal "order" seems to go beyond the simpler language of the text.[29] Since nothing is said about the procedure for enrollment, such a list must already have existed, and Paul is simply giving instructions about how this list was to be regulated.

To be enrolled on the list, a widow had to be someone who was "really in need" and did not have family support (5:3–4). She could not be someone who

---

28. Towner, *1–2 Timothy & Titus*, 120.
29. See Fee, *1 and 2 Timothy, Titus*, 119.

lived "for pleasure" (5:6) and was thus morally unworthy.[30] A widow enrolled on this list could expect regular support from the church and might also have enjoyed a certain status in the church. This did not mean that the church did not help younger widows or widows who did not meet all these requirements. But it seems that the church had entered a "permanent arrangement"[31] with certain qualified widows.

Paul spells out the qualifications for enrollment on the widows' list. The widow had to be "over sixty" years old (5:9), the recognized point of transition to old age in those times; in addition, it was "beyond the age at which a person might reasonably be thought able to provide for their own needs."[32] Paul did not want to discourage remarriage as a normal course of action for a widow (5:14), and being enrolled in the widows' list would have made remarriage more difficult (5:12). But at sixty, remarriage was unlikely. Since Paul mentions age first, this was clearly an important prerequisite (5:9).

In applying this passage in today's world, we must be conscious that life expectancy and limitations imposed by age vary from society to society. Men and women now live longer and are active longer. People also tend to remarry at an older age than was previously thought appropriate. So Paul's criterion of sixty years must be read contextually today, and we must recognize that many people have the capacity for active and creative leadership well past sixty-five. A growing number of Asian women are also rejecting the belief that a widow must depend on others and embracing the idea that she can take responsibility for her own well-being and growth.

Across Asian societies, the role expected of widows varies. In some Chinese societies – and this includes Chinese people living or working overseas, who are trying to safeguard the central values of their tradition – even a young widow is often expected to remain unmarried. In many Asian countries, widows – like single women – have successfully established their own business or professional careers and are providing not only for their children's care and education but sometimes even for parents-in-law in their old age. Therefore, local churches must carefully reevaluate who needs the church's assistance as they consider the guidelines given in 1 Timothy 5.

---

30. Dibelius and Conzelmann note that the "widow in need" in verses 3 and 5 is the same as the "widow" in verse 9. Dibelius and Conzelmann, *The Pastoral Epistles*, 74.
31. See Knight, *The Pastoral Epistles*, 223.
32. Marshall, *The Pastoral Epistles*, 593.

To qualify for enrollment in the list, a widow had to have been "faithful to her husband" (5:9). This phrase is also translated "married only once" (NRSV) – literally, a "one-man woman" – or "the wife of one husband" (ESV), which is sometimes taken to mean that the widow should have been married only once. However, since Paul permits and even advises younger widows to remarry (5:14), it is unlikely that he would have excluded from the list a widow who had remarried and then become a widow again. The requirement here is probably sexual fidelity within marriage, whether or not a widow had remarried. Paul imposes a similar requirement for overseers, deacons, and elders (3:2, 12; Titus 1:6).

To be placed on the list, a widow must have demonstrated godliness by a life of Christian service and so was required to be "well known for her good deeds" (5:10); this idea is repeated at the end of the verse, where Paul says that a widow should have been "devoting herself to all kinds of good deeds." In between these two statements, Paul gives practical examples of such good deeds, some of which a widow might have done in better times, while her husband was alive.

Paul's list of good deeds is not prescriptive but simply gives examples of the kinds of good deeds a widow might have done. The first item is "bringing up children" (5:10). In both the Greco-Roman world and in Jewish thought, successfully raising children was one of the characteristics of the ideal woman. If the widow had brought up her own children, then these children would have been obliged to look after her (see 5:4), in which case she would not be among the widows who were "really in need," although of course it is possible that all her children had died or were not living nearby. But it is more likely that "bringing up children" refers to bringing up orphans.[33]

Hospitality was a highly prized virtue in the ancient world, and a widow who had shown "hospitality" (5:10) was likely to have extended such hospitality to traveling Christians, especially itinerant teachers, and preachers.[34] The widow was also expected to wash "the feet of the Lord's people" (5:10) or "the saints' feet" (NRSV). In the NT, "saints" is often used of Christians in general.[35] Washing the feet recalls Jesus washing the feet of his disciples (John 13:1–17; compare 1 Sam 25:41). Knight suggests that foot washing had not

---

33. See Dibelius and Conzelmann, *The Pastoral Epistles*, 75.
34. See Matthew 10:40; 25:35; Romans 12:13; 16:23; Hebrew 13:2; 1 Peter 4:9; 3 John 5–8.
35. See for example, Acts 9:13, 32; Romans 8:27; 12:13; 2 Corinthians 1:1. On "saints" see Trebilco, *Self-designations and Group Identity in the New Testament* (Cambridge: Cambridge University Press), 122–63.

become part of the liturgy of the Lord's Supper because if it had, it would not have served as a unique qualification;[36] rather, this probably refers to acts of care for weary travelers. A gracious host would see that this humble, servile task, which concretely demonstrated hospitality, was carried out (see Luke 7:44–46). Towner notes that the meaning goes beyond the literal: "Figuratively, the term includes the sense of performing all manner of humble tasks for the benefit of others."[37]

"Helping those in trouble" (5:10) might have involved providing financial or personal support for others in times of difficulty or persecution. In all this, it is the attitude of humility and service that is important, not that a widow had carried out each of the "good deeds" Paul mentions.

The list concludes, "devoting herself to all kinds of good deeds" (5:10). That the widow was "devoting" herself suggests that she was eager to find opportunities for doing good. The term "all kinds" makes the list broad and inclusive since it includes every kind of good work that God requires of his people.

Does this stress on Christian service imply that the enrolled widows had a part in ministry or that they were expected to perform certain duties? Knight suggests that if the need arose, the church might have entrusted to the widow tasks which she had already performed in the past.[38] Hanson thinks that "those who joined the order were expected to perform certain duties in return for the support which the church gave them, notably intercessory prayer and assistance in the entertainment of the church's guest."[39] However, although the commendation for good deeds could suggest that these women were serving the church in some way at the time, it does not require this interpretation.[40] Since the text does not explicitly say that the widows continued to do the good works mentioned, verse 10 does not seem to set up a list of present duties. Rather, the widow must *already* have been "well known" for such deeds.

Paul then turns to the subject of younger widows (5:11–14). He begins by saying that younger widows should not be put on the "list of widows." A possible reason for this prohibition was that the church in Ephesus might have previously enrolled younger widows, who had later sought to leave the group because they wanted to remarry, which might have led to scandal in the

---

36. Knight, *The Pastoral Epistles*, 224.
37. Towner, *1–2 Timothy & Titus*, 119.
38. Knight, *The Pastoral Epistles*, 225.
39. Hanson, *The Pastoral Epistles*, 96.
40. See Fee, *1 and 2 Timothy, Titus*, 115.

community.⁴¹ In the context of chapter 5, "younger" means less than sixty, but verse 14 implies that these widows were still able to bear children.

Why were younger widows not to be enrolled? Paul gives two reasons. The first is that "when their sensual desires overcome their dedication to Christ, they want to marry" (5:11). The desire to marry because of the impulse of sensual desire might have caused them to set aside their commitment to serve Christ as widows. Thus marrying would "bring judgment on themselves, because they have broken their first pledge" (5:12). Since enrollment on the list seems to have involved a pledge to remain a widow and serve Christ in that capacity, remarriage would violate that pledge and thus they would fall under judgment.⁴²

There are other suggestions about what this pledge refers to.⁴³ First, a widow might have been seen as breaking her pledge to her first husband if she remarried. However, in view of the counsel that young widows should remarry (5:14), this interpretation is unlikely, for Paul would hardly have advised a widow to break her pledge. Second, Fee suggests that remarriage might involve abandoning Christ if a widow married an unbeliever and, following the social custom of the time, adopted his religious beliefs and abandoned her own.⁴⁴ This view takes the word "pledge" (*pistis* in Greek), to mean "faith" – as it does elsewhere in the Pastorals (1 Tim 1:19; 5:8) – and interprets this verse to mean that the widow would be violating her first "faith." However, this interpretation introduces a new element – an unbelieving husband – into the text. Further, while the marriage itself seems to be the problem for an enrolled widow, marriage is actively encouraged for the widow who is not enrolled (5:14). So here, the problem does not lie with *who* a widow marries but with the fact that the marriage breaks the pledge to serve Christ as an enrolled widow.

Paul then gives a second reason for refusing enrolment to a young widow. In their single state, some of the younger widows had grown accustomed to "being idle and going about from house to house," and had "become idlers, but also busybodies who talk nonsense, saying things they ought not to" (5:13). For Paul, idleness contradicts the Christian calling to serve God (compare 2 Thess

---

41. Hanson notes that remarriage was difficult for a destitute widow "since normally a father, or at least a male relative, was needed to arrange the marriage." Hanson, *The Pastoral Epistles*, 98.
42. Bassler notes that "since ordinary marriage is regarded very positively in these letters, the condemnation or judgment (Greek, *krima*) of those widows who desire to marry indicates the uniqueness and gravity of their vow." Bassler, *1 Timothy, 2 Timothy, Titus*, 97.
43. See Knight, *The Pastoral Epistles*, 226.
44. Fee, *1 and 2 Timothy, Titus*, 121–22.

3:6–12).⁴⁵ In addition, these women were going "from house to house" – which probably means from house church to house church – not merely being idle but also either wasting other people's time or misusing opportunities. The latter option seems most likely. Dibelius and Conzelmann see "house to house" as referring to "pastoral house calls," which they suggest were among the widows' duties.⁴⁶ Fee, however, notes that the activities of the women entitled to be on the widows' list – prior to their being enrolled on the list – centered on their own homes.⁴⁷ So it seems unlikely that these younger widows had formal duties such as paying pastoral house calls.

Fee suggests that since these younger widows are described as "busybodies who talk nonsense, saying things they ought not to," they might have been disrupting the activities of the various worshiping communities in Ephesus. Although "talk nonsense" is also rendered "gossips" (NRSV), Fee thinks the latter translation is misleading. The term does not refer to talking about others' affairs but means

> to talk nonsense, or foolishness, and is used most often in contexts of speaking something foolish or absurd in comparison to truth. Thus, the young widows are described in terms very much like the false teachers, whose talk is foolish (1:6) and empty (6:20), and who are also saying things they ought not to (compare 1:6–7; 4:7; 6:3–4). It is probably as the "idle" purveyors of the false teachings that they are busybodies, and this becomes one of the reasons they are to be in all submissiveness and not to teach (2:11–12).⁴⁸

A key reason for the younger widows' problematic behavior in the church was that some of them had adopted the doctrines advocated by the false teachers and were promoting it from house (church) to house (church). These activities by the widows also "had the potential of creating a negative reaction in the wider society, which expected women to follow a more domestic and less public pattern of behavior."⁴⁹

Having described what younger widows should *not* do (5:11–13), Paul now describes what they should do: "So I counsel younger widows to marry,

---

45. Note that Paul is not talking about the necessity to be in paid employment here.
46. Dibelius and Conzelmann, *The Pastoral Epistles*, 75.
47. Fee, *1 and 2 Timothy, Titus*, 122.
48. Fee, *1 and 2 Timothy, Titus*, 122.
49. Bassler, *1 Timothy, 2 Timothy, Titus*, 94.

to have children, to manage their homes and to give the enemy no opportunity for slander" (5:14). Paul not only had no objection to a second marriage, but he also actively encouraged these young widows to remarry, be involved in family life, and so remove the occasions for temptation. In marrying and having a family they would also emulate the "good deeds" of the older, godly widows (5:10). Further, by marrying, the young widows would cease going about from house to house and so would stop promulgating false teachings. As Fee notes, in this way "the satanically induced problems of the Ephesian church would tend to be brought to an end."[50]

Paul instructs the younger widows to "have children" and to "manage their homes" (5:14), which was the "socially normative role of the homemaker" in that culture.[51] Indonesian scholar R. Budiman underlines the positive emphasis of this section. He sees Paul encouraging each person within the congregation to find and understand their own role, "beginning with the closest environment, their own family."[52] A well-ordered family life is a powerful witness. The reason given for remarriage and having children is that this would "give the enemy no opportunity for slander" (see also 3:6; 5:8). "The enemy" seems to be a reference to hostile opponents who seek to slander (see Titus 2:8), rather than to the devil. Since some of these younger widows seemed to have been on the "list of widows" who were receiving financial support from the church, their actions (5:13) could have been seen as being financially subsidized by the church and thus damaging to the church's reputation among outsiders. Obeying Paul's instructions concerning younger widows would have helped to protect the church from such misconceptions and criticisms.

By saying that "some have in fact already turned away to follow Satan" (5:15), Paul adds urgency to his instructions. Clearly, Paul is not describing a hypothetical situation but one that really existed in the church at Ephesus.

---

50. Fee, *1 and 2 Timothy, Titus*, 123. Singleness is commended in 1 Corinthians 7:7–8, 28, 32–35, even for widows (1 Cor 7:39–40). In 1 Corinthians, Paul recognizes that the decisive thing is whether God has given the person the gift of singleness. "The application in 1 Timothy 5 . . . is that he now recognizes more clearly that being married before (i.e. being a widow) is, as a general rule, an indicator of how God has gifted one with reference to marriage and thus a reason to counsel remarriage (compare 1 Cor 7:9)." Knight, *The Pastoral Epistles*, 228. Fee, too, draws a similar contrast: "There [1 Cor 7] Paul said she is *free* to remarry (a believer), but it is *better* to remain single. Here he still holds that it is *better* to be single (5:9, 12), but the situation in Ephesus has now caused him to *advise* remarriage." Fee, *1 and 2 Timothy, Titus*, 123.
51. Towner, *1–2 Timothy & Titus*, 122.
52. Budiman, *Tafsiran Alkitab*, 50–51.

Once again, we note the link with the false teachers who were associated with "deceiving spirits" and "demons" (4:1).

In verse 16, Paul returns to the responsibility believers have for widows as he addresses women who were caring for older widows. Paul probably had in mind a scenario where a Christian woman showed hospitality by sheltering needy widows in her home, as Tabitha did (Acts 9:36–42). Bassler notes that "Christian women of means, perhaps themselves widows, provided material support – food, housing, or clothing – to other widowed women in their congregation."[53]

Fee suggests that the problem might have been a specific case of a younger widow of means refusing to care for a widowed mother or grandmother.[54] In any case, Paul wanted Christians to care for the needy widows without burdening the church. In that way, the church would have been able to focus on those needy widows who had no one to care for them (5:16b).

In many Asian societies there is a very strong cultural expectation that relatives will care for elderly or other needy members of the extended family. One of the authors attended a funeral in New Zealand. A Chinese man had died, leaving a widow who had no close relatives to assist her. The author asked a distant relative – who had come from overseas for the funeral – what the local community could do to assist the widow. He was told, "Her relatives in Canada already have the matter in hand." To fail to care for family – even if they are distantly related or live far away – would invite sharp criticism and result in a loss of standing in the community. Here again the teaching of this letter is in harmony with and reinforces important cultural values.

When believers take responsibility for the care of widows – those in their own family, their extended family, or others – this frees the church to care for widows who are truly alone. In 1 Timothy 5, the support in view seems to be financial assistance, which suggests that the local church had a fund of some sort for this purpose. But since the congregation did not have unlimited resources, they could only support a limited number of widows.

Widows must be cared for – either by their own families or by the church. This passage defines the qualifications for enrollment on the list of widows and makes it clear that such widows were expected to reflect godly characteristics.[55]

---

53. Bassler, *1 Timothy, 2 Timothy, Titus*, 96.
54. See Fee, *1 and 2 Timothy, Titus*, 124.
55. See Knight, *The Pastoral Epistles*, 230.

Younger widows were not to be enrolled on the list but were given instructions about how to live.

5:17–25 THE ELDERS

Having dealt with widows, Paul now deals with elders, who serve as leaders in the community. Marshall notes several connections with the preceding section about widows: Respect, recognition, and tangible financial support are to be given to both groups and there is a danger of unworthy people being involved in both groups.[56]

A church office such as elder, deacon, or pastor may enhance a person's social status. Even those outside the church may applaud such a position as an achievement and give undue honor to these leaders. As a result, people sometimes seek to hold office in the church for selfish or unworthy motives. The Pastorals lay down important criteria that must be met before a person is entrusted with leadership responsibilities in the church.

Fee thinks that this passage is related to the false teachers' desire to be elders and gain wealth,[57] which led to Paul's charge to Timothy concerning his responsibilities in such a situation (4:6–16), followed by "instructions about how to deal with the two specific groups who are the problem element – some young widows (5:3–16) and their 'captors,' the straying elders (this section)."[58] The fact that some elders seemed to have followed the false teachers (or were themselves "false teachers") also helps to explain the placement of this material in the letter.

The broad structure of this section (5:17–25) mirrors what was said about widows (5:3–16): Paul's words about caring for elders (5:17–18) parallel his instructions about caring for widows (5:3–8), while the cautions given in relation to appointing elders and disciplining sinning elders (5:19–22, 24–25) are mirrored by Paul's warnings about younger widows (5:9–16). Verse 23 is a digression, which might have been prompted by verse 22, in the light of the asceticism of the false teachers.

5:17–18 Caring for Elders

Paul begins, "The elders who direct the affairs of the church well are worthy of double honor, especially those whose work is preaching and teaching." The

---

56. Marshall, *The Pastoral Epistles*, 609.
57. Fee, *1 and 2 Timothy, Titus*, 127–28.
58. Fee, *1 and 2 Timothy, Titus*, 127–28.

word translated "direct" means "to exercise a position of leadership, rule, direct, be at the head (of)."[59] The verb translated "work" is used by Paul in relation to the difficult and demanding activities of leadership, which requires considerable effort.[60] The use of both "direct" and "work" in verse 17 confirm that the Greek word *presbuteros* – earlier used in the nontechnical sense of "older man" (5:1) – is used here in a technical sense with reference to leadership.

The term "especially" (5:17) is better translated "namely," which would then identify "the elders who direct" with "those whose work is preaching and teaching."[61] As Marshall notes, "With the author's stress on the importance of teaching, he is likely to have regarded the outstanding elders as those who performed this duty."[62]

This means that two different groups of "elders" are envisaged in the church at Ephesus: first, those who do not rule, but are "older" in age; second, those who rule and labor in preaching and teaching, and who were given the official title "elder." But older men did not automatically become leaders ("elders") in the early church, as is evident from the qualifications expected of church leaders and the requirement that potential leaders be tested (3:1–13; 5:22).

In view of the clear reference to financial support – "the worker deserves his wages" (5:18) – the word "honor" (5:17) seems to involve financial compensation or "pay," although perhaps an honorarium rather than a fixed salary is in view.[63] However, it is unlikely that "double honor" meant "double" the amount received by widows.[64] It is far more likely that "double honor" means "twofold honor" – that is, the honor and respect due to those in leadership in addition to their remuneration.[65] Hence, "honor" here has the same double sense as the related verb "recognition" which was used in relation to widows (5:3) – both honor (or recognition) and an honorarium. The term "double" thus refers to this twofold meaning of the word.[66]

---

59. W. Bauer, revised and edited by F. W. Danker, *A Greek-English Lexicon of the New Testament and Other early Christian Literature*, 3rd ed. (Chicago: University of Chicago Press, 2000), 870.
60. See Romans 16:12; 1 Corinthians 15:10; Galatians 4:11; Philippians 2:16; Colossians 1:29; 1 Thessalonians 5:12. It clearly implies that preaching and teaching are demanding works.
61. See Marshall, *The Pastoral Epistles*, 612. The word has this sense of "namely" in 1 Timothy 4:10; 2 Timothy 4:13; Titus 1:10–11.
62. Marshall, *The Pastoral Epistles*, 612.
63. Dibelius and Conzelmann, *The Pastoral Epistles*, 78.
64. The real widows, who were destitute, needed full support; it is very unlikely that the elders received twice this amount.
65. See Witherington, *A Socio-Rhetorical Commentary on Titus, 1–2 Timothy and 1–3 John*, 273–74.
66. See Knight, *The Pastoral Epistles*, 232; Collins, *1 & II Timothy and Titus*, 144.

We should not, however, think of remuneration as meaning a salary or an income sufficient to live on.[67] The word translated "honor" is never used of an ongoing salary.[68] The honorarium in view might have been quite modest, and it is best to think of honor given in some tangible form.[69]

Paul's injunction for the church to doubly honor elders does not mean the same amount of salary or honorarium in all countries and in all contexts. This is especially true in the diverse economic and demographic contexts of Asia. In many urban centers in Asia, where churches are affluent, it goes without saying that many elders are well paid and well supported by their churches. But there are also many urban poor centers in Asia where churches are unable to offer their elders the same salary that churches in richer countries pay. In some cases, a church may be so small that it can only pay its elders a part-time salary. However, all churches are mandated to give "double honor" to their elders within their means.

Paul notes that the work of the elders "is preaching and teaching." The term translated "preaching" can mean "speaking" and here, in conjunction with "teaching," most likely means preaching in the sense of exhortation. Marshall notes that "preaching and teaching" are "two broadly separable but not altogether distinguishable activities, possibly evangelistic and edificatory respectively."[70] The attempt to distinguish too sharply between these two activities in a congregational setting may lead to unexpected outcomes. For example, in the 1970s, one of the writers was rebuked by the elders of an Indonesian city congregation for using a blackboard and chalk to illustrate points in a sermon because, they said, "using a blackboard is 'teaching' not 'preaching.'" Today's preachers probably use PowerPoint presentations without a second thought. Teaching and preaching involve the use of Scripture (2 Tim 3:16) and seek to pass on sound teaching (2 Tim 2:2).

Paul supports what he says about financial remuneration for elders by appealing to what "Scripture says" (5:18). The term "Scripture" is used in the NT exclusively of the OT. Paul uses the present tense ("says") to indicate the present relevance of the Scripture he cites. The quotation, "Do not muzzle an

---

67. Marshall notes that there is no evidence for a "paid clergy" before the end of the second century. Marshall, *The Pastoral Epistles*, 614. After preaching in Indonesian village churches, one writer came home with anything from a live hen to a long unprocessed sugar cane.
68. Marshall, *The Pastoral Epistles*, 613.
69. That some form of gift was given is shown by 1 Corinthians 9:7–14; 2 Corinthians 11:8; Galatians 6:6; Didache 13.
70. Marshall, *The Pastoral Epistles*, 612.

ox while it is treading out the grain," comes from the OT (Deut 25:4) and is also cited by Paul in 1 Corinthians 9:9.[71] As Marshall notes, "The allusion is to the practice of driving oxen over a threshing floor to trample the corn with their hooves, separating the wheat from the chaff. The law laid down that the farmer must not prevent the animal from taking its share of the harvest."[72] Just as the ox must be permitted to obtain sustenance from its labors, so should an elder who preaches and teaches.

The second statement – "The worker deserves his wages" – is not taken from the OT but are the words of Jesus (Luke 10:7) and is connected to the first quotation by a simple "and."[73] Would Paul have referred to the words of Jesus as "Scripture"? In 1 Corinthians, Paul regards Jesus's teaching as authoritative (1 Cor 7:10). In 1 Timothy, too, Paul treats this saying of Jesus as authoritative. But some scholars think that this second quotation is given as an addition to back up the first quotation, with the reference to "Scripture says" only applying to the first quotation. In this case, it would not be necessary to conclude that Paul thought the second quotation was "Scripture."[74] But it is also possible that Paul considered Jesus's words here under the formula "Scripture says," meaning that these words were as authoritative as the OT. As Marshall notes, if this is the case, "this is early evidence for the conferral of scriptural status on a collection of sayings of Jesus."[75] In any case, the saying regards the worker as a real laborer who is entitled to wages.

What prompted Paul to make this statement about remuneration? Were some elders not being paid? Since the false teachers thought that godliness (and hence probably the teaching of godliness) was "a means to financial gain" (6:5), in reaction to this, some people might have suggested that elders not be paid at all. But the problem with the false teachers was greed and dishonest gain (3:3; Titus 1:7). Paul makes it clear that elders who rule "well" – that is, doing honest work and not for dishonest gain – deserve pay for the work they do.

In churches that do not have a great deal of experience to call upon, the issue of honoring those who preach and teach presents two sharply contrasting kinds of problems. On the one hand, an impractical and self-loathing piety

---

71. In 1 Corinthians 9:9–10 Paul explicitly says that this verse applies to humans.
72. Marshall, *The Pastoral Epistles*, 615–16.
73. The wording in Matthew 10:10 (which parallels Luke 10:7) is slightly different.
74. Fee argues that the term "Scripture" meant only the OT for Christians until the end of the second century. He compares Mark 1:2, where Mark writes, "it is written in Isaiah the prophet," and then cites Malachi and Isaiah. Fee, *1 and 2 Timothy, Titus*, 134.
75. Marshall, *The Pastoral Epistles*, 615.

may assume that material reward is unworthy or inappropriate, leaving those who labor in the ministry with the dilemma of how to offer significant time to their ministry tasks while engaging in an occupation that enables them to support their dependents. On the other hand, elders and ministers may be tempted to focus more and more on the need to earn income and less and less on the fulfilllment of their designated role, resulting in a commercialization of their function. During Indonesia's New Order era in 1966 to 1998, the expression *komersialisasi jabatan* – which refers to exploiting one's position for personal gain – was frequently used with reference to civil and military officials whose concern about income – "Will I get paid for this?" – determined priorities and choices. The simple lifestyle and relative poverty of most ministers and priests in Indonesia have saved churches, for the most part, from this accusation and is in its own way a positive witness to the life of faith.

5:19–25 Cautions About Elders

Paul gives instructions about dealing carefully with accusations against elders (5:19) and the proper discipline of elders found guilty of wrongdoing (5:20), and then commands Timothy not to be intimidated by anyone as he impartially judges the sinning elders (5:21). Since those in leadership are constantly under the scrutiny of others, they are likely to face criticism. But Paul warns that accusations against elders must not be entertained unless due process is followed, whereby the accusation is supported by the required number of witnesses (a reference to Deuteronomy 17:6 and Matthew 18:16). This is an attempt to avoid the problem of false or unfounded accusations, which could cause significant problems for an elder. It is also part of the "honor" or respect due to elders (5:17). The warning that an accusation against an elder must be supported "by two or three witnesses" before it is accepted – and hence investigated – endorses an OT principle (see Deut 17:6; 19:15).[76]

Some have argued that verses 20–21 are speaking about sinners and not elders.[77] But there is no radical break after verse 19, and the passage makes good

---

76. Note Deuteronomy 19:15: "One witness is not enough to convict anyone accused of any crime or offense they may have committed. A matter must be established by the evidence of two or three witnesses." This principle is also applied in Matthew 18:16. The same principle applies for any church member, according to John 8:17, 2 Corinthians 13:1, and Hebrew 10:28. With regard to what is behind this, Collins suggests that it may imply "that the community may have faced a troubling situation in which false teachers were unjustly accusing the community's elders." Collins, *1 & II Timothy and Titus*, 146.
77. Dibelius and Conzelmann, *The Pastoral Epistles*, 80; Hanson, *The Pastoral Epistles*, 103. This suggestion does mean that the verse would continue to be about discipline.

sense if verses 20–21 are interpreted as still speaking about elders. So, since the principle about public rebuke applies to elders, if an accusation against an elder is found to be true and such an elder persists in sin, the person is to be reprimanded in public.

"Sinning" – the present participle of the verb "to sin" – indicates ongoing sin. If "an accusation against an elder" is found to be true, the first step in church discipline is to confront and reprimand the sinning elder in private before "two or three witnesses" (5:19). But if this attempt fails, and there is no repentance, such sins should not be covered up, and the elder who persists in sin must be rebuked in public.

The reproof is "before everyone." Although two or three witnesses might bring accusations against an elder, when the elders are satisfied that there is sufficient evidence for these accusations, they must rebuke the sinning elder before the whole congregation. This procedure is in line with Jesus's own instructions about church discipline (Matt 18:15–17; see also 1 Cor 5:1–8).

In Asia's shame-oriented cultures, the idea of publicly rebuking an elder seems unthinkable, particularly if the one tasked with rebuking the elder is a younger person. But the public rebuke Paul recommends here is not the kind that takes place casually in a store or out on the street. Rather, what is envisaged is a prescribed disciplinary process within the local church, in accordance with what Christ himself has set out, which should help to reassure Asian readers and ease their discomfort and hesitancy over rebuking an elder in the church.

The purpose of the rebuke is so that "the others may take warning." While "the others" here would have included the other elders, the disciplinary action also had the rest of the congregation in view. The reason for the rebuke was that they "may take warning," where "warning" means fear, alarm, or fright. In the OT, the accusation that is "established by the testimony of two or three witnesses" (Deut 19:15) also ensures that "the rest of the people will hear of this and be afraid, and never again will such an evil thing be done among you" (Deut 19:20). A public rebuke reminds the community of both the seriousness of sin and the unpleasant disciplinary consequences that would follow. Fee helpfully relates this to the situation in Ephesus. Timothy was to expose those who persisted in sin – and some specific elders seem to have been in view. The emphasis is thus on verse 20, rather than on verse 19. But Timothy is "not to be on a vendetta, so Paul begins with the caution – no private or unsupported charges."[78]

---

78. Fee, *1 and 2 Timothy, Titus*, 130.

A proper exercise of discipline has been regarded as important by the Christian church through the ages. But churches have not always been careful to exercise church discipline as they should. For example, in cases of sexual or physical abuse, churches have frequently remained silent and failed to give proper attention to the cries of victims. Victims of abuse have felt further betrayed when the faith community has failed to deal appropriately with their accusations on the basis that there were "no witnesses." Another problem is the tendency of the church and church officials to attempt to resolve issues in ways that safeguard the good name of the church. Instead of a transparent process, leading – where justified – to open rebuke and even dismissal of the offender, the outcome of complaints has often been quiet transfer of the offender to another post and a confidential settlement for the victim. As a result, another congregation is put at risk of abuse and the victim is likely to become disillusioned and feel alienated.

In the last few decades, the Western church has demonstrated greater openness in discussing and dealing with the moral lapses of its leaders. Asian churches have slowly begun to follow suit, setting aside their natural and cultural reticence about such matters, and acknowledging both the importance of justice and the urgent need to reestablish the moral credibility of the church in a world where vigilant media have made it increasingly difficult to cover up serious moral lapses of leaders. Dealing justly and openly with complaints is the best way to ensure that we "give the enemy no opportunity for slander" (5:14b).

The issue of discipline also arises when a Christian leader repents openly before the congregation. Spiritually, such an act of repentance has great significance for the person's relationship with God and the congregation. But if, as it sometimes does, this leads to the congregation protecting offenders from the legal or social consequences of their wrongdoing, such an action is misguided, may hinder closure for victims and even the offender, and invites justifiable criticism from wider society.

Paul's solemn charge emphasizes the seriousness of the matters under discussion: "I charge you, in the sight of God and Christ Jesus and the elect angels, to keep these instructions without partiality, and to do nothing out of favoritism" (5:21). Since "these instructions" is plural, Paul was probably referring to his earlier instructions (5:19–20), which emphasize the gravity of sinning by elders – since they had considerable influence on the community.[79]

---

79. Fee, *1 and 2 Timothy, Titus*, 131.

This seems to reflect a specific historical situation rather than being general instructions for dealing with elders.

The charge to Timothy ("I charge you" is singular) to carry out these instructions without partiality or favoritism is accompanied by the reminder that Timothy was not alone, and that the heavenly tribunal stood with him. "In the sight of God" means that the charge is given in the context of God's heavenly court, and the appeal to three witnesses – "God, Christ, and the elect angels" – emphasizes the solemnity of the charge. This

> is a reminder that one is living and acting in the very presence of the God who gives life to all and before whom one is responsible . . . and of the awesome reality that it is God who will be the Judge of one's actions (compare 2 Tim 4:1).[80]

"Christ Jesus" is joined to "God" in a clause using a Greek word translated "in the sight of" (see also 6:13; 2 Tim 4:1),[81] pointing to the implicit high Christology which shows Jesus as being intimately connected to God.

The addition of "the elect angels" adds further solemnity to the charge. In Scripture, angels are God's good messengers, associated with Christ's return and his work of judging.[82] "Elect" is not used elsewhere of angels, but perhaps Paul used it here as a contrast to "fallen angels" (2 Pet 2:4; Jude 6) who might have been behind the false teachers' false teachings. The "elect" angels are agents of God who carry out God's will, including God's judgment.

The instructions given in verses 19 and 20 are to be followed "without partiality," meaning that guilt or innocence must not be decided in advance of a fair hearing. Further, when dispensing discipline, nothing is to be done "out of favoritism." In dealing with accusations and administering public rebuke, the proper process must be followed, and matters must be handled with fairness.

After encouraging Timothy to deal correctly with accusations against elders and to properly discipline sinning elders, Paul cautions him against the hasty appointment of elders (5:22). The reason for this caution is the possibility of sin; not only are some sinning in the present (5:20) but not all sins are readily apparent (5:24). If someone is ordained too quickly, some sins may not be known, and then those who set the person apart for this position will share

---

80. Knight, *The Pastoral Epistles*, 238.
81. 2 Timothy 4:1: "In the presence of God and of Christ Jesus, who will judge the living and the dead, and in view of his appearing and his kingdom."
82. See Luke 9:26; 12:9; 2 Thessalonians 1:7.

responsibility for their sins; delaying the appointment may avoid this problem. Similarly, 1 Timothy 3:10 speaks of testing potential deacons.

"The laying on of hands" (5:22) describes the public ceremony by which a person was set apart for office (see 4:14; 2 Tim 1:6). In the NT, the laying on of hands may signify God's blessing (Mark 10:16), God's healing (Mark 5:23), the gift of the Spirit (Acts 8:17–19; 19:6), or commissioning for a role within the church (Acts 6:6; 13:3). Here in 1 Timothy 5:22, it involves commissioning for leadership.

"Do not share in the sins of others" (5:22) is a warning against partnering in the sins of others by knowingly or unknowingly ordaining an unsuitable person as an elder. This could happen if the laying on of hands happened too quickly, before the character of the potential elder became clear. Knight notes:

> By placing a person in an office that has as one of its qualifications that the person be "above reproach" (3:2), the one laying on hands will seem to be condoning the sins that that person commits ["sins" referring back to the "persisting in sin" of 5:20]. The sins are those of others . . . , but Timothy and the other elders will become responsible for those sins when they lay hands on too hastily.[83]

The importance of not partnering with sin is underlined by the exhortation to Timothy to keep himself "pure," that is, free from sin. As Johnson notes, "Staying pure means not associating with the corruption of the elders under charges."[84] This would not have been only for Timothy's own sake but also so that he could, with integrity, be involved in maintaining discipline in the church.

Paul's instructions to carefully evaluate a person before ordaining them to a ministry – "Do not be hasty in the laying on of hands" (5:22) – could prove difficult in areas where churches are growing rapidly. In today's world, where travel is usually quick and convenient, one option is to "borrow" an experienced elder or deacon from another church. Nevertheless, local church leaders have a responsibility to investigate, as far as possible, the background, call, and motivation of Christian workers before appointing them to key ministries by "the laying on of hands."

---

83. Knight, *The Pastoral Epistles*, 239.
84. L. T. Johnson, *The First and Second Letters to Timothy. A New Translation with Introduction and Commentary.* AB (New York: Doubleday, 2001), 281.

Paul has a personal word to Timothy concerning wine: "Stop drinking only water, and use a little wine because of your stomach and your frequent illnesses" (5:23). The connection between this instruction and what precedes it may not be immediately clear. It seems likely that Paul was clarifying the word "pure" (5:22). Timothy might have abstained from wine for religious reasons. To drink only water "among Jews as well as Greeks belongs to the pious life, the life full of renunciation."[85] But Paul explains that being "pure" does not mean total abstinence from wine.[86] Marshall notes that "avoidance of sin need not be misunderstood as requiring a continuing total abstinence from wine, even when it could be helpful health-wise."[87] Knight also thinks that since Paul knew that Timothy was "feeling the pressure and demands of the preceding verses, he pauses to express his concern for Timothy as a person and for his health."[88] Paul does not criticize abstinence from wine but he also encourages a little wine for medicinal reasons. The verse is a reminder that just as spiritual health is important – "keep yourself pure" – so is physical well-being.

In NT times, wine was widely used for medicinal purposes; even today, it is marketed as a health food in some Asian countries. Paul encouraged Timothy to drink "a little" wine – thus distinguishing this from any excess (compare 3:3, 8; Titus 1:7) – for medicinal purposes – "because of your stomach and your frequent illnesses." Paul's words seem to be personal advice to Timothy, not general guidance about alcohol consumption. However, prudence in the use of alcohol is always appropriate, particularly for church leaders, who often serve as role models for those in their congregations.

Paul then explains the reasons for not being "hasty" in the decision to ordain a person as an elder (5:24–25). In some instances, a person's sins and flaws are "obvious" and can be identified early – so it would be possible to assess, early on, whether they are suitable candidates to be elders. In other cases, people's faults "trail behind them" and become evident only after some time, and so delaying ordination of elders would allow sufficient time for such sins to become clear and prevent the appointment of unsuitable leaders. This in turn would minimize the need to discipline and rebuke ordained church leaders. Paul does not specify what sins the elders are accused of or guilty of.

---

85. Dibelius and Conzelmann, *The Pastoral Epistles*, 81. Note Luke 1:15 and the Nazirite vow of Numbers 6:1–4; note also that drunkenness is spoken of in 1 Timothy 3:3, 8 and Titus 2:3.
86. See Fee, *1 and 2 Timothy, Titus*, 132.
87. Marshall, *The Pastoral Epistles*, 608.
88. Knight, *The Pastoral Epistles*, 240.

Perhaps hidden sins such as pride, jealousy, and avarice were in view since Paul speaks of such sins in the next chapter (see 6:3–5).

Some people's sins are conspicuous. "Reaching the place of judgment ahead of them" means that these sins are obvious to human judgment. Of greater concern is those whose sins are not so obvious, those whose sins "trail behind them" or "follow them" (NRSV) to judgment. These sins become obvious only later. But how much later? And is this a reference to God's final judgment?[89] But Mounce notes, "The context requires that the sins be obvious now so Timothy can make decisions about leadership."[90] Since it is necessary to associate with people for some time before their sins become evident, it is wise not to be hasty in ordaining an elder (5:22).

What is true of sins is also true of "good deeds" – some are conspicuous, and some are not (5:25). For Paul, good deeds are characteristic of the Christian community, "a sign that they have heard the message and live accordingly."[91] But even when good deeds are not evident, they cannot be hidden forever, either from God or from others. Thus good deeds that are not evident now will become obvious eventually. This statement parallels Paul's reference to sins which are obvious and sins which are hidden (5:24).

When does Paul think good deeds will no longer be hidden? Possibly at the final judgment, but it is more likely that Paul is referring to verse 22 – that is, if they do not lay hands on someone hastily but give them time, good deeds (that are now not so obvious) will become clear and so worthy people will come to the fore.

These two verses (5:24–25) thus make the same point, first about sin and then about good deeds. The point is that delaying the laying on of hands on a potential elder can make it easier to detect those whose worthiness is not immediately clear.

---

89. In this case, verse 24 would be suggesting that some elders' sins will not be known until judgment day; hence they cannot be anticipated even by a long period of probation and will be disclosed only when everything is made clear.
90. Mounce goes on: "The next verse must also refer to the same time of judgment. It may be that Timothy's present judgment is a precursor to God's judgment; Timothy sees the sins – which show that God's judgment rests, and will rest, on them – and on this basis does not commission elders." Mounce, *The Pastoral Epistles*, 320.
91. Collins, *1 & II Timothy and Titus*, 151.

1 TIMOTHY 6

In this closing chapter, Paul exhorts Timothy to "fight the good fight of the faith" and gives final instructions to Timothy about various groups in the church – slaves, false teachers, and the wealthy.

6:1–2 INSTRUCTIONS FOR SLAVES

The theme of "respect" or "honor" links this section (6:1–2) with the previous chapter, where Paul emphasized the importance of giving due "recognition" or "honor" to widows and elders (5:3, 17). However, while honoring widows and elders has financial implications, the respect due from slaves does not involve either remuneration or financial assistance; in addition, while it is the local church that is required to show honor to widows and elders, here slaves are to honor their masters.

Were Paul's instructions to slaves prompted by the false teaching that was spreading in Ephesus? Fee thinks that this was likely since this section (6:1–2) is preceded by instructions about widows and elders – which are linked to false teachers – and followed immediately by a section that directly addresses false teaching (6:3–10).[1] Paul's emphasis seems to be on right attitudes among believers who were slaves. Fee notes that

> perhaps problems have arisen among some Christian slaves and their attitudes toward Christian masters similar to those among the younger widows. Has an over-realized eschatology or an elitist spirituality caused them to disdain the old relationships that belong to the age that is passing away? One cannot have certain answers to such questions, of course, but such a reconstruction does make sense of Paul's instructions.[2]

Alternatively, it might simply be that Paul's teaching about oneness in Christ (see Gal 3:28) "was causing some slaves to move faster than the Christian or secular societies could cope with."[3] Budiman points out that contemporary society could not cope, either socially or economically, with a revolutionary

---
1. Fee, *1 and 2 Timothy, Titus*, 137.
2. Fee, *1 and 2 Timothy, Titus*, 137. The over-realized eschatology was probably caused by the false teachers' belief that the resurrection had already taken place (see 2 Tim 2:18).
3. Marshall, *The Pastoral Epistles*, 627.

ending of slavery and that Christians – who were an insignificant minority in society at the time – were incapable of initiating such a change and would also have been aware that they would face severe repercussions if they tried to do so.[4] This problem would have been aggravated if some of these slaves were elders in the church and their masters were not. Such a situation was not as unlikely as it may seem to some Asian readers. The slaves under consideration here were not like the brutalized laborers of the North American plantations, familiar to many of us through books and films. In the Greco-Roman world, slaves often held responsible positions, and some of them even practiced professions. Such people could easily have been leaders of church congregations. Whatever the actual situation in Ephesus, it is clear that there were tensions in the master-slave relationship, and so Paul addresses these concerns just as he dealt with concerns related to widows and elders.

The emphasis here is on the evangelistic and apologetic aspect of the Christian slave's behavior. It seems clear that some Christian slaves had non-Christian masters (6:1–2; Titus 2:9–10). Considerable weight is given to the need for slaves to exemplify a Christian lifestyle so that their unbelieving masters would not be put off by Christianity.[5]

Paul's words to slaves – given in a very different context – should not be interpreted as signifying acceptance of the institution of slavery either in later times or in the modern world. This issue of slavery in NT times – like the question of the caste system in India, which has some parallels with slavery – brings out the truth of this ethical maxim:

> . . . new occasions teach new duties
> Time makes ancient good uncouth . . .[6]

The early Christians never imagined themselves being able to abolish slavery. But, over time, the church gradually realized that slavery was morally unacceptable and worked to abolish it. We should never return to slavery claiming

---

4. Budiman, *Tafsiran Alkitab*, 56–58.
5. Paul includes instructions concerning slaves in addressing different groups in the local church (Eph 6:5–9; Col 3:22–4:1; compare Titus 2:9–10; 1 Pet 2:18–20), and the topic is also addressed in 1 Corinthians 7:20–22 and Philemon 10–21, where Paul encourages slaves to gain their freedom if they can and encourages masters to free their slaves. The instruction given here is closest to that in the prison epistles (see Eph 6:5, 7; Col 3:22–23), focusing on the attitude of slaves to their masters.
6. From the Hymn "Once to Every Man and Nation" written in 1845 by the American poet James Russell Lowell (1819–1891) as a protest to the American war with Mexico, which he considered unjust; an extension of American territory, he considered, would only enlarge the area in which (at that time) slavery was practiced.

that the Scriptures authorize it. The Scriptures do not condone slavery but only help Christians to respond appropriately in the particular political or social situation in which they find themselves. The same is true of many other social evils. For example, many Indian Christians have taken a firm stand on the Dalit issue and are fighting against the social injustice that takes place because of a caste system invented by human beings. The teaching in 1 Timothy 6:1–2 must be read as a responsible stance taken within the political and social environment of the time.

The section begins with instructions to those "who are under the yoke of slavery" (6:1). The word "yoke" – widely used in relation to slavery but also to signify tyranny in politics or oppressive rule by another nation – recognizes that slaves have no personal freedom but must obey their masters. In such circumstances, slaves might well have felt justified in doing the bare minimum of work for their masters. Further, Christian slaves who considered themselves "free" (Gal 3:28) might have felt that they were under no obligation to treat their masters respectfully. Paul disagrees.

It is not because their masters were "worthy" of respect that Paul instructs slaves to be respectful but because "masters are in authority in the sphere of work . . . and thus it is appropriate to recognize that position as worthy of respect."[7] "Full respect" would imply that honor is expressed through a respectful attitude as well as by wholehearted service (see 6:2).

The reason for showing such respect is "so that God's name and our teaching may not be slandered" (6:2). If Christian slaves behaved badly or were disloyal to their masters, this could have led to God and the gospel being criticized by non-Christians. If the disobedient slave was an elder in the church, this was even more likely to bring the church into disrepute. Paul was eager both to avoid such criticism of the church and to ensure that slaves, by their hard work, loyalty, and trustworthiness, would "make the teaching about God our Savior attractive" (Titus 2:10). Although Paul does not explicitly state that evangelism was his goal, given the emphasis on salvation and the general missionary thrust of the Pastorals (1 Tim 2:3–4; 2 Tim 2:10; Titus 2:10–11), this seems likely.

---

7. Knight notes that the teaching concerning honor is in keeping with the NT understanding of Christian behavior as servanthood, and of existence as eschatological. Knight, *The Pastoral Epistles*, 245; Fee, *1 and 2 Timothy, Titus*, 138. Since the form of the world is passing away, present status is irrelevant (1 Cor 7:17–24, 29–31).

Paul's instructions are for slaves of Christian masters as well as slaves of non-Christian masters. If Christian slaves failed to honor their non-Christian masters, those masters might have reacted negatively to Christianity, assuming that it was their Christian faith that made these slaves less respectful or less hardworking. If Christian slaves failed to honor their Christian masters, this was likely to have created a negative impression on their non-Christian neighbors. As part of his recurring concern about how the church was viewed by outsiders, Paul warns slaves not to let their attitudes or actions bring disrepute to God or the gospel (see 3:7; 5:14).

Paul warns slaves with believing masters not to be disrespectful "just because they are fellow believers" (6:2). It appears that Christian slaves in Ephesus were treating their Christian masters less respectfully just because they were members of the church.[8] The term "fellow believers" includes both men and women, and there would have been both slaves and slaveowners of both genders among these believers. Spiritually, slaves and slaveowners were members of the family of God and thus brothers or sisters of one another. So a slave might well have claimed, "In Christ, I am now an equal with my master, so I should be treated differently." Perhaps some slaves even treated their masters disdainfully because they regarded them as equals. But Paul does not condone such actions. In fact, he commands slaves to "serve them even better because their masters are dear to them as fellow believers." The NRSV translates this, "they must serve them all the more, since those who benefit by their service are believers and beloved." The term "beloved" ("dear" in the NIV) is often used in the NT to describe being loved by God (Mark 1:11; Rom 1:7; 11:28). Because someone is loved by God, that person should also be regarded by others as "beloved." As Knight comments, "God's love for both slave and master has made them brothers and brought them to regard one another as 'beloved.'"[9]

Paul describes believing masters as being "devoted to the welfare of their slaves" (6:2) – that is, they cared for their slaves. On the other hand, this phrase may also be translated "benefit from their service" (see NIV footnote) – that is, the slaves were benefiting their Christian masters. The word "devoted" (*euergesia*) is usually associated with the actions of someone in authority acting as a benefactor to others. But here, Paul describes what slaves do for their masters

---

8. See Mounce, *The Pastoral Epistles*, 328.
9. Knight comments: "What Paul intends is that these masters are believers and therefore part of the brotherhood who are 'beloved.'" Knight, *The Pastoral Epistles*, 247. As Fee, *1 and 2 Timothy, Titus*, 139.

as a "benefaction" or "that which is good and beneficial to someone."[10] Paul "turns the service of a slave into an act of bestowing good on another, even his master. Paul has thereby made the difficult role of a slave the means by which the slave can benefit his master."[11] This offers a whole new perspective on what slaves do, transforming "servitude" into the giving of a worthwhile benefit and subverting the typical way in which the slave-master relationship was understood.[12] In addition to encouraging slaves to see themselves as "benefactors," this perspective would presumably have encouraged masters, too, to view slaves differently, as benefactors who should be treated well. Mounce comments, "The master should view the labors of the slave not as a demanded responsibility but as acts of kindness."[13] This radically different perspective, whereby slaves were called to see their masters as "believers and beloved" (6:2 NRSV), might also have led to masters viewing and treating their slaves as "beloved." While this did not lead to an immediate end to slavery, it might have encouraged Christian slaveowners to see their Christian slaves differently. It was "in effect an indirect injunction to them to live out their faith."[14] We see an example of a more direct injunction to masters in Paul's instruction to Philemon to receive Onesimus back "no longer as a slave, but better than a slave, as a dear brother" (Philemon 16).

Paul does not directly address Christian masters. This was probably because he was not writing about relationships in general – which would have required discussing both sides of the master-slave relationship – but about the behavior of Christian slaves that was causing offense in society and damaging the reputation of the church (5:14; 6:1).[15] So Paul was not laying down instructions for all time on the matter of slave-master relationships and, as Marshall notes, "no change in the social system is envisaged."[16] Instead, here in 1 Timothy, "slaves are treated along with elders and widows, where the significance of the actions of these groups for the community is of paramount importance."[17]

---

10. Towner argues that seeing the masters as benefactors complicates the logic of the text where Paul is primarily addressing the slaves. Towner, *The Letters to Timothy and Titus*, 387.
11. Knight, *The Pastoral Epistles*, 247.
12. See Marshall, *The Pastoral Epistles*, 633.
13. Mounce, *The Pastoral Epistles*, 325.
14. Marshall, *The Pastoral Epistles*, 628.
15. Bassler notes that the Romans were suspicious of groups like the early Christians who "disrupted proper social relations and customs. Thus, to silence such criticism and to address the social tensions within the church, Christian writers reinforced the patterns of social behavior that the wider society expected of all its members." Bassler, *1 Timothy, 2 Timothy, Titus*, 104.
16. Marshall, *The Pastoral Epistles*, 628.
17. Bassler, *1 Timothy, 2 Timothy, Titus*, 104.

The verse ends with an admonition: "These are the things you are to teach and insist on" (6:2c; compare 4:11). "The things" could refer either to what precedes – all the teaching in the letter thus far or just the material in 1 Timothy 5:3–6:2 – or to what follows. To "insist on" means to exhort those being taught to apply the teaching to their lives. What Timothy is commanded to "teach and insist on" is contrasted, in the next section (6:3–10), with the teaching of the false teachers.

CONTEMPORARY RELEVANCE OF PAUL'S INSTRUCTIONS TO SLAVES

If we accept that Paul's teaching about the duties of slaves speaks to a historical context different from our own, we may wonder what relevance these instructions have for us today. While slavery has no place in the modern world, Christians still find themselves in situations where they are bound in duty and loyalty to superiors who may or may not share their faith. Examples of such servitude in modern days include the military service, the police force, and public servants who may be subject to oppressive hierarchical systems that demand loyalty without argument. Although some Christians have resisted involvement in these areas, believers have important contributions to make in wider society and, today, usually enjoy the protection afforded by constitutional and legal provisions that prevent them from being compelled to carry out illegal or immoral actions. Christian men and women who fulfill their vocation in military or civil service sectors will invariably have to grapple with issues of loyalty and conscience as they carefully carry out their duties with integrity and in ways that honor God's name and uphold gospel values.

The principles underlying Paul's words to Christian slaves in Ephesus apply to Christian employees in today's workplace. One need not be a slave to find Paul's words relevant. Witnessing in the workplace does not mean that Christians should be overly zealous and become a nuisance to their superiors or to their workmates. The Christian faith speaks most powerfully through a transformed life – manifested in a good work ethic, honesty, and exemplary behavior.

There are many heartening stories of Christian employees in China who have integrated their faith with their work. Hui Wen, a Christian sales executive in the city of Shenzhen in southern China, says this: "Some non-Christians like to grumble and complain. For example, they

> might be dissatisfied when the boss gives the year-end bonus, saying that this year's bonus doesn't match last year's, or they will compare who gets more and less. But for us [Christians], we tend to be more understanding. I may feel that it's okay to have a bit less bonus, because business this year hasn't been good, and this is helpful for the boss's business. Or, when we encounter some minor problems, we try to be more accommodating, and to touch others with our loving care. Some non-Christians have bad habits, after arriving they will first make coffee, surf the internet, and start their work in the afternoon. We focus on doing our job well first thing in the morning."[1]
>
> ---
> 1. F. K. G. Lim, "'Serving the Lord': Christianity, Work, and Social Engagement in China," *Religion* 10 (2019): 7.

6:3–10 FALSE TEACHERS AND THEIR LOVE OF MONEY

What should be a Christian's attitude toward money and material possessions? This is an important discipleship question for followers of Christ. In many parts of the world, particularly in Asia, there is a widening gulf between the rich and the poor. In the Philippines, for example, some people are extremely wealthy, while others are extremely poor. What has God to say to these people? As economies boom in many places in Asia, there is rejoicing because millions of people are being lifted out of poverty. But, in today's society, we are also seeing more and more of what Paul describes as "the love of money" (6:10). Religion does not shield people from the vice of being lovers of money. In times past, it was mainly sectarian church groups and leaders who peddled the "prosperity gospel" and pursued abhorrently lavish lifestyles. Today, the "prosperity gospel" is being peddled by many in Asia, Africa, and worldwide, both in poor and wealthy countries. Paul's warnings about wealth are very relevant for the Asian church today.

In this section, Paul's indictment of the false teachers (6:3–5) is followed by a discussion of true contentment (6:6–8) and the dangers of desiring wealth (6:9–10). The false teachers are in view throughout this section.

Although issues related to false teachings have been present throughout the letter, Paul returns explicitly to the subject of the false teachers for the third time (6:3–5; compare 1:3–11; 4:1–5). The general principle is stated first

(6:3), but it is clear from the shift to the plural "they" that Paul had specific teachers in mind.

Paul begins by expressing the heart of the problem: "If anyone teaches otherwise and does not agree to the sound instruction of our Lord Jesus Christ" (6:3). The verb *heterodidaskaleō* (to teach otherwise) is found only here and in 1 Timothy 1:3, showing that the discussion is about the same teachers Paul referred to earlier. In fact, there are several echoes here of what was said in 1 Timothy 1:3–11. The false teachers teach a doctrine that is completely different from the apostolic teaching and thus should be regarded as false. As Marshall notes, what is said here in verse 3 "gives support to the view that a major theme of the epistle is the need for right teaching as the antidote to false teaching"[18] – that is, teaching that does not conform to "the sound instruction of our Lord Jesus Christ" (6:3). "Sound" here means "healthy" and points to the positive effects of this teaching.

What is meant by "the instruction of our Lord Jesus Christ"? While Paul sometimes quotes the actual words of Jesus (1 Cor 11:23–25; 1 Tim 5:18), he also uses this sort of language to refer more generally to the gospel (1 Thess 1:8). This latter usage seems to fit the sense here better since the emphasis is on the false teachers having abandoned the truth of the gospel – that is, the truth concerning Jesus – rather than Jesus's actual words. The authority of the teaching about Jesus is thus placed in opposition to the false teaching. The full designation of Jesus as "our Lord Jesus Christ" is used in 1 Timothy to underline the authority and power of Christ (1:2, 12; 6:3, 14). The false teachers, however, do not submit to Christ's authority.

The false teachers also do not agree with "godly teaching" (6:3). In terms of its content and outcome, "godly teaching" is not something different from "the sound instruction of our Lord Jesus Christ." It is teaching that accords with and promotes godliness. Godliness describes "a life totally consecrated to God."[19] Paul affirms the strong link between theology and ethics, between correct teaching and right practice. Sound words lead to godliness, but false teachings lead to all kinds of chaos.

Just as there is a link between sound teaching and godliness (6:3, 6), which involves leading a moral life, false teaching is linked with and leads to what could be called "moral chaos . . . [which] appears almost exclusively as antisocial attitudes and activities that destroy the social cohesion of the household

---

18. Marshall, *The Pastoral Epistles*, 638.
19. Mounce, *The Pastoral Epistles*, 336.

of God."[20] Paul describes the character qualities of those who turn away from sound teaching (6:4–5). Marshall sees three basic qualities here: "empty pride, ignorance and disputatiousness."[21]

Paul describes the false teachers as "conceited" (6:4; see also 3:6; 2 Tim 3:4) or "puffed up with conceit" (RSV). In his letter to the Corinthians, Paul uses a similar term in speaking about people who "think they know something" but do not really "know as they ought to know" (1 Cor 8:1–2). The false teachers do not agree with "the sound instruction of our Lord Jesus Christ" (6:3); as such, they "understand nothing" (6:4). These teachers also have "an unhealthy interest in controversies and quarrels about words" (6:4). The term "unhealthy interest" (*nosos*) is literally "to be sick or ailing," in contrast to the "sound" words of Jesus (6:3).

The craving for controversy and verbal disputes leads to several undesirable consequences involving both attitudes and actions – "envy, strife, malicious talk, evil suspicions and constant friction" (6:4–5) – that disrupt harmony in the community. "The implication is that, if people lose hold on the truth of the gospel, they become corrupt in mind and turn to quarrels that engender strife."[22]

The false teachers' "corrupt" thinking seemed to have led to their mistaken belief that "godliness is a means to financial gain" (6:5), and their actions were probably motivated by greed. They "simply do not understand what godliness is all about."[23] Paul had previously warned that church leaders should not be controlled by a love of money (3:3, 8; compare 6:9–10; 2 Tim 3:2; Titus 1:7). In Crete, false teachers had been "disrupting whole households by teaching things they ought not to teach," and this was "for the sake of dishonest gain" (Titus 1:11). In other words, these teachers had been trying to gain more followers simply to profit from them. In such a situation, it seems likely that their teachings might have been tailored to cater to whatever the audience wanted to hear (see 2 Tim 4:3–4). Today, we are well aware of televangelists who use the gospel as a basis for operating international "businesses" that bring great wealth ("blessing") not only for their ministries but also personally. However, even ordinary Christians can be tempted to pursue "dishonest gain." The

---

20. Bassler, *1 Timothy, 2 Timothy, Titus*, 109.
21. Marshall, *The Pastoral Epistles*, 639.
22. Marshall, *The Pastoral Epistles*, 642.
23. Collins, *1 & II Timothy and Titus*, 156.

Pastoral Epistles affirm the need to reward faithful workers without making money the focus of one's ministry.

When Christian workers fail to guard against self-serving practices and make wealth their goal, or sometimes even embezzle funds, they evoke widespread criticism in the media. Where the local church fails to make adequate provision for its workers and their dependents, this is viewed with disfavor by the community. But when church workers put service and ministry before self-interest this is a powerful witness. A village headman in North Sumatra, commenting on a church-managed rural development program in his area, said to one of the writers, "It is easy to see that the ministers managing this program are not taking off anything for themselves; they look as poor now as they were when the project began!"

We have already noted that the elders in the church received an honorarium (5:17–18) – and perhaps the false teachers also expected such remuneration and charged their followers for the instruction they provided. But, as Mounce notes, given that Paul encourages his addressees to pay leaders, "his concern [in 6:5] is not that there is money involved. However, from verses 6–10 it is obvious that the love of money and the central place it holds in the opponents' lives constitute the real problem."[24] Since the false teachers were still members of the local church – and some may have been church officers who handled money – they might have risked charges of embezzlement.[25] Much of what Paul says in these verses (6:3–5) echoes the qualifications he lists for leaders (3:2–12) and his concern that they remain morally pure.[26] Knight concludes:

> The indictment of the false teachers is thus multifaceted and comprehensive. It begins with their heterodoxy (v. 3), which is correlated with their conceit and lack of real understanding (v. 4a) and their sick interest in mere controversy (v. 4b), turns to the maliciousness of life that flows from these characteristics (v. 4c), roots all this in spiritual blindness (v. 5a), and ends with their materialistic motivation (v. 5b). It is given to warn the church against such people.[27]

Paul then picks up the word "gain" (6:5) and goes on to speak about appropriate gain (6:6–8). He says that "godliness with contentment is great

---

24. See Mounce, *The Pastoral Epistles*, 340.
25. See Hanson, *The Pastoral Epistles*, 107.
26. See Fee, *1 and 2 Timothy, Titus*, 142.
27. Knight, *The Pastoral Epistles*, 252–53.

gain" (6:6). Godliness gives a true perspective to the material side of life, helping us to distinguish between what is important and what is secondary. False teachers worked to gain wealth. But godly people serve without focusing on gaining wealth.

Whereas the false teachers viewed godliness as a "means to financial gain" (6:5), Paul teaches that contentment along with godliness is "great gain" (6:6). By including the words "contentment" and "great," Paul moves beyond a material sense of gain to a spiritual sense.[28] As Bassler notes, although Paul does not spell out what this gain is, he has already done so earlier on:[29] "godliness has value for all things, holding promise for both the present life and the life to come" (4:8). The word "great" (6:6) also serves to underline the fact that such spiritual gain is real gain or gain that really matters.

"Godliness" is indeed the way to great (spiritual) gain, provided it is accompanied by contentment and satisfaction with what one has. The word translated "contentment" (*autarkeia*) was a favorite virtue of the Cynics and Stoics – ancient philosophical schools – who interpreted that word as "sufficiency" or "self-sufficiency."[30] Paul does not promote such self-sufficiency but, rather, "contentment" – "the quality of the person who has enough and is not longing for more."[31] Paul implies that with "godliness" – which is associated with Christ – a person has been given all that is necessary. It is wrong, therefore, to look for material wealth over and above God's provision. As Witherington notes, "Paul believes in God-sufficiency not self-sufficiency . . . Paul is referring to someone who is content with having the necessities of life and has found sufficiency in God."[32] There is probably an allusion to 1 Timothy 4:4: "Everything God created is good, and nothing is to be rejected if it is received with thanksgiving." As Collins notes, "What is necessary for human sustenance is a gift from God that believers are to use but for which they are also to give thanks."[33]

The basis for this contentment that should accompany godliness is given in verse 7: "For we brought nothing into the world, and we can take nothing

---

28. See Marshall, *The Pastoral Epistles*, 644.
29. See Bassler, *1 Timothy, 2 Timothy, Titus*, 110. She goes on to say that godliness "enhances the present life and leads to eternal life."
30. Dibelius and Conzelmann quote the saying of Epictetus: "The art of living well . . . is contingent upon self-control, self-sufficiency, orderliness, propriety, and thrift." Dibelius and Conzelmann, *The Pastoral Epistles*, 84.
31. Marshall, *The Pastoral Epistles*, 645.
32. Witherington, *A Socio-Rhetorical Commentary on Titus, 1–2 Timothy and 1–3 John*, 285.
33. Collins, *1 & II Timothy and Titus*, 157.

out of it." We have nothing that we have not received from God. And there is no point in striving to accumulate material possessions that we cannot take with us. Since these things are temporary, not eternal, we should strive for godliness "with contentment." Paul is citing proverbial truth, echoing Job 1:21 and Ecclesiastes 5:15.[34] As Knight notes, "All humans have satisfactorily begun life without bringing with them any material things."[35] They can also continue life with only the necessities (6:8). At death, too, no one can take any of their possessions with them. So the acquisition of things brings no final benefit.

Paul acknowledges that human beings do have needs in the present age. He writes, "But if we have food and clothing, we will be content with that" (6:8). In saying "we," Paul includes all Christians. "Food" clearly refers to nourishment, and Budiman, in his Indonesian commentary,[36] draws attention to the basic meaning of *skepasmata* (*skepas*: "a covering or shelter"), translated here as "clothing." While clothing is included, he suggests that covering should be understood in a more general sense as including a place to live – "food, clothing, and a roof over our heads," we might say in modern English (or, in Indonesian, *alat penutup*). We are to be "content" with necessities and embrace a simple lifestyle, avoiding worry and greed and, instead, being grateful for God's good gifts (4:3–5; 6:17; compare Phil 4:12).[37]

The issue of a simple lifestyle is an important criterion in the modern Christian context where there are often strongly held beliefs about acquiring material wealth. Many groups teach and believe that the accumulation of wealth by pastors and others is a sign of blessing and something to be sought as a sign of God's endorsement of their ministry. This blinds people to the moral and ethical issues of pursuing what would be viewed as a luxurious lifestyle in communities where many others suffer the effects of poverty, unemployment, and other social disadvantages. Unbiblical teachings about wealth and prosperity divert people from the path of truly costly discipleship and undermine the credibility of the gospel in communities that can see through the professed motives of these wealthy teachers. Teaching people, and adopting for oneself an appropriate lifestyle is a powerful witness to the teaching not only of Jesus but also of the Hebrew prophets and the mainstream of Christian discipleship. As Jesus himself said, "You cannot serve both God and money" (Matt 6:24).

---

34. See the list of parallels in Towner, *The Letters to Timothy and Titus*, 399.
35. Knight, *The Pastoral Epistles*, 254.
36. Budiman, *Tafsiran Alkitab*, 61.
37. This reflects the teaching of Jesus (see Matt 6:24–34; Luke 12:16–32).

1 Timothy 6

Paul contrasts the godly who find contentment (6:6–8) with those whose greed for riches leads to ruin and destruction (6:9–10). Those who "want to get rich" and are "eager for money" may find themselves ensnared by "foolish and harmful desires" that plunge them deeper into temptation and sin. Ultimately, this leads to destruction. Bassler notes that by "ruin and destruction" Paul does not mean "financial or moral ruin but eschatological, that is, final ruin (see 1 Thess 5:3)."[38]

Paul then cites a common proverb – which has many parallels in other literature of the period[39] – to explain the dangers of the desire for wealth: "For the love of money is a root of all kinds of evil" (6:10). Paul does not say "the" root but "a" root of all kinds of evil. So the proverb is not saying that the love of money is the root of *all* evil, nor that every known evil has the love of money at its root. Like most proverbs, it exaggerates for effect. What it means is that "greed is a trap full of many hurtful desires that lead to all kinds of sin."[40] Paul also does not say that the root of evil is "money" but, rather, the "love of money," which refers to a reaching out for or a craving after money that involves covetousness. It is this wanting, loving, and reaching out for wealth that has such terrible consequences.

Paul then illustrates the truth of his warnings about the danger of riches (6:9–10a) by pointing out that "some people" in the church at Ephesus had "wandered from the faith" (6:10). Giving in to greed had led to their ultimate apostasy. Paul probably had in mind the false teachers, who even viewed godliness as a means to financial gain (6:5). As a result of their love of money, some people had endured great tragedy, for they had "pierced themselves with many griefs."

A few years ago, a huge scandal rocked the church in Singapore, making headlines across the globe. The senior pastor of one of the largest churches in Singapore – a proponent of "prosperity theology" – along with five other leaders from the same church were sentenced to jail for embezzling fifty million US dollars from the church. This scandal brought grief and shame not just to those five leaders, their families, and their local church, but also to the name of Christ. Paul's warnings about greed continue to be valid today.

---

38. Bassler, *1 Timothy, 2 Timothy, Titus*, 111.
39. See Witherington, *A Socio-Rhetorical Commentary on Titus, 1–2 Timothy and 1–3 John*, 287–88.
40. Fee, *1 and 2 Timothy, Titus*, 145.

6:11–21 FINAL CHARGE TO TIMOTHY

In his final charge to Timothy, Paul begins with a personal word to Timothy (6:11–16), followed by a word to wealthy believers (6:17–19), and then concludes with a final command to Timothy and a prayer for grace to be with the whole community (6:20–21).

6:11–16 A Word to Timothy

This section is addressed to Timothy and concerns his own conduct. In contrast to those who let their eagerness for money lead them to wander from the faith (6:10), Timothy is urged to pursue Christian virtues that would help him remain firm in faith.

In 1 Timothy, each of Paul's indictments of the false teachers is followed by a personal word to Timothy, encouraging him to resist the false teachers and be a good example in the church (compare 1:3–7 with 1:18–20 and 4:1–5 with 4:6–16). Paul often reminds Timothy of his special calling to ministry (1:18; 4:14). This pattern is repeated here, where Paul's indictment of the false teachers (6:3–10) is followed by an exhortation to Timothy (6:11–20), which includes four imperatives (6:11–12), a solemn charge (6:13–14), and a final doxology (6:15–16) that places "the whole of the appeal . . . against the backdrop of Christian eschatological certainties."[41]

Paul writes, "But you, man of God, flee from all this, and pursue righteousness, godliness, faith, love, endurance and gentleness" (6:11). Paul exhorts Timothy to shun the greed of the false teachers (6:9–10) and probably also their false doctrines and destructive controversies (6:3–4). Timothy is called a "man of God" (2 Tim 3:17), setting him apart from the false teachers (6:3–5) and from those who pursued riches rather than God (6:9–10). Since the OT uses the phrase "man of God" to designate a servant or messenger of God,[42] using this designation for Timothy might have emphasized his leadership of God's people and his dedication to God. But the phrase "man of God" – or "servant of God" (2 Tim 3:17) – could also refer to all Christians. Marshall notes that "Timothy is addressed as a leader whose way of life is to be an example to all believers, and what is said to him can be applied to them all."[43]

---

41. Fee, *1 and 2 Timothy, Titus*, 148.
42. For example, Moses (Deut 33:1; Josh 14:6), David (2 Chr 8:14), or a prophet (1 Sam 9:6; 1 Kgs 13:1; 2 Kgs 23:17).
43. Marshall, *The Pastoral Epistles*, 657.

While the vices of the false teachers lead to ruin and destruction (6:9–10), the virtues that Paul urges Timothy to pursue reflect the gospel and will lead to eternal life (6:12, 19). These six virtues – "righteousness, godliness, faith, love, endurance and gentleness" (6:11) – are fundamental spiritual and ethical qualities for the Christian. "Righteousness" refers to uprightness of conduct or doing what is right (Phil 1:10–11); "godliness" refers to "a life fully consecrated to God."[44] "Faith" and "love" appear on many such lists of virtues in the Pastoral Epistles (1 Tim 1:5, 14; 2:15; 4:12; 6:11; 2 Tim 1:13; 2:22; 3:10; Titus 2:2).[45] "Endurance" and "gentleness" are clearly appropriate in the context of an appeal to Timothy to lead a church that seemed to be facing many problems.

This leads to a call for perseverance: "Fight the good fight of the faith" (6:12). "Fight" is a metaphor drawn from athletics – for example, contests between gladiators or boxing matches – but it also has military overtones (see 2 Tim 4:7). The "fight of the faith" relates to "faith as the characteristic quality of the Christian life that must be maintained to the end."[46] The Christian life is a present struggle in which Timothy is to persevere.

Timothy is then told to "take hold of the eternal life" (6:12). In 1 Timothy 1:16, Paul said that eternal life is the result of belief in Christ, something Timothy had experienced from the day he believed. Here, Paul speaks of eternal life as something to be taken hold of *now* – for the command to do this clearly implies a present action – as well as something at the end of the contest. Hence the tension between the "already" and the "not yet," so often found in the NT, is present here. The believer must "take hold of" eternal life now, although its final consummation lies in the future. Paul also says that Timothy was "called" to this eternal life. God's action is prior, but there is also a necessary human response to God's call.

"The good confession in the presence of many witnesses" (6:12b) refers to bearing testimony on some specific occasion – possibly Timothy's call to ministry, his "ordination vows," or some occasion of persecution when he made a confession of faith. However, since the verse speaks of being "called" to "eternal life" rather than to a ministry, it seems more likely that Paul was

---

44. Mounce, *The Pastoral Epistles*, 354.
45. Elsewhere in Paul's writings we note that love is both a fruit of the Spirit (Gal 5:22) and something to be pursued (1 Cor 14:1; see also Col 3:12–17). Accordingly, the fact that some of these qualities can be seen as given by God does not mean that the Christian cannot also be called to "pursue" them.
46. Marshall, *The Pastoral Epistles*, 659.

referring to a "confession" made at the time of conversion or baptism. Fee writes: "Thus the imperatives [of vv. 11–12] exhort Timothy to persevere both in his life in Christ and his ministry (the present), and thereby to secure the awaited prize (the future), by being reminded of his beginnings – God's call and his own response (the past)."[47] That the confession is "good" means that it was approved by God. The reference to "witnesses" points to both the gravity and the binding nature of the confession. The content of the confession is not given since the emphasis is on Timothy's faithfulness to it. Marshall notes, "There is no indication that it was anything more than a confession of Jesus Christ as Lord."[48]

The imperatives of verses 11 and 12 lead to a "charge" in verses 13 and 14. That this charge is given "in the sight of God" and "Christ Jesus" emphasizes that it is a solemn command. God is described as the one who "gives life to everything" – "everything" refers to the universe (see also Eph 1:23) and emphasizes God's role as creator and sustainer. God's omnipotence is thus in view. That the verb "gives life" is in the present tense "is consistent with the idea of God's continuous activity in the universe rather than merely the initial act of creation."[49]

The charge to Timothy is also in the sight of Christ Jesus, which is particularly appropriate since Jesus himself "made the good confession" (6:13) at his trial before Pontius Pilate (see John 18:36–37). Johnson notes, "The explicit mention of Pilate also reminds us that the author was fully aware of the grimmer possibilities of dealing with the Roman Empire than are suggested by the positive commands of 2:1–7."[50] The emphasis here is on Jesus's faithfulness as he faced death. As Timothy faced difficulties, both within and outside the church, Jesus himself was to be the model who inspired him to remain steadfast, persevere, and "fight the good fight." Although the false teachers viewed godliness as a means to financial gain (6:5), true godliness often leads to suffering and hardship.

The actual charge to Timothy is given in verse 14: "Keep this command without spot or blame" – that is, in an unblemished way that is above reproach. The "command" Paul had in view was probably the instructions given to

---

47. Fee, *1 and 2 Timothy, Titus*, 150. Note that there are no contemporary parallels to a confession at ordination.
48. Marshall, *The Pastoral Epistles*, 661.
49. Marshall, *The Pastoral Epistles*, 662.
50. Johnson, *The First and Second Letters to Timothy*, 308.

Timothy in the letter as a whole (see also 1:3, 18).[51] Thus, this charge summarizes the basic thrust of the letter and implies that "Timothy will best stem the tide of the false teachers as he himself is steadfast in his faith and calling."[52]

"Until the appearing of our Lord Jesus Christ" (6:14) emphasizes the need for perseverance, while also offering encouragement because of the certainty of Christ's return. The word "appearing" refers to "a visible and frequent sudden manifestation of a hidden divinity, either in the form of a personal appearance, or by some deed or power . . . by which its presence is made known."[53] In the Pastoral Epistles, the word is used to refer both to the first coming and the second coming of Christ (see 2 Tim 1:10; 4:1, 8; Titus 2:11, 13). While the word "appearing" was sometimes used in Hellenistic Judaism to refer to the manifestation of God's power, it was also used regularly in Hellenistic religions to describe the "appearance" of a deity. The doxology in verses 15–16 stresses that God is invisible. The use of the word "appearing" here in verse 14 "may also stress the significance of the epiphany of Jesus through whom the invisible, unapproachable God may be seen and approached."[54]

Paul expresses certainty about the second coming "which God will bring about in his own time" (6:15). Just as Christ's first coming was at "the proper time" or "appointed season" (Gal 4:4), the timing of his second coming also lies in God's sovereign control and cannot be calculated ahead of time.

This leads to a series of striking epithets about God: "the blessed and only Ruler, the King of kings and Lord of lords" (6:15). "Taken together they sound a note for the transcendent majesty of the Eternal God matched in the NT only by the splendid imagery of Revelation 4."[55] The word "Ruler" was used for human rulers as well as for God. Phrases similar to "King of kings and Lord of lords" are found in the OT (Deut 10:17; Ps 136:3; Dan 2:37). The emphasis is on God's complete sovereignty over all powers.[56]

The doxology continues, "who alone is immortal and who lives in unapproachable light, whom no one has seen or can see" (6:16). Marshall notes that "immortality is a Hellenistic way of stating that God alone has and can

---

51. The word "command" (*entolē*) can also mean "commission," which fits the context here well. For a discussion, see Fee, *1 and 2 Timothy, Titus*, 151–52; Marshall, *The Pastoral Epistles*, 664–65; Knight, *The Pastoral Epistles*, 266–68.
52. Fee, *1 and 2 Timothy, Titus*, 152.
53. W. Bauer, revised and edited by F. W. Danker, *A Greek-English Lexicon of the New Testament and Other Early Christian literature*, 385.
54. Marshall, *The Pastoral Epistles*, 654.
55. Fee, *1 and 2 Timothy, Titus*, 153.
56. See Fee, *1 and 2 Timothy, Titus*, 153.

confer life ... It is not a description of God that is found in Hellenistic Judaism and has therefore been taken over from the language used of gods and emperors."[57] But the point here is that God alone is immortal and free from death, not the emperor.

Further, God dwells in "unapproachable light" and can never be seen by humans. The place of God's dwelling is envisaged as glorious, brilliant light (Ps 104:2). This echoes the Jewish emphasis that God is so infinitely holy that sinful humanity can never see him and live (see Exod 33:18–23), rather than the Greek idea that God is unknowable. The doxology concludes appropriately, "To him be honor and might forever. Amen" (6:16).

Why is there a doxology here? Budiman points out that Paul, when deeply moved by God's action, often breaks off his discussion to offer praise (doxology) and then resumes his theme.[58] The doxology also functions as a means of bolstering Timothy's faith: If this kind of all-powerful, unique, and transcendent God is for Timothy, who can be against him? This doxology also reflects some of Paul's teachings from earlier in this section – God being unique and transcendent (6:15–16) and God giving life to everything (6:13). As Johnson notes, "Paul emphasizes the otherness of God precisely in order to praise the astonishing reality that God has chosen to cross over the boundary and enter into relationship with humans."[59] Fee notes that there is yet another reason for the doxology:

> It begins in a context emphasizing the certainty of the Second Advent to be brought about by the Mighty God. Is this to reinforce courage in Timothy to persevere in the difficult situation in Ephesus? Perhaps. But it is probably for the sake of the church as well. Ephesus was not only the haven of Artemis, but an early center of emperor worship as well. This doxology, therefore, is Paul's parting shot that the God with whom the church has to do in the gospel of Christ is none other than the supreme Ruler of the universe, the Lord over all other lords.[60]

---

57. Marshall, *The Pastoral Epistles*, 667.
58. Budiman, *Tafsiran Alkitab*, 65–66.
59. Johnson, *The First and Second Letters to Timothy*, 314.
60. Fee, *1 and 2 Timothy, Titus*, 154.

6:17–19 A Word to the Rich

After his unexpected doxology (6:15–16), Paul resumes his discussion on riches, which had been primarily with reference to the false teachers (6:3–10). But since there were some in the Ephesian church who were already rich (6:17), it might be that Paul now speaks to them "lest they feel condemned by verses 6–10"[61] or perhaps to prevent the congregation turning against the wealthy in their midst. In this section (6:17–19), Paul gives instructions both about overcoming some of the temptations associated with being wealthy and about using wealth wisely. He shows what "godliness with contentment" (6:6) should look like.

Paul speaks to "those who are rich in this present world" (6:17). These wealthy people were clearly part of the congregation. Those who are rich in this present world may become "arrogant" – either by looking down on those who are less wealthy or by trusting in riches rather than in God. But wealth belongs to this age. Riches cannot be taken with us into the next age (6:7); they are temporary and offer no permanent security, and so the wealthy must be warned "not to be arrogant nor to put their hope in wealth, which is so uncertain" (6:17). As Marshall notes, "The dangers against which the rich are warned thus stem from the recognition that this world is transitory and that they must live as those who already belong to the world to come."[62] The wealthy, like everyone else (4:10; 5:5), must "put their hope in God." It is wise to put our hope in God since God can be relied on to provide "richly" or lavishly for all our needs.

Paul was no ascetic, and he does not reject wealth. He writes that God "richly provides us with everything" (6:17). The word "everything" is "used in the limited sense of 'everything we get' or perhaps 'everything we need.'"[63] God's generous provision is "for our enjoyment" – the things God gives are inherently good, and he intends them for our pleasure. Everything God gives may be enjoyed because everything (including wealth) is a gift from God (see 4:3–5). But enjoyment is not self-indulgence (compare 5:6). Marshall notes, "The implication is that the letter has to deal with two opposing tendencies, the asceticism which forbade enjoyment of the good gifts of God and the self-sufficiency which was based on greed for possessions."[64]

---

61. Fee, *1 and 2 Timothy, Titus*, 156.
62. Marshall, *The Pastoral Epistles*, 671.
63. Marshall, *The Pastoral Epistles*, 672.
64. Marshall, *The Pastoral Epistles*, 672.

Those who have enjoyed God's generosity must also give generously. They are "to do good, to be rich in good deeds, and to be generous and willing to share" (6:18). The wealthy are called to use their wealth for the benefit of others. To be "rich in good deeds" involves being "generous and willing to share." Those who do this mirror God's own example of generous giving, and the actions outlined in verse 18 flow from the recognition that everything we have is a gift from God. "Hence true 'riches' is found in the giving, not in the having."[65] When Paul writes of being "generous and willing to share," he probably has in view the support of needy relatives (5:4, 8, 16) as well as others in the congregation.

Several years ago, a new church was being planted among an urban poor community in Manila, and one of the authors was working with this community. There were huge needs, both in the congregation and in the wider community. A benevolence fund was set up, as part of the church's annual budget, so that the church could extend financial assistance to needy people in the congregation. In addition, some of the more well-to-do people in the congregation began to reach out to help the poorer members. For instance, one of the local church leaders volunteered to pay a year's university fees on behalf of a young person whose parents could not afford it. His generosity encouraged others to participate in giving toward the needy, and the church grew as a result.

By being generous with their riches (6:18), believers "lay up treasure for themselves as a firm foundation for the coming age" (6:19). By speaking of "treasure," Paul continues to use the metaphor of riches, but by referring to "the coming age" he extends the metaphor eschatologically.[66] While good deeds cannot earn salvation, such actions are part of the practical outworking of faith. With reference to the rich doing good and being generous, Mounce comments: "The result of – not the reason for – doing this is that they will store up treasures for themselves."[67] It is by sharing our earthly riches that we gain true and enduring spiritual riches. To give riches away is not to suffer loss but to lay up treasure of a different kind – a firm foundation for the coming age (compare Luke 12:32–33).

---

65. Fee, *1 and 2 Timothy, Titus*, 158.
66. Fee notes, "In doing so, he makes what appear to be some very un-Pauline comments (as in 2:15). But the awkwardness is the result of the metaphor(s), not of a theological shift. Salvation is to put one's hope in God; it is not achieved by 'buying shares in heaven'!" Fee, *1 and 2 Timothy, Titus*, 158.
67. Mounce, *The Pastoral Epistles*, 367.

Traditional houses built by the Toba Batak people of North Sumatra are large enough to accommodate eight or more families. These houses – with their high, pitched roofs, supported by great beams made of whole tree trunks, which require careful engineering and, above all else, a solid foundation – have given rise to the saying:

Molo sala mendasor, sega luhutan

which means,

If the foundation is wrong everything will come to ruin.

What is the nature of this "treasure"? It is "the life that is truly life" (6:19b), a goal common to all believers (1:16; 4:8; 6:12), a treasure celebrated in the Asian hymn "The Great Love of God" by D. T. Niles:

It's yours, it is ours,
O how lavishly given!
The pearl of great price,
and the treasure of heaven.[68]

This treasure of "the life that is truly life" is the result of putting one's hope in God, which in turn results in good works.

There is a play on the word "riches," which occurs four times in 1 Timothy 6:17–18 in different forms. Fee comments, "'*The rich*' are not to trust in '*riches*,' but in God who *richly* gives all things, and therefore are *to be rich* in good deeds, which then, to extend the metaphor, is their way *to lay up . . . treasure* for the future."[69] Despite the love of money being "a root of all kinds of evil" (6:10), wealth is not seen as inherently evil. In fact, the wealthy have the advantage of special opportunities to do good deeds. But the true reward for their benefactions is in the next life, rather than in this one, and this reward is not public acclamation, but the reward given by God.

6:20–21 Final Word to Timothy

There are no final greetings from Paul and his co-workers to the recipients of the letter (compare 2 Tim 4:19–21; Titus 3:15). Instead, Paul repeats his initial charge to Timothy, forming an *inclusio* with chapter 1 (1:3; 6:20–21):

---

68. Words by Daniel Thambyrajah Niles (d. 1970), Tune "Thailand" by Charoen Vijaya, 1960, orig. in *EACC Hymnal*, 1963.
69. Fee, *1 and 2 Timothy, Titus*, 159, emphasis original.

1 Timothy

Timothy must guard the truth of the gospel and resist the false teaching that is so dangerous.

Paul writes, "Timothy, guard what has been entrusted to your care" (6:20). This is the third such charge to Timothy (compare 1:18–19; 6:13–16). It literally reads "guard the deposit." This metaphor of guarding a deposit reflects "the highest kind of sacred obligation in ancient society, namely, being entrusted with some treasured possession for safekeeping while another is away. A person so entrusted was under the most binding sacred duty to keep 'the deposit' safe."[70] Thus the emphasis is on faithfulness in guarding what has been entrusted to a person. Paul concludes his letter by placing Timothy (and, by implication, the other recipients) under such a trust. In the context of the whole letter, the deposit "entrusted" to Timothy is clearly the gospel, although also in view would be the exposition of the gospel as it is found in the letter. Timothy is to guard the gospel (which means preserving it unharmed), by resisting the false teachers, so that he can pass it on to others.

Paul concludes with a final charge to resist the false teachers: "Turn away from godless chatter and the opposing ideas of what is falsely called knowledge" (6:20). Since Gnosticism taught that salvation was through "knowledge," Paul's focus on the false teachers who claimed to teach "knowledge" has sometimes been interpreted to mean that some form of Gnosticism was present in Ephesus. But other key ingredients of Gnosticism – such as speculation about spiritual hierarchies and the soul finding salvation through knowledge – are not found in the Pastorals. Further, the term "knowledge" was widely used by a variety of groups and does not by itself point to Gnosticism. For example, although there were people in Corinth who opposed the gospel in the name of "knowledge" (1 Cor 8:1–10), Gnosticism in the way that it developed later was not present in Corinth at the time.

Sincere and devoted Christians have sometimes rejected the authority of all knowledge apart from Scripture, particularly those elements of modern scientific and philosophical inquiry that initially appear difficult to reconcile with the teachings of Scripture. There is a rapidly growing body of knowledge, particularly scientific knowledge, discovered and tested by our God-given gifts of intellect and critical inquiry. This body of knowledge is, by its own nature, open to review and correction, and Christians must come to terms with such knowledge if we are going to be able to share our faith coherently with our contemporaries. It is not this kind of self-critical knowledge that Timothy and

---

70. Fee, *1 and 2 Timothy, Titus*, 160.

his associates are to reject but "what is falsely called knowledge." In today's world, "what is falsely called knowledge" may include the strange mixture of unreconciled elements of traditional wisdom, mysticism, and nature religions that we call New Age thought.

What happened to some people in Ephesus was tragic: "some have . . . departed from the faith" (6:21). By following what was "falsely called knowledge," some had missed the mark regarding the faith. Clearly, the false teachers and their followers are in view here. As Johnson notes, the false teachers

> have thought to add on to their profession by claims to knowledge and the imposition of legalism and asceticism; by so doing, Paul says, they have missed entirely the nature of this life, which is the response of the human person to the living God in *pistis* – faith, trust, obedience, commitment, love.[71]

Then follows the typical Pauline benediction: "Grace be with you all" (6:21). The "you" is plural, which shows that Paul intended that the letter be read aloud in the church. The benediction is a prayer, asking that God's undeserved favor and blessing would be with all the recipients of this letter.

---

71. Johnson, *The First and Second Letters to Timothy*, 312.

CONCLUDING REMARKS

We have reached the end of our journey through 1 Timothy. The letter contains many rich theological insights, which continue to be relevant in today's world. We consider some of these briefly below.

Timothy teaches about the Triune God. God the Father's greatness is emphasized – he is "the King eternal, immortal, invisible, the only God" (1:17), and "the blessed and only Ruler, the King of kings and Lord of lords, who alone is immortal and who lives in unapproachable light, whom no one has seen or can see" (6:15–16). However, God is not distant from us, but is the Savior (1:1; 2:3; 4:10), the creator (4:3; 6:13) and the sanctifier (4:5) on whom we are to set our hope (4:10; 5:5; 6:17).

The pre-existent Christ came to save sinners (1:15) by giving himself as a ransom for all people (2:6), who was then vindicated and ascended in glory. He is the only mediator between God and humanity (2:5). The Gospel is the Gospel of Christ, and it is to be preached to the nations and believed in throughout the world as stated in the powerful creed in 1 Timothy 3:16. Jesus Christ, in his grace and mercy, had "the utmost patience" (1:16) with Paul, the worst of sinners (1:15), and it is clear that such grace and mercy is available to all (1:15–16). Our Lord Jesus Christ will be coming again at the right time (6:14–15). The Spirit, who vindicated Christ at his resurrection, forewarns believers about false teachers and gives God's people the gifts of prophecy and leadership (3:16; 4:1, 14).

Timothy also has a strong emphasis on the true gospel – often called "sound doctrine," "the truth," or "good teaching" (1:10; 2:4, 4:6) – which nourishes God's people. Timothy, the elders, and "the household of God" are all charged with guarding this gospel which was under attack by the false teachers (1:3–7; 3:1–13, 15; 4:1–3). Some women (2:9–15), including some widows (5:13), seem to be propagating the false teaching, which leads Paul to require them to be silent until they learn the truth, to curb the spread of the false teaching (2:11–15; 5:3–16).

Timothy also gives various instructions about overseers and deacons, probably because some of the false teachers are leaders in the Christian community. Overseers and deacons play a vital role in leading the church and in guarding the true faith (6:20). The key attributes and requirements for those in leadership and ministry are outlined, with the work of preaching and teaching noted as being especially significant (3:1–13; 4:6–16; 5:17–19).

Church leaders must not only preach and teach God's word faithfully but live exemplary lives that gain the respect of those within the church as well as those in wider society (3:5–6). Paul is anxious to avoid a situation where outsiders might regard the church with reproach, since this would lead to such outsiders writing off the Christian Gospel (3:7). Paul is also concerned to avoid the situation where the behavior of slaves would lead to God's name and Christian teaching being slandered (6:1); again, this would lead to the Gospel being disregarded. This is in keeping with the strong emphasis on salvation and mission in 1 Timothy (1:1, 15; 2:3–6, 15; 4:10, 16). In addition, both the role of faith (1:4–5, 14, 19; 2:7, 15; 3:9, 13; 4:6, 12; 5:8; 6:11–12, 21) and the response of "good works" (2:10; 5:10, 25; 6:18) are often spoken of. Rich Christians, in particular, are to be "rich in good works," by being generous and willing to share with others (6:17–19). But Paul's call for an exemplary lifestyle is not limited to Christian leaders; *all* Christians – old and young, men and women, the married, the single, and the widowed, slaves and masters, rich and poor – are called to live godly lives with contentment.

Finally, 1 Timothy calls us today to worship and serve the Triune God, who has given us this glorious Gospel about the appearance in the flesh of the Lord Jesus Christ; this is the sound and health-giving teaching. We are called to guard this Gospel from the many elements of false teaching today that would also cause a shipwreck of the faith. Leaders have a special role in guarding, preserving, and passing on this true Gospel, and in preaching and teaching it faithfully. Leaders are also to care for the household of God, the church, just as they would for their families. All people within the church are called to have faith in the Lord Jesus and to live out our faith in many good works, which are acts of love for those in the household of God and beyond. We are all called to "Fight the good fight of the faith. Take hold of the eternal life to which you were called when you made your good confession in the presence of many witnesses" and "to keep this command without spot or blame until the appearing of our Lord Jesus Christ" (6:12, 14).

SELECTED BIBLIOGRAPHY

Andres, T. Q. D. and P. C. Lada-Andres, *Making the Filipino Values Work for You.* Makati: St. Paul Publication, 1988.

Aquinas, Thomas, *Summa Theologiae: Latin Text and English Translation, Introduction, Notes, Appendices and Glossaries*, 61 volumes. London: Blackfriars with Eyre & Spottiswoode, 1964–66.

Bailey, K. E. "Women in the New Testament: A Middle Eastern Cultural View." *Evangelical Review of Theology* 22 (1998): 208–26.

Barrett, C. K. *The Pastoral Epistles in the New English Bible, with introduction and commentary.* New Clarendon Bible. Oxford: Clarendon Press, 1963.

Bassler, J. M. *1 Timothy, 2 Timothy, Titus.* Abingdon New Testament Commentaries. Nashville: Abingdon Press, 1996.

Bauer, W., revised and edited by F. W. Danker, *A Greek-English Lexicon of the New Testament and Other Early Christian Literature.* 3rd Edition. Chicago: University of Chicago Press, 2000.

Bray, G. *The Pastoral Epistles.* ITC. London: Bloomsbury T&T Clark, 2019.

Bruce, F. F. *The Epistle of Paul to the Galatians.* NIGTC. Exeter: Paternoster Press, 1982.

Budiman, R. *Tafsiran Alkitab: Surat-surat Pastoral I, II Timotius dan Titus.* Jakarta: BPK Gunung Mulia, 1997.

Chandran, R. "Widows of Suicide Farmers to Get Land Titles in Indian State." *Reuters*, June 21, 2019, https://www.reuters.com/article/us-india-landrights-women-idUSKCN1TM14R (accessed April 18, 2022).

Dave, R. "Widowhood: The Problems and Challenges Faced by Widows in India." *International Journal of Advanced Research in Commence, Management & Social Sciences* 3.4 (2020): 34–36.

Davies, M. *The Pastoral Epistles.* Epworth NT Commentaries. London: Epworth, 1996.

Diamante, D. J. R., A. E. C. Ruiz, R. E. M. Apad, J. P. A. C. Ferrer, and A. M. Fillone, "Crowd Estimation of the Black Nazarene Procession in Manila, Philippines." *Philippine Journal of Science* 150 (2021): 883–93.

Dibelius, M. and H. Conzelmann. *The Pastoral Epistles.* Hermeneia. Philadelphia: Fortress Press, 1972.

Fee, G. D. *1 and 2 Timothy, Titus.* Understanding the Bible Commentary Series. Grand Rapids: Baker Books, 2011.

Fohrer, G. and W. Foerster, "σωτήρ." In *TDNT.* Volume 7. Edited by G. Friedrich, 1003–21. Grand Rapids: Eerdmans, 1971.

Freedman, D. N. *The Nine Commandments: Uncovering the Hidden Pattern of Crime and Punishment in the Hebrew Bible.* Anchor Bible Reference Library. New York: Doubleday, 2000.

Gloer, W. H. *1 & 2 Timothy-Titus.* Smyth & Helwys Bible Commentary. Macon: Smyth & Helwys, 2010.

Gloer, W. H. and P. L. Stepp. *Reading Paul's Letters to Individuals. A Literary and Theological Commentary on Paul's Letters to Philemon, Titus, and Timothy.* Reading the New Testament. Macon: Smyth & Helwys, 2013.

Hanson, A.T. *The Pastoral Epistles.* New Century Bible. Grand Rapids: Eerdmans, 1982.

Harding, M. *What Are They Saying About the Pastoral Epistles.* New York: Paulist Press, 2001.

Harper, A. C. *Understanding the Iglesia ni Christo.* Eugene, OR: Wipf & Stock, 2017.

Hirano, K. "Don't be afraid to become a minority." *Faith and Leadership*, https://faithandleadership.com/katsuki-hirano-dont-be-afraid-become-minority. Retrieved on April 18, 2022.

Houlden, J. L. *The Pastoral Epistles.* Pelican New Testament Commentaries. Harmondsworth: Penguin Books, 1976.

Huizenga, A. B. *1–2 Timothy, Titus.* Wisdom Commentary Volume 53. Collegeville: Liturgical Press, 2016.

Hultgren, A. J. "I-II Timothy, Titus," in *I-II Timothy, Titus, II Thessalonians*, by A. J. Hultgren and R. Aus, 9–189. Augsburg Commentary on the NT. Minneapolis: Augsburg, 1984.

Johnson, L. T. *Letters to Paul's Delegates: 1 Timothy, 2 Timothy, Titus.* The NT in Context. Valley Forge: TPI, 1996.

———. *The First and Second Letters to Timothy. A New Translation with Introduction and Commentary.* AB. New York: Doubleday, 2001.

Karris, R. J. "The Background and Significance of the Polemic of the Pastoral Epistles." *JBL* 92 (1973): 549–64.

———. *The Pastoral Epistles.* New Testament Message 17. Wilmington: Michael Glazier, 1979.

Kelly, J. N. D. *A Commentary on The Pastoral Epistles.* Black's New Testament Commentaries. London: A & C Black, 1963.

Kidd, R. M. *Wealth and Beneficence in the Pastoral Epistles.* SBL Dissertation Series 122. Atlanta: Scholars Press, 1990.

Knight, G. W. *The Pastoral Epistles. A Commentary on the Greek Text.* NIGTC. Grand Rapids: Eerdmans, 1992.

Kümmel, W. G. *Introduction to the New Testament*, Rev. ed. London: SCM Press, 1975.

Selected Bibliography

Lim, F. K. G. "'Serving the Lord': Christianity, Work, and Social Engagement in China," *Religion* 10 (2019): 1–17.

MacDonald, M. Y. *The Pauline Churches. A Socio-historical Study of Institutionalization in the Pauline and Deutero-Pauline Writings*. Society for New Testament Studies Monograph Series 60. Cambridge: Cambridge University Press, 1988.

Marshall. C. "What did you say, Paul? 'Let A Woman Learn': 1 Timothy 2:8–15 in Context," *Today's Christian* 1989, no. 9, 43–51.

———. *The Pastoral Epistles*. ICC. 2nd edition. Edinburgh: T&T Clark, 2004.

Meier, J. P. "*Presbyteros* in the Pastoral Epistles." *CBQ* 35 (1973): 323–45.

Mounce, W. *The Pastoral Epistles*. WBC. Nashville: Thomas Nelson, 2000.

Oepke, A. "μεσίτης, μεσιτεύω." In *TDNT*. Volume 4. Edited by G. Kittel, 598–624. Grand Rapids: Eerdmans, 1967.

Procksch, O. "ἁγιάζω." In *TDNT*. Volume 1. Edited by G. Kittel, 111–12. Grand Rapids: Eerdmans, 1964.

Rae, S. H. *Breath Becomes the Wind: Old and New in Karo Religion*. Dunedin: Otago University Press, 1994.

Robert, D. L. *Gospel Bearers, Gender Barriers: Missionary Women in the Twentieth Century*. Maryknoll, NY: Orbis Books, 2002.

Saarinen, R. *The Pastoral Epistles with Philemon & Jude*. Brazos Theological Commentary on the Bible. Grand Rapids: Brazos Press, 2008.

Skeat, T. C. "'Especially the Parchments': A Note on 2 Tim 4.13." *JETS* 30 (1979): 173–77.

Spurgeon, A. B. "1 Timothy 2:13–15: Paul's Retelling of Genesis 2:4–4:1." *JETS* 56 (2013): 543–56.

Starr, C. *Chinese Theology: Text and Context*. New Haven: Yale University Press, 2016.

Stiefel, J. H. "Women Deacons in 1 Timothy: A Linguistic and Literary Look at 'Women Likewise . . .'." *New Testament Studies* 41 (1995): 442–57.

Stott, J. R. W. *The Message of 1 Timothy and Titus*. BST. Leicester: Inter-Varsity Press, 1996.

Tiatco, A. P. and A. Bonifacio-Ramolete, "Cutud's Ritual of Nailing on the Cross: Performance of Pain and Suffering." *Asian Theatre Journal* 25 (2008): 58–76.

Torres, J. "Bible is the most read book among Filipinos," in *Godgossip*, October 29, 2018, http://www.godgossip.org/article/bible-is-most-read-book-among-filipinos (accessed May 3, 2022).

Towner, P. H. *1–2 Timothy & Titus*. IVP NT Commentary Series. Downers Grove: InterVarsity Press, 1994.

———. *The Goal of Our Instruction: The Structure of Theology and Ethics in the Pastoral Epistles*. JSNTSup 34. Sheffield: JSOT Press, 1989.

———. *The Letters to Timothy and Titus*. NICNT. Grand Rapids: Eerdmans, 2006.
Trebilco, P. R. *Self-designations and Group Identity in the New Testament*. Cambridge: Cambridge University Press, 2012.
Vellaram, S. "Kerala Church Starts Matrimonial Site to Help Widows, Middle-Aged Men Find Life Partners." *The News Minute*, November 19, 2019, https://www.thenewsminute.com/article/kerala-church-starts-matrimonial-site-help-widows-middle-aged-men-find-life-partners-112566 (accessed April 18, 2022).
Wall, R. W., with R. B. Steele, *1 & 2 Timothy and Titus*. Two Horizons New Testament Commentary. Grand Rapids: Eerdmans, 2012.
Witherington, B. *A Socio-Rhetorical Commentary on Titus, 1–2 Timothy and 1–3 John*. Volume 1 of *Letters and Homilies for Hellenized Christians*. Downers Grove: IVP Academic, 2006.
Wu Ching-tzu, *The Scholars*. E.T. by Hsien-yi and Gladys Yang. Peking: Foreign Languages Press, 3rd ed., 1973.
Yarbrough, R. W. *The Letters to Timothy and Titus*, Pillar New Testament Commentary. Grand Rapids: Eerdmans, 2018.
Yeoman, S. *Is Anyone in Charge Here? A Christian Evaluation of the Idea of Human Domination Over Creation*. Eugene OR: Pickwick Publications, 2019.
Young, F. *The Theology of the Pastoral Letters*. Cambridge: Cambridge University Press, 1994.

Asia Theological Association
54 Scout Madriñan St. Quezon City 1103, Philippines
Email: ataasia@gmail.com Telefax: (632) 410 0312

OUR MISSION
The Asia Theological Association (ATA) is a body of theological institutions, committed to evangelical faith and scholarship, networking together to serve the Church in equipping the people of God for the mission of the Lord Jesus Christ.

OUR COMMITMENT
The ATA is committed to serving its members in the development of evangelical, biblical theology by strengthening interaction, enhancing scholarship, promoting academic excellence, fostering spiritual and ministerial formation and mobilizing resources to fulfill God's global mission within diverse Asian cultures.

OUR TASK
Affirming our mission and commitment, ATA seeks to:

- **Strengthen** interaction through inter-institutional fellowship and programs, regional and continental activities, faculty and student exchange programs.
- **Enhance** scholarship through consultations, workshops, seminars, publications, and research fellowships.
- **Promote** academic excellence through accreditation standards, faculty and curriculum development.
- **Foster** spiritual and ministerial formation by providing mentor models, encouraging the development of ministerial skills and a Christian ethos.
- **Mobilize** resources through library development, information technology and infra-structural development.

To learn more about ATA, visit www.ataasia.com or facebook.com/AsiaTheologicalAssociation

Langham Literature, along with its publishing work, is a ministry of Langham Partnership.

Langham Partnership is a global fellowship working in pursuit of the vision God entrusted to its founder John Stott –

> *to facilitate the growth of the church in maturity and Christ-likeness through raising the standards of biblical preaching and teaching.*

Our vision is to see churches in the Majority World equipped for mission and growing to maturity in Christ through the ministry of pastors and leaders who believe, teach and live by the word of God.

Our mission is to strengthen the ministry of the word of God through:
- nurturing national movements for biblical preaching
- fostering the creation and distribution of evangelical literature
- enhancing evangelical theological education

especially in countries where churches are under-resourced.

Our ministry

Langham Preaching partners with national leaders to nurture indigenous biblical preaching movements for pastors and lay preachers all around the world. With the support of a team of trainers from many countries, a multi-level programme of seminars provides practical training, and is followed by a programme for training local facilitators. Local preachers' groups and national and regional networks ensure continuity and ongoing development, seeking to build vigorous movements committed to Bible exposition.

Langham Literature provides Majority World preachers, scholars and seminary libraries with evangelical books and electronic resources through publishing and distribution, grants and discounts. The programme also fosters the creation of indigenous evangelical books in many languages, through writer's grants, strengthening local evangelical publishing houses, and investment in major regional literature projects, such as one volume Bible commentaries like the *Africa Bible Commentary* and the *South Asia Bible Commentary*.

Langham Scholars provides financial support for evangelical doctoral students from the Majority World so that, when they return home, they may train pastors and other Christian leaders with sound, biblical and theological teaching. This programme equips those who equip others. Langham Scholars also works in partnership with Majority World seminaries in strengthening evangelical theological education. A growing number of Langham Scholars study in high quality doctoral programmes in the Majority World itself. As well as teaching the next generation of pastors, graduated Langham Scholars exercise significant influence through their writing and leadership.

To learn more about Langham Partnership and the work we do visit **langham.org**

www.ingramcontent.com/pod-product-compliance
Lightning Source LLC
Chambersburg PA
CBHW070538170426
43200CB00011B/2460